Investigating Disinformation & Fake News with OSINT

Algoryth Ryker

In the digital age, truth itself is under attack. Governments, corporations, extremist groups, and cybercriminals have weaponized misinformation, using fake news, deepfakes, AI-generated propaganda, and social media manipulation to influence public opinion, disrupt elections, and incite division.

Disinformation campaigns are no longer limited to shadowy intelligence operations—they are now part of global conflicts, political battles, and online culture wars. From viral fake news stories and bot-driven trends to meme warfare and deepfake videos, the lines between fact and fiction are deliberately blurred.

But Open-Source Intelligence (OSINT) is the antidote. This book is your playbook for identifying, analyzing, and countering disinformation, equipping you with the tools and methodologies used by intelligence agencies, journalists, and cybersecurity professionals to expose falsehoods and defend truth.

Through real-world case studies, you'll uncover how fake news spreads, how state-sponsored disinformation operates, and how AI-generated fakes manipulate perceptions. You'll learn how to trace the origins of viral misinformation, investigate deepfake videos, map coordinated disinformation networks, and track bot armies used for influence campaigns.

If you've ever wondered who is behind fake news, how deepfakes are detected, or how social media manipulation works—this book will take you inside the world of modern information warfare.

Chapter Breakdown

1. Understanding Disinformation & Influence Campaigns

- Defining disinformation, misinformation, and malinformation
- The psychological manipulation tactics used in fake news
- How influence campaigns shape public perception
- The differences between propaganda and disinformation
- Examining major historical disinformation operations

📌 **Case Study**: How Disinformation Has Shaped Public Opinion

2. Identifying Fake News & Deepfakes

- How to spot fake news articles and sensationalist content
- Investigating clickbait tactics and false narratives
- Using reverse image and video search for verification
- Detecting deepfake videos and AI-generated content
- Understanding the rise of synthetic media manipulation

📌 **Case Study**: Investigating a Viral Deepfake Video

3. Social Media Disinformation Tactics

- How fake news spreads through social media algorithms
- Identifying manipulated hashtags and viral disinformation
- Investigating sock puppets, troll farms, and astroturfing
- Analyzing coordinated disinformation attacks

📌 **Case Study**: A Social Media Disinformation Operation Exposed

4. Fact-Checking Tools & Methods

- The science behind fact-checking and source verification
- Investigating claims with OSINT tools
- Using metadata analysis to verify images and videos
- Cross-referencing suspicious information with trusted sources
- Challenges in debunking viral misinformation

📌 **Case Study**: How OSINT Debunked a High-Profile Hoax

5. Tracking Bots & Coordinated Networks

- Understanding how bot networks amplify disinformation
- Identifying bot behavior and fake engagement
- Mapping coordinated social media disinformation campaigns
- OSINT tools for tracking automated activity

📌 **Case Study**: Exposing a Bot-Driven Disinformation Operation

6. Identifying State-Sponsored Disinformation

- How nation-states use disinformation as a weapon
- Investigating foreign influence operations
- Analyzing leaked government documents and propaganda
- Intelligence methods for countering state-backed misinformation

📌 **Case Study**: How a Government-Backed Disinformation Campaign Was Exposed

7. Investigating Propaganda Campaigns

- Identifying propaganda techniques in media
- Investigating news bias and controlled narratives
- How propaganda influences elections and public policy
- Tracking media manipulation across platforms

📌 **Case Study**: OSINT Unveiling a State-Run Propaganda Machine

8. Analyzing Memes & Viral Trends

- The power of memes in influence campaigns
- Tracking viral memes to their origin
- Decoding hidden messages and symbolism in memes
- How memes are weaponized for political manipulation

📌 **Case Study**: A Meme-Driven Disinformation Campaign

9. Countering Disinformation with OSINT

- Strategies for debunking and neutralizing disinformation
- Collaborating with fact-checkers and investigative journalists
- Educating the public on media literacy and OSINT skills
- Tools for proactive disinformation monitoring

📌 **Case Study**: How OSINT Helped a Community Combat Fake News

10. Case Study: Disinformation in Elections

- How election disinformation campaigns operate
- Investigating fake accounts and vote manipulation tactics
- Tracking election-related misinformation on social media
- The impact of deepfakes and false endorsements

✦ **Case Study**: OSINT in Action Against Election Disruption

11. Ethical Dilemmas in Disinformation Investigations

- The ethics of exposing fake news creators
- The fine line between censorship and fact-checking
- Privacy concerns in identifying disinformation actors
- How OSINT investigators become targets of disinformation

✦ **Case Study**: Ethical Challenges in a High-Stakes Disinformation Probe

12. The Future of OSINT in Media Verification

- How AI and machine learning will change fact-checking
- The role of blockchain and cryptographic proof in media verification
- The evolution of disinformation tactics
- The future battle against synthetic media and AI-generated fakes
- How global collaboration can counter disinformation

✦ **Preparing for the Future:** Skills & Tools for the Next Generation of OSINT Investigators

Final Thoughts

The battle against disinformation is one of the most critical fights of the digital age. Every day, governments, corporations, and malicious actors flood the internet with fake news, propaganda, and deepfake content designed to manipulate minds and shape global events.

But disinformation can be exposed. Using OSINT techniques, analysts can trace the origins of fake news, identify propaganda networks, and debunk viral falsehoods before they cause real-world harm.

This book equips you with the skills, tools, and investigative techniques to fight back against misinformation warfare—whether you're a journalist, intelligence analyst, cybersecurity expert, or digital investigator.

If you're ready to uncover who is behind fake news, how deepfakes deceive millions, and how social media is weaponized for information warfare—this book will teach you how to expose the truth.

1. Understanding Disinformation & Influence Campaigns

In the digital age, disinformation and influence campaigns have become powerful tools used to manipulate public perception, sway opinions, and shape societal narratives. This chapter delves into the mechanisms behind these malicious operations, exploring how false information is spread, often through sophisticated networks and coordinated efforts. We'll examine the psychological tactics that make disinformation effective, the various platforms used to disseminate it, and the role of both state and non-state actors in driving these campaigns. By understanding the anatomy of disinformation and influence campaigns, we lay the foundation for using Open-Source Intelligence (OSINT) to uncover the truth and counter these digital threats.

1.1 Defining Disinformation, Misinformation & Malinformation

In today's hyper-connected digital world, the spread of false information has become one of the most significant challenges to public trust, democracy, and social cohesion. It is essential to understand the different types of harmful information that circulate across various platforms to properly address their impact. While terms like disinformation, misinformation, and malinformation are often used interchangeably, they each have distinct meanings, implications, and methods of dissemination. This section will define and differentiate these terms, explore their consequences, and explain why distinguishing between them is crucial for anyone working in the field of Open-Source Intelligence (OSINT) and media verification.

Misinformation: False Information without Malicious Intent

Misinformation refers to the dissemination of false or inaccurate information, but crucially, it is spread without the intent to deceive or cause harm. People may share misinformation unknowingly or unintentionally, often in good faith, believing the content to be true. This category can encompass a wide variety of situations, such as when someone shares a misleading headline without checking the facts or when an outdated study or statistic is cited in a post.

The spread of misinformation can occur in several ways. For example, a viral Facebook post might claim that a particular food is proven to cure a common illness, when in reality the claim is based on a misinterpreted or outdated study. Another example might involve an image or video shared on Twitter that inaccurately depicts an event, such as a natural disaster or political rally, but the person sharing it believes it to be accurate because it fits the narrative they want to believe.

Though misinformation may not be intentional, its consequences can still be significant. It can create confusion, spread anxiety, and contribute to the erosion of trust in credible sources of information. When individuals share false information, they unintentionally amplify its reach, allowing the misinformation to spread further and faster. This is particularly problematic on social media platforms, where posts can go viral within minutes. However, misinformation often fades as quickly as it spreads once it is corrected or clarified.

In the context of OSINT, misinformation presents a challenge for analysts who must discern whether information is the result of simple errors or if it is part of a larger, more coordinated campaign. Investigating misinformation requires an understanding of human behavior, cognitive biases, and the dynamics of information flow in the digital space.

Disinformation: Deliberate Falsehoods for Deceptive Purposes

Unlike misinformation, disinformation is intentionally created and spread to deceive others. Disinformation campaigns are orchestrated with the specific goal of manipulating public opinion, distorting facts, or serving a political, ideological, or financial agenda. The creators of disinformation may intentionally craft false narratives to mislead the public, sow discord, or destabilize societal structures.

One of the most common vehicles for disinformation is social media, where individuals, groups, or even governments exploit the viral nature of posts to amplify their messages. Disinformation can take many forms: fabricated news articles, manipulated images or videos (including deepfakes), and false narratives propagated through fake accounts or bots. The purpose of these campaigns is often to create confusion, manipulate emotions, and influence decision-making, such as swaying elections, discrediting political opponents, or inciting social unrest.

A classic example of disinformation is the spread of fake news articles designed to promote a particular political viewpoint. During elections, disinformation campaigns might spread fabricated stories about candidates, accusing them of corruption or scandal, regardless of their truthfulness. Disinformation is often tailored to appeal to specific audiences, using targeted messaging that resonates with their beliefs or fears, making it particularly effective in shaping public discourse and influencing behavior.

In an OSINT investigation, identifying disinformation is crucial because it has the potential to cause widespread harm. Analysts must be able to track the origin and trajectory of false information, uncover coordinated efforts behind disinformation campaigns, and determine the intent behind the spread. The challenge lies in the sophistication of disinformation strategies, which often include misleading metadata, fake social media profiles, and other deceptive tools designed to obfuscate the truth.

Malinformation: Truth Used with Harmful Intent

Malinformation is distinct from both misinformation and disinformation in that it involves the sharing of truthful information, but with the intent to cause harm or damage someone's reputation, privacy, or safety. While misinformation and disinformation rely on falsehoods or manipulations, malinformation capitalizes on truth in a malicious context, often selectively presenting information to achieve a particular agenda. The intent behind malinformation is key—it is designed to cause damage rather than inform or educate.

An example of malinformation might include the release of a private individual's personal information (doxxing), such as addresses, phone numbers, or private conversations, with the aim of causing harm to that individual. Malinformation can also be seen in the release of true but highly damaging information about someone, such as a politician or public figure, that is intended to damage their reputation. This can include sharing a truthful but private piece of information, like a politician's personal relationship issues, that is irrelevant to their public role but is used to scandalize or discredit them.

The distinction between malinformation and disinformation is subtle yet important. While disinformation manipulates or fabricates falsehoods for a harmful purpose, malinformation takes truthful information and weaponizes it for personal, political, or social gain. In the context of OSINT, malinformation presents its own challenges. Analysts must be able to distinguish between the truthful dissemination of private information, which may be legally or ethically harmful, and the manipulation of that information for a specific purpose. The investigation of malinformation often involves considering privacy laws, ethical boundaries, and the broader social consequences of releasing certain types of information.

The Impact of Disinformation, Misinformation, and Malinformation

The spread of disinformation, misinformation, and malinformation can have far-reaching consequences for society. These forms of false information undermine trust in media, public institutions, and even scientific research. When people cannot distinguish between true and false information, they become more susceptible to manipulation, polarized thinking, and the erosion of democratic processes.

Misinformation, while often unintentional, can contribute to confusion and delay important societal responses to issues like health crises, political events, and natural disasters. Disinformation, on the other hand, can have a much more damaging impact, intentionally deceiving large groups of people and potentially altering political landscapes or public sentiment. Malinformation, while based in truth, can cause harm by selectively exposing information for malicious purposes, leading to invasions of privacy or reputational damage.

Understanding the distinctions between these three types of harmful information is critical for OSINT analysts, journalists, and anyone working in the field of media verification. By recognizing the intent behind the information and examining its dissemination patterns, it becomes possible to effectively combat the spread of these harmful types of content.

In conclusion, while disinformation, misinformation, and malinformation may all share the common characteristic of spreading false or misleading content, they differ significantly in intent and impact. Misinformation is the unintentional spread of inaccurate information, disinformation is deliberately crafted to deceive, and malinformation involves the use of truthful information with harmful intent. Distinguishing between these types of content is essential for those working to combat the digital threats posed by false information. As the digital world continues to evolve, so too must our ability to identify, understand, and respond to these varied forms of harmful content, utilizing OSINT and other tools to safeguard truth and integrity in the information landscape.

1.2 The Psychology Behind Fake News & Manipulation

The spread of fake news and disinformation is not just a technological or political issue—it is deeply rooted in human psychology. People are not merely passive consumers of information; they actively interpret, share, and react based on their biases, emotions, and cognitive limitations. Understanding the psychological mechanisms that drive the consumption and spread of fake news is crucial for OSINT analysts, journalists, and anyone working to combat disinformation. This chapter explores the cognitive biases, emotional triggers, and social influences that make individuals susceptible to fake news and manipulation.

Cognitive Biases and Why People Believe Fake News

Humans rely on cognitive shortcuts, or heuristics, to process the vast amounts of information they encounter daily. While these mental shortcuts help us make quick decisions, they can also make us vulnerable to misinformation and manipulation. Some of the most influential cognitive biases in the spread of fake news include:

1. Confirmation Bias

Confirmation bias is the tendency to seek out, interpret, and remember information in a way that supports our existing beliefs while ignoring or dismissing contradictory evidence. This bias is one of the primary reasons people believe and share fake news. When an article, meme, or video aligns with what someone already believes—whether about politics, health, or social issues—they are more likely to accept it as truth without critical evaluation.

For example, during an election, supporters of a particular candidate may be more likely to believe and share stories that portray their preferred candidate positively while rejecting negative reports—even if those reports are accurate. This creates an environment where misinformation thrives because people are less willing to challenge or verify information that fits their worldview.

2. Availability Heuristic

The availability heuristic refers to our tendency to judge the likelihood of an event based on how easily examples come to mind. If we frequently encounter a certain type of information—such as news stories about violent crime, corruption, or conspiracy theories—we may overestimate its prevalence or significance. Fake news exploits this by flooding social media with sensationalized or exaggerated claims, making them seem more common or urgent than they are in reality.

For example, if someone sees repeated reports of vaccine side effects, even if the information is misleading or taken out of context, they may overestimate the risks and develop an irrational fear, leading them to reject scientific consensus.

3. Illusory Truth Effect

The illusory truth effect occurs when people start believing false information simply because they have been exposed to it multiple times. Repetition increases familiarity, and familiarity creates the illusion of truth. This is why disinformation campaigns often rely on spreading the same narratives repeatedly across different platforms and in different formats.

Social media algorithms contribute to this effect by continuously exposing users to similar content, reinforcing their beliefs. Even if an individual encounters fact-checks debunking a claim, their repeated exposure to the falsehood can make it feel true over time.

4. Authority Bias

People are more likely to believe and share information that comes from perceived authority figures, even if those figures are not experts in the field. Disinformation campaigns often exploit this by using fake experts, misleading credentials, or influential personalities to spread false narratives.

For instance, during health crises, misinformation about treatments or cures often spreads when celebrities or social media influencers endorse them, even if real medical experts refute their claims. The presence of a confident, authoritative voice can make false information seem more credible.

Emotional Manipulation in Fake News

Disinformation is not just about presenting false facts—it is designed to trigger strong emotions that override rational thinking. Fake news creators understand that emotional content spreads faster and is more likely to be believed. Some of the most common emotional triggers include:

1. Fear and Panic

Fear is one of the most powerful emotions that influence decision-making. Misinformation often exaggerates threats—whether related to health, safety, or politics—to create panic and drive engagement. During crises such as pandemics, natural disasters, or elections, fake news spreads rapidly because fear makes people more likely to share alarming information without verification.

For example, during the COVID-19 pandemic, fake news about hospitals being overwhelmed, exaggerated death rates, or false cures spread widely, leading to real-world consequences such as panic-buying and vaccine hesitancy.

2. Outrage and Moral Superiority

Disinformation often appeals to outrage by framing events or people as threats to societal values. Political and ideological fake news frequently uses moralistic language to make individuals feel superior to the opposing side. This sense of moral superiority encourages engagement, as people feel compelled to share the information to "educate" others or express their anger.

For instance, manipulated videos or out-of-context quotes from political figures are often used to provoke outrage, even if the full context tells a different story. Social media algorithms amplify outrage-driven content, making emotionally charged disinformation spread faster than factual, neutral reports.

3. Tribalism and Group Identity

People have a deep psychological need to belong to social groups, and disinformation campaigns exploit this by reinforcing in-group loyalty and distrust of outsiders. Fake news often frames information in ways that pit one group against another—whether based on political affiliation, nationality, religion, or ideology.

For example, propaganda campaigns may frame news stories as "us vs. them" narratives, encouraging people to distrust mainstream media, experts, or other groups. When people feel their identity is under threat, they become more likely to accept and defend disinformation that supports their side.

4. Nostalgia and Idealization of the Past

Fake news and conspiracy theories often appeal to nostalgia by presenting a romanticized version of the past while claiming that the present is corrupt or dangerous. This tactic is frequently used in political messaging, where disinformation campaigns suggest that society was better before certain policies, people, or events.

For example, disinformation narratives might falsely claim that a country was safer, more prosperous, or morally superior in the past, blaming modern problems on specific groups or changes. This manipulation taps into people's desire for stability and simpler times, making them more receptive to misleading claims.

Social Media's Role in Psychological Manipulation

Social media platforms play a key role in amplifying the psychological effects of fake news. Algorithms prioritize content that generates engagement, meaning emotionally charged misinformation spreads more rapidly than neutral or fact-based information.

Some of the ways social media enhances psychological manipulation include:

- **Echo Chambers**: People are often exposed only to information that aligns with their existing beliefs, reinforcing biases and making them more resistant to correction.
- **Bots and Fake Accounts**: Automated accounts spread disinformation, making it appear more popular or credible than it actually is.
- **Virality Over Veracity**: Misinformation spreads faster than corrections because emotionally charged content generates more shares, comments, and reactions.

Fake news and disinformation are not just about false claims; they exploit fundamental aspects of human psychology to manipulate perception, emotion, and behavior. Cognitive biases such as confirmation bias and the illusory truth effect make individuals more susceptible to misinformation, while emotional triggers like fear, outrage, and tribalism drive engagement and spread. Social media platforms, with their engagement-driven algorithms, further amplify these effects, making it even harder to counter false narratives.

For OSINT analysts, understanding the psychology behind fake news is critical in developing effective strategies to detect, counter, and mitigate disinformation. By recognizing how and why people fall for manipulation, analysts can design better tools and methods to promote digital literacy, encourage critical thinking, and reduce the influence of false information in society.

1.3 Tactics Used in Influence Campaigns

Influence campaigns are carefully orchestrated efforts designed to shape public opinion, manipulate behavior, and achieve political, economic, or ideological goals. These campaigns leverage psychological, technological, and strategic tools to spread disinformation, create confusion, and control narratives. Whether state-sponsored or conducted by private actors, influence campaigns can disrupt democratic processes, fuel polarization, and erode trust in institutions. This section explores the most common tactics used in influence operations and how OSINT analysts can detect and counter them.

1. Exploiting Social Media Algorithms

Modern influence campaigns thrive on social media platforms, where algorithms prioritize engagement over accuracy. Disinformation spreads rapidly when it provokes strong emotional reactions, leading to more shares, comments, and visibility.

Key Strategies:

- **Viral Amplification**: Creating sensational content that triggers fear, outrage, or curiosity to maximize engagement.
- **Hashtag Hijacking**: Injecting disinformation into trending hashtags to increase visibility.
- **Echo Chambers & Filter Bubbles**: Encouraging ideological isolation by reinforcing one-sided narratives through selective content promotion.

Example:

During elections, bot networks and coordinated trolls may flood platforms with misleading information about voter fraud, creating the illusion of widespread irregularities even when none exist.

2. Botnets & Troll Farms

Influence campaigns frequently use automated bots and human-operated troll accounts to amplify messages, drown out dissenting voices, and manipulate public discourse.

Key Strategies:

- **Astroturfing**: Creating fake grassroots movements to simulate organic support.
- **Brigading**: Coordinating mass reporting of opposing voices to silence critics.
- **Amplification Loops**: Bots retweet, like, and comment on content to give it artificial popularity.

Example:

During the COVID-19 pandemic, bot networks promoted conspiracy theories about vaccines, making them appear more widely accepted than they actually were.

3. Disinformation Laundering

This tactic involves spreading false information through a network of seemingly credible sources, making it harder to trace back to its origin.

Key Strategies:

- **Fake Experts & Think Tanks**: Using fabricated credentials to make disinformation appear legitimate.

- **Circular Reporting**: Publishing false claims across multiple platforms so they reinforce each other.
- **Leak Manipulation**: Seeding selective leaks to mislead the public while maintaining plausible deniability.

Example:

A state-sponsored campaign may publish an unverified intelligence "leak" about an adversary's election interference, which is then reported by news outlets without verification.

4. Deepfakes & Media Manipulation

Advancements in artificial intelligence have enabled the creation of highly realistic fake videos, images, and audio clips. These tools can deceive audiences, damage reputations, and fabricate events.

Key Strategies:

- **Synthetic Media**: Creating fake speeches or manipulated footage to discredit individuals.
- **Cheapfakes**: Editing real videos deceptively to alter their meaning.
- **Fake Fact-Checking**: Producing false fact-checks to discredit legitimate reporting.

Example:

A deepfake video of a political candidate making inflammatory remarks could be used to sway public opinion before an election.

5. Meme Warfare & Visual Propaganda

Memes are powerful tools for influence campaigns because they are easily shareable, emotionally charged, and often evade fact-checking.

Key Strategies:

- **Humor as a Shield**: Using satire to spread disinformation while avoiding accountability.
- **Dog-Whistle Messaging**: Embedding hidden messages that resonate with specific audiences.

- **Demonization**: Portraying opponents as villains to reinforce tribalism.

Example:

During social movements, adversarial actors may spread divisive memes that exaggerate tensions between different communities.

6. Manipulating Search Engine Results (SEO Warfare)

Influence campaigns often use search engine optimization (SEO) tactics to push misleading content to the top of search results, ensuring that false narratives reach wider audiences.

Key Strategies:

- **Keyword Stuffing**: Creating misleading content optimized for trending search terms.
- **Content Farms**: Producing large volumes of low-quality articles to manipulate rankings.
- **Google Bombing**: Coordinating efforts to associate negative terms with a public figure.

Example:

By flooding search engines with misleading articles about a public health crisis, bad actors can distort the public's understanding of the issue.

7. Psychological Manipulation & Fearmongering

Fear is a powerful motivator, and influence campaigns frequently use it to shape public perception and decision-making.

Key Strategies:

- **Crisis Exploitation**: Using emergencies (e.g., pandemics, wars) to spread disinformation.
- **Scapegoating**: Blaming specific groups for societal problems to incite division.
- **Apocalyptic Narratives**: Predicting catastrophic outcomes to create urgency and compliance.

Example:

A campaign might spread false claims that a financial collapse is imminent, causing panic and economic instability.

8. Sock Puppets & Fake Personas

Creating fake identities allows influence campaigns to appear more credible and widespread than they actually are.

Key Strategies:

- **Fake Whistleblowers**: Fabricating anonymous insiders to leak "classified" information.
- **Influencer Infiltration**: Placing operatives in activist communities to steer narratives.
- **Multi-Platform Manipulation**: Using the same personas across multiple sites for credibility.

Example:

A fake environmental activist account might be used to push misleading narratives about climate change policies.

9. Controlled Opposition & False Flags

Influence campaigns sometimes create fake opposition movements or stage events to manipulate public perception.

Key Strategies:

- **Controlled Dissent**: Setting up fake protest groups to discredit real activists.
- **Provocateur Tactics**: Infiltrating movements to incite violence or illegal activities.
- **Fake Cyberattacks**: Staging cyber incidents to justify crackdowns or retaliatory actions.

Example:

A government might create a fake "rebel group" to justify increased surveillance or military actions.

10. Narrative Warfare & Strategic Framing

The way information is framed can shape how people perceive it, making narrative control a key tactic in influence campaigns.

Key Strategies:

- **Selective Omission**: Presenting only part of the story to mislead audiences.
- **Loaded Language**: Using emotionally charged words to sway opinions.
- **Reframing Events**: Shifting blame or redefining issues to serve an agenda.

Example:

An authoritarian regime might label pro-democracy protests as "foreign interference" to justify a crackdown.

Influence campaigns are highly sophisticated operations that exploit human psychology, social media algorithms, and technological advancements to manipulate public opinion. By understanding these tactics, OSINT analysts can better detect and counter disinformation, ensuring that truth and transparency prevail. Recognizing patterns of influence, tracing information flows, and exposing coordinated efforts are critical skills in the fight against digital deception. As influence operations evolve, so too must our methods for uncovering and dismantling them.

1.4 Disinformation vs. Propaganda: Key Differences

The terms "disinformation" and "propaganda" are often used interchangeably, but they represent distinct concepts with unique goals, methods, and historical contexts. Both are tools of influence that shape public perception and behavior, yet their intent, scale, and execution differ. Understanding the distinctions between disinformation and propaganda is crucial for OSINT analysts investigating influence campaigns, media manipulation, and geopolitical information warfare. This chapter explores their definitions, key differences, overlaps, and real-world examples.

Defining Disinformation and Propaganda

What is Disinformation?

Disinformation is false or misleading information deliberately created and spread to deceive an audience. Unlike misinformation, which may be incorrect but not intentionally deceptive, disinformation is crafted with the goal of manipulating perceptions, sowing confusion, or achieving a specific agenda.

Key Characteristics of Disinformation:

- **Intentional Deception**: The creators of disinformation knowingly produce falsehoods.
- **Targeted Manipulation**: It is often used to influence political, social, or economic decisions.
- **Fabrication or Distortion**: It can involve completely false stories or the manipulation of real information to mislead.
- **Short-Term Tactical Impact**: Disinformation is often designed to achieve immediate influence, such as swaying public opinion before an election or crisis.

Example of Disinformation:

During the COVID-19 pandemic, false claims that vaccines contained microchips were deliberately spread by malicious actors to create fear and distrust in public health systems.

What is Propaganda?

Propaganda is the systematic dissemination of information, ideas, or narratives designed to promote a particular ideology, political agenda, or cause. While propaganda can involve disinformation, it does not always rely on falsehoods—it may selectively present facts, use emotional appeals, or frame events in a biased way to shape public opinion.

Key Characteristics of Propaganda:

- **Ideological or Political Motivation**: Propaganda serves a larger narrative, often aligned with government or institutional goals.
- **Emotional and Psychological Influence**: It frequently appeals to patriotism, fear, or morality to persuade audiences.
- **Long-Term Influence**: Unlike short-term disinformation, propaganda is often a sustained effort aimed at shaping cultural or national identity.
- **State and Institutional Backing**: Governments, political groups, and large organizations frequently use propaganda to control narratives.

Example of Propaganda:

During World War II, Allied and Axis powers used posters, films, and radio broadcasts to rally public support for the war effort, demonize the enemy, and boost national morale.

Key Differences Between Disinformation and Propaganda

Feature	Disinformation	Propaganda
Intent	To deceive and manipulate for a specific goal	To promote an ideology, cause, or agenda
Truthfulness	Often entirely false or misleading	Can include selective truths, exaggerations
Tactics Used	Fake news, deepfakes, doctored evidence	Emotional appeals, repetition, framing
Longevity	Short-term, designed for immediate impact	Long-term, shaping cultural or national views
Primary Users	State actors, cybercriminals, influence groups	Governments, political parties, institutions
Examples	Election meddling, fake health cures, hoaxes	War propaganda, nationalistic education

Overlap Between Disinformation and Propaganda

While disinformation and propaganda are distinct, they frequently intersect. Propaganda campaigns often use disinformation to strengthen their narratives, while disinformation efforts can serve broader propaganda goals.

Examples of Overlap:

- **State-Sponsored Disinformation**: Governments may use disinformation (e.g., fake news about an adversary) as part of a larger propaganda effort to shape public perception.
- **Media Manipulation**: Propaganda can selectively amplify disinformation by featuring misleading stories in state-controlled media.
- **False Narratives in War**: During conflicts, both sides may spread disinformation to undermine the enemy while reinforcing their own propaganda.

Case Study: Russia's Influence Operations

Russia's state-run media and social media influence campaigns often combine disinformation (e.g., false reports about Western interference) with broader propaganda efforts that frame Russia as a defender of traditional values against "Western decadence."

How OSINT Analysts Can Distinguish Between the Two

For OSINT investigators, differentiating between disinformation and propaganda is crucial for identifying influence campaigns and their objectives. Analysts can use the following techniques:

Source Analysis:

- Check if the information originates from state-controlled or anonymous sources.
- Identify whether media outlets have a history of bias or misinformation.

Content Examination:

- Assess whether the message is designed to deceive (disinformation) or persuade (propaganda).
- Look for selective framing, emotional appeals, and omitted context.

Network Analysis:

- Trace the spread of information across platforms to identify coordinated efforts.
- Detect bot activity, fake accounts, and state-sponsored amplification.

Historical Context:

- Investigate whether the message aligns with long-standing ideological narratives.
- Compare past propaganda efforts to detect recurring themes.

While disinformation and propaganda are closely related, they serve different functions in influence operations. Disinformation is primarily about deception and short-term manipulation, whereas propaganda seeks to instill long-term ideological beliefs. However, the two often work in tandem to shape public perception on a massive scale. OSINT analysts must remain vigilant in identifying, dissecting, and countering these tactics to preserve information integrity in an increasingly complex digital landscape.

1.5 Major Historical Disinformation Campaigns

Disinformation is not a new phenomenon. Throughout history, governments, intelligence agencies, and other actors have used false or misleading information to manipulate public perception, destabilize enemies, and achieve strategic goals. From wartime propaganda to Cold War deception and modern digital influence operations, historical disinformation campaigns provide valuable lessons for OSINT analysts. This chapter examines some of the most significant disinformation efforts and their lasting impact on geopolitics, media, and public trust.

1. Operation INFEKTION (1980s) – The AIDS Hoax

Origin: Soviet Union (KGB)

- **Goal**: Undermine U.S. credibility and create global distrust in American institutions
- **Method**: Spreading false claims that the U.S. military created HIV/AIDS

During the Cold War, the Soviet Union's intelligence agency, the KGB, launched "Operation INFEKTION," one of the most infamous disinformation campaigns. The KGB planted a story in an Indian newspaper, The Patriot, falsely claiming that the U.S. military had developed HIV/AIDS as a biological weapon at Fort Detrick, Maryland. The story gained traction, spreading to African and Western media outlets, fueling anti-American sentiment, and worsening the stigma around AIDS.

Impact:

- The false narrative persisted for years, even after the Soviet Union collapsed.
- It contributed to conspiracy theories about Western governments and medical science.
- It demonstrated the effectiveness of media infiltration and narrative amplification in disinformation campaigns.

2. The Dreyfus Affair (1894) – A Nation Divided by Lies

- **Origin**: France (French military and anti-Semitic factions)
- **Goal**: Wrongfully convict a Jewish officer to protect military leadership

Method: Forged documents and media manipulation

Captain Alfred Dreyfus, a Jewish officer in the French army, was falsely accused of espionage and sentenced to life imprisonment based on forged documents. The French military intelligence service fabricated evidence and manipulated public perception by leaking misleading information to the press. The case divided France, with pro-Dreyfus intellectuals (such as writer Émile Zola) battling anti-Semitic factions that supported the false charges.

Impact:

- The scandal exposed how disinformation could be used to protect institutions at the cost of justice.
- It fueled widespread anti-Semitism in France and beyond.
- It eventually led to reforms in the French military and judicial system after Dreyfus was exonerated.

3. Nazi Propaganda & Disinformation (1930s–1945)

- **Origin**: Nazi Germany (Joseph Goebbels, Ministry of Public Enlightenment and Propaganda)
- **Goal**: Control public perception, justify war, and demonize enemies

Method: State-controlled media, fabricated reports, and racial pseudoscience

The Nazi regime under Adolf Hitler engaged in one of the most sophisticated disinformation campaigns in history. Led by Joseph Goebbels, Nazi propaganda portrayed Germany as a victim of international conspiracies, justified aggression against neighboring countries, and spread falsehoods about Jewish people, Roma communities, and political dissidents. The regime used newspapers, radio broadcasts, and films to manipulate public opinion.

Impact:

- Disinformation played a critical role in justifying the Holocaust and other war crimes.
- The tactics used by Nazi propagandists influenced modern political communication strategies.
- The legacy of Nazi disinformation continues to fuel extremist ideologies today.

4. The Zinoviev Letter (1924) – Fake Soviet Threat in Britain

- **Origin**: British intelligence operatives (possibly with foreign involvement)
- **Goal**: Undermine the Labour Party before an election

Method: Forged document attributed to a Soviet official

Just days before the 1924 British general election, the British press published a letter supposedly written by Soviet leader Grigory Zinoviev, urging British communists to incite revolution. The letter was later proven to be a forgery, likely created by British intelligence operatives or foreign actors to discredit the Labour Party and prevent it from forming a government.

Impact:

- The scandal contributed to Labour's defeat and reinforced fears of communist influence in Britain.
- It showcased the power of fabricated documents in shaping political outcomes.
- The incident remains one of the earliest examples of election-related disinformation.

5. Operation CHAOS (1967–1974) – CIA Domestic Disinformation

- **Origin**: United States (CIA)
- **Goal**: Discredit anti-war activists and civil rights leaders

Method: Fake news, infiltration, and psychological operations

During the Vietnam War era, the CIA launched Operation CHAOS, an extensive domestic surveillance and disinformation campaign aimed at discrediting anti-war activists, civil rights leaders, and left-wing organizations. The agency planted false stories in the media, fabricated evidence against activists, and conducted covert psychological operations to undermine protest movements.

Impact:

- Led to public distrust in government institutions when exposed in the 1970s.
- Contributed to legal restrictions on domestic intelligence operations.
- Highlighted the ethical concerns surrounding state-sponsored disinformation.

6. The Kuwait Incubator Hoax (1990) – A PR Fabrication for War

- **Origin**: U.S. public relations firm (Hill & Knowlton) and Kuwaiti government
- **Goal**: Justify U.S. intervention in the Gulf War

Method: Fake witness testimony and emotional manipulation

Before the U.S. launched Operation Desert Storm in 1991, a shocking testimony was presented to Congress: a young Kuwaiti girl claimed she had witnessed Iraqi soldiers killing babies in hospital incubators. The story fueled global outrage and helped justify military intervention. However, it was later revealed that the girl was the daughter of the Kuwaiti ambassador to the U.S., and her testimony had been orchestrated by a public relations firm.

Impact:

- The false narrative played a crucial role in rallying public support for war.
- It demonstrated how emotional manipulation can be a powerful disinformation tool.
- It led to greater scrutiny of war-related propaganda efforts.

7. Russian Disinformation in the 2016 U.S. Election

- **Origin**: Russia (Internet Research Agency, state-sponsored actors)
- **Goal**: Influence U.S. political discourse and undermine trust in democracy

Method: Social media manipulation, fake news websites, and hacking leaks

During the 2016 U.S. presidential election, Russian operatives launched an extensive disinformation campaign to influence voters. The Internet Research Agency (IRA) created fake social media accounts, spread divisive content, and amplified conspiracy theories. Additionally, Russian hackers leaked emails from political figures to manipulate public perception.

Impact:

- Increased polarization in American society.
- Raised awareness of foreign influence operations in elections.
- Led to social media reforms and increased scrutiny of political advertising.

Historical disinformation campaigns reveal a pattern of deliberate manipulation, often using emotional appeals, false evidence, and media infiltration to achieve strategic goals. Whether state-sponsored or conducted by private actors, these campaigns have had profound consequences on politics, warfare, and public trust. For OSINT analysts, studying these cases provides valuable insights into the evolving tactics of disinformation and the critical need for verification, critical thinking, and digital literacy in the modern information landscape.

1.6 Case Study: How Disinformation Has Shaped Public Opinion

Disinformation has repeatedly influenced public opinion, shaping societal beliefs, political decisions, and even historical events. Whether through government propaganda, digital influence campaigns, or manipulated media narratives, disinformation has the power to shift perspectives on a massive scale. This case study examines real-world examples of how disinformation has shaped public perception, the methods used to disseminate false narratives, and the lasting impact of these efforts.

Case Study 1: Weapons of Mass Destruction (WMDs) & the 2003 Iraq War

Background

In the early 2000s, the U.S. government, alongside its allies, justified the invasion of Iraq by claiming that Saddam Hussein's regime possessed weapons of mass destruction (WMDs). High-ranking officials and intelligence agencies presented this as a certainty, influencing global public opinion and securing support for military action.

Disinformation Tactics Used

- **Manipulated Intelligence**: Selective use of intelligence reports to support the claim of WMDs.
- **Government & Media Amplification**: Press briefings, speeches, and mainstream media coverage reinforced the narrative.
- **Fear-Based Messaging**: Emphasizing the potential catastrophic threat of WMDs to justify preemptive military action.

Impact on Public Opinion

- The majority of Americans initially supported the Iraq War, believing the WMD claims.

- Many allied nations backed the war effort due to the perceived legitimacy of the intelligence.
- Trust in media and government declined significantly when WMDs were never found.

Long-Term Consequences

- Destabilization of the Middle East: The war led to years of instability, insurgency, and the rise of extremist groups.
- Erosion of Trust in Institutions: The revelation that the WMD claim was misleading damaged the credibility of intelligence agencies and political leaders.
- Increased Skepticism Toward Future Military Interventions: Many citizens and policymakers became more critical of government justifications for war.

Case Study 2: The Cambridge Analytica Scandal & Election Manipulation (2016 U.S. Presidential Election & Brexit)

Background

Cambridge Analytica, a political consulting firm, harvested data from millions of Facebook users without their consent. This data was used to create hyper-targeted political advertisements designed to influence voter behavior in the 2016 U.S. presidential election and the Brexit referendum in the UK.

Disinformation Tactics Used

- **Microtargeted Fake News**: Users were shown highly personalized disinformation campaigns tailored to their fears, biases, and beliefs.
- **Emotional Manipulation**: Ads focused on divisive topics such as immigration, national security, and economic fears.
- **Coordinated Social Media Manipulation**: Fake accounts, bots, and troll farms amplified misleading narratives.

Impact on Public Opinion

- Created deep divisions among voters, reinforcing ideological bubbles.
- Influenced key swing voters by manipulating emotions rather than presenting factual arguments.
- Fueled distrust in democratic institutions, with many questioning the legitimacy of election outcomes.

Long-Term Consequences

- **Increased Regulation of Big Tech**: Governments introduced stricter policies on data privacy and political advertising.
- **Mistrust in Social Media as a News Source**: People became more skeptical of online political content.
- **Greater Awareness of Digital Manipulation**: The scandal raised awareness about psychological profiling and voter manipulation tactics.

Case Study 3: COVID-19 Disinformation & Vaccine Hesitancy

Background

The COVID-19 pandemic saw an explosion of disinformation related to the virus, treatments, and vaccines. Conspiracy theories spread rapidly, leading to widespread public confusion and resistance to health measures.

Disinformation Tactics Used

- **Fabricated Scientific Claims**: False information about vaccine ingredients (e.g., microchips, DNA alteration).
- **Exploitation of Fear and Uncertainty**: Narratives that vaccines were rushed and unsafe.
- **Influence from Alternative Media & Social Media**: Disinformation was spread through fringe websites, YouTube videos, and viral social media posts.

Impact on Public Opinion

- Millions of people refused vaccination, prolonging the pandemic and increasing death tolls.
- Trust in public health institutions declined.
- Political and ideological divisions deepened, with vaccine beliefs becoming highly partisan.

Long-Term Consequences

- **Stronger Fact-Checking Efforts**: Social media platforms implemented stricter content moderation policies.

- **Health Misinformation Became a Global Threat**: Governments and health organizations recognized the dangers of viral medical disinformation.
- **Public Distrust in Future Health Crises**: Many people remain skeptical of future medical guidance due to past disinformation.

These case studies highlight the immense power of disinformation in shaping public opinion, influencing elections, justifying wars, and impacting public health. Whether through state actors, private firms, or viral misinformation campaigns, the ability to manipulate truth has profound societal consequences. OSINT analysts must remain vigilant, developing methods to detect, debunk, and counter disinformation before it further erodes public trust and democratic stability.

2. Identifying Fake News & Deepfakes

The rise of digital media has made distinguishing fact from fiction increasingly difficult, with fake news and deepfakes at the forefront of this challenge. In this chapter, we explore the various forms of fake news, from misleading headlines to entirely fabricated stories, and the methods used to create and propagate them. We also dive into the world of deepfakes—hyper-realistic, AI-generated videos and audio that can deceive even the most discerning viewers. By learning how to spot the red flags and employing OSINT techniques to analyze sources, metadata, and patterns, this chapter equips readers with the skills to uncover deception and defend against the harmful impact of fake news and deepfakes.

2.1 Common Characteristics of Fake News Articles

Fake news is designed to mislead, manipulate, or provoke emotional reactions, often spreading rapidly on social media and other digital platforms. Understanding the common characteristics of fake news articles helps OSINT analysts, journalists, and the general public recognize and debunk misinformation effectively. Below are key features that define fake news and make it distinguishable from credible journalism.

1. Sensationalist & Clickbait Headlines

Fake news articles often use exaggerated, misleading, or emotionally charged headlines to grab attention and encourage clicks. These headlines typically:

- Use all caps or excessive punctuation (e.g., "SHOCKING! You Won't Believe What Happened Next!!!").
- Contain emotionally charged words like "horrifying," "terrifying," or "mind-blowing."
- Make extreme claims without providing evidence (e.g., "Scientists Confirm the Earth Will Explode in 2025!").

Example

- **Legitimate headline**: "Scientists Warn About Climate Change Risks"
- **Fake news headline**: "CLIMATE CHANGE HOAX EXPOSED! ELITES CAUGHT LYING TO CONTROL YOU!!!"

2. Lack of Credible Sources & Anonymous Authors

A major red flag in fake news articles is the absence of credible sources or citations from unverified, anonymous, or biased individuals. Fake news articles often:

- Reference unnamed "experts" or "insiders" without proof.
- Use vague sources like "a source close to the situation" or "some scientists say".
- Rely on fringe websites, blogs, or social media posts instead of academic or journalistic sources.

Example

- **Legitimate article**: "According to the World Health Organization, COVID-19 vaccines are safe and effective."
- **Fake news article**: "A Facebook user named 'TruthWarrior99' exposed that vaccines are dangerous, but the media is covering it up!"

3. Poor Grammar, Spelling Errors, & Unprofessional Layout

Many fake news sites lack editorial oversight, leading to frequent grammatical errors, typos, and unpolished website layouts. Warning signs include:

- Random capitalization and punctuation mistakes.
- Poorly formatted text with excessive bolding or italics.
- Overuse of exclamation points or ALL CAPS.

Example

- **Legitimate news site**: A structured, professional website with clearly cited sources and proper spelling.
- **Fake news site**: A cluttered webpage full of ads, broken links, and articles with obvious spelling mistakes.

4. Strong Bias & Lack of Objectivity

Fake news often promotes one-sided narratives that align with a particular ideology or agenda. These articles:

- Contain no counterarguments or alternative viewpoints.
- Frame stories in an "us vs. them" mentality.
- Use emotionally charged language to provoke outrage or fear.

Example

- **Legitimate article**: "New Tax Policies Proposed by Congress: Pros and Cons"
- **Fake news article**: "The Government Wants to STEAL YOUR MONEY with a NEW TAX SCAM!!!"

5. Manipulated or Out-of-Context Images & Videos

Fake news often uses misleading images or videos to support false claims. These include:

- Photoshop alterations to change the meaning of an image.
- Recycled images from old events passed off as new ones.
- Deepfake videos that manipulate real footage.

Example

- **Legitimate image**: A news article shows an image with proper attribution and context.
- **Fake news image**: A viral post claims a natural disaster just happened but uses an old, unrelated image.

6. Overreliance on Emotional Appeal

Fake news exploits emotions like fear, anger, or excitement to bypass critical thinking. Articles often:

- Use fearmongering ("This new law will DESTROY your freedoms!").
- Invoke anger and outrage ("Politicians are secretly giving your tax dollars to criminals!").
- Appeal to hope or too-good-to-be-true stories ("A simple trick to cure cancer that doctors don't want you to know!").

Example

- **Legitimate news**: "New Study Shows Increase in Crime Rates in Certain Areas."
- **Fake news**: "The GOVERNMENT IS ALLOWING CRIMINALS TO TAKE OVER YOUR CITY!"

7. Fake or Impersonated Websites

Many fake news sources impersonate legitimate news organizations to appear credible. This includes:

- Mimicking domain names (e.g., "CNN-news.com" instead of "CNN.com").
- Copying website designs of trusted media outlets.
- Using misleading social media handles (e.g., @BBCBreakingReal instead of @BBCBreaking).

Example

- **Legitimate site:** BBC.com/news/world
- **Fake site**: BBCnews.co/global-breaking-news

8. Lack of Verifiable Facts or Cited Studies

Fake news articles do not provide verifiable evidence for their claims. Instead, they:

- Cherry-pick data to fit a specific narrative.
- Reference nonexistent studies or reports.
- Misinterpret or misquote scientific findings.

Example

- **Legitimate claim**: "A peer-reviewed study published in the Journal of Medicine found a 10% reduction in heart disease risk."
- **Fake news claim**: "Studies prove that eating chocolate every day cures cancer!" (No source given).

9. Rapid & Widespread Sharing Without Fact-Checking

Fake news spreads quickly on social media because:

- It triggers emotional reactions, making people share it impulsively.
- Bots and coordinated networks amplify false narratives.
- People trust headlines alone without reading full articles.

Example

- **Legitimate news**: A well-researched investigative report that gains traction over time.
- **Fake news**: A viral meme claiming "5G towers spread COVID-19," shared by thousands in hours.

Recognizing fake news requires critical thinking and careful analysis. By identifying sensationalist headlines, lack of credible sources, emotional manipulation, and false imagery, OSINT analysts and the public can mitigate the impact of disinformation. Fact-checking, cross-referencing with reputable sources, and analyzing the credibility of news outlets are essential skills in the fight against misinformation.

2.2 Detecting Clickbait & Sensationalist Content

In the digital era, where information is abundant and attention spans are short, clickbait and sensationalist content have become pervasive tools used to capture eyeballs and drive engagement. However, these tactics often serve as gateways to misinformation and fake news, making it imperative for OSINT analysts and the public alike to learn how to detect them. This subchapter examines the defining characteristics of clickbait and sensationalist content, explores the psychological and technical mechanisms behind their success, and outlines practical methodologies—rooted in open-source intelligence (OSINT)—for identifying and mitigating their impact.

Understanding Clickbait and Sensationalism

At its core, clickbait is designed to exploit human curiosity and emotional impulses. Articles with clickbait titles often promise dramatic revelations or shocking content but fail to deliver on those expectations. Sensationalist content, meanwhile, employs exaggerated language and dramatic imagery to provoke strong emotional responses—fear, anger, or excitement—without necessarily being factually substantiated.

Key Characteristics Include:

- **Exaggerated Headlines**: Titles that make bold, often unverified claims designed to provoke an emotional reaction, such as "You Won't Believe What Happens Next!" or "This Shocking Discovery Will Change Your Life!"
- **Ambiguous or Vague Promises**: Headlines that intentionally withhold key details to entice readers into clicking to satisfy their curiosity.
- **Overuse of Punctuation and Capitalization**: Excessive exclamation points, capital letters, or rhetorical questions intended to grab immediate attention.

- **Emotional Manipulation**: Content crafted to trigger emotional responses rather than present balanced information, often bypassing critical reasoning.

These elements are not merely stylistic choices; they are deliberate tactics to increase click-through rates and generate advertising revenue. In the broader ecosystem of digital media, the incentives for using clickbait and sensationalism are intertwined with social media algorithms that reward engagement, regardless of factual accuracy.

Psychological Drivers Behind Clickbait

Understanding the psychological underpinnings of why people click on sensationalist headlines is crucial for developing effective detection strategies. Several cognitive biases contribute to the success of clickbait:

- **Curiosity Gap**: Humans have an innate desire to fill gaps in their knowledge. A headline that hints at extraordinary information without fully revealing it exploits this gap, compelling readers to click.
- **Emotional Arousal**: Sensationalist headlines often elicit strong emotions, and emotionally charged content is more likely to be shared and remembered.
- **Confirmation Bias**: Readers may be more inclined to engage with content that reinforces their preexisting beliefs, even if the claims are exaggerated or misleading.
- **Social Validation**: When sensational headlines become viral, the sheer volume of engagement can lead others to believe that the information must be important or true.

By understanding these biases, OSINT analysts can better appreciate the appeal of clickbait and design strategies that not only detect but also contextualize such content within the larger information landscape.

Methodologies for Detecting Clickbait and Sensationalism

OSINT offers a range of techniques to identify and analyze clickbait and sensationalist content. The following methods can be integrated into a systematic approach:

Headline Analysis Tools:

- **Linguistic Pattern Recognition**: Automated tools can analyze headlines for patterns typical of clickbait, such as excessive punctuation, hyperbolic adjectives, and vague promises. These tools compare the headline against known clickbait databases to assign a "clickbait score."

- **Sentiment Analysis**: Natural language processing (NLP) algorithms can evaluate the emotional tone of headlines. Overly emotional or polarized language often indicates sensationalism.

Source Credibility Assessment:

- **Domain Verification**: Checking the domain registration and history of the website hosting the content can reveal red flags. Impersonated or newly established domains often correlate with lower credibility.
- **Cross-Referencing With Reputable Outlets**: OSINT analysts can compare the sensationalist content with reports from established news organizations. A lack of corroboration from multiple trusted sources is a strong indicator of clickbait.

Engagement and Network Analysis:

- **Social Media Footprint**: Analyzing how and where a piece of content is being shared can offer insights into its authenticity. Content predominantly circulated through bot networks or by accounts with low credibility should be scrutinized.
- **Content Dissemination Patterns**: Mapping the spread of an article through social media networks can reveal whether the engagement is organic or artificially amplified. High rates of sharing among closely linked groups may suggest coordinated efforts to boost visibility.

Metadata Examination:

- **Image Verification**: Sensationalist articles often use manipulated or recycled images. Tools such as reverse image search (e.g., Google Images, TinEye) can help trace the origins of images and determine whether they are being used out of context.
- **Publication Timestamp Analysis**: Inconsistencies between the publication date and current events can indicate that an article is either outdated or intentionally rehashed to mislead readers.

User Engagement Patterns:

- **Comment Analysis**: Examining the comments section can provide clues about the article's credibility. A disproportionate number of highly emotional responses, without substantive discussion or evidence, can be symptomatic of clickbait.

- **Feedback Loops**: Monitoring user reports and fact-checks on platforms that allow community flagging can help identify and devalue sensational content.

Case Example: The Role of OSINT in Unmasking a Sensationalist Story

Consider a hypothetical example where an online article claims, "Secret Government Program Reveals Alien Life on Earth!" A cursory glance might prompt curiosity-driven clicks, but an OSINT analyst would employ several strategies to evaluate the claim:

- **Headline Analysis**: An automated tool flags the headline for excessive sensationalism due to the use of phrases like "Secret Government Program" and "Alien Life."
- **Source Verification**: A domain lookup reveals that the website was registered only a few months ago and has no history of credible reporting. Cross-referencing with established news outlets shows no corroborating evidence for such a claim.
- **Social Media Analysis**: The article's dissemination is largely confined to a network of accounts that have been flagged for disseminating conspiracy theories, further reducing its credibility.
- **Metadata Check**: Reverse image searches of any accompanying visuals reveal that the images are taken from unrelated science fiction movies, not actual government leaks or credible sources.
- **User Engagement Analysis**: Comments are overwhelmingly emotional with little substantive critique, suggesting that the content is intended more to provoke than inform.

This multi-layered approach, which leverages OSINT tools and techniques, helps analysts cut through the hype and identify content that is not only misleading but potentially harmful if left unchecked.

Mitigating the Impact of Clickbait

While detection is the first step, mitigating the influence of clickbait and sensationalist content is equally important. Strategies include:

- **Educational Campaigns**: Promoting digital literacy and critical thinking among the public can reduce susceptibility to sensationalist headlines.
- **Platform Accountability**: Encouraging social media platforms and search engines to refine their algorithms to prioritize verified content over clickbait can help curb the spread of misinformation.

- **Collaborative Fact-Checking**: Integrating OSINT findings with community-based fact-checking initiatives can create a robust defense against sensationalist narratives.

Detecting clickbait and sensationalist content is a critical component of the broader fight against disinformation and fake news. By understanding the linguistic cues, psychological drivers, and technical patterns associated with these tactics, OSINT analysts can develop sophisticated tools and methodologies to identify and neutralize misleading content. As digital media continues to evolve, a vigilant, multi-pronged approach that combines automated tools with human expertise will be essential to safeguard public discourse and ensure that the truth prevails in an increasingly noisy information landscape.

Through rigorous analysis and proactive countermeasures, it is possible to reduce the impact of clickbait and sensationalism, ultimately fostering a more informed and resilient society.

2.3 Reverse Image & Video Searching for Verification

In an era where misinformation spreads rapidly through manipulated images and videos, reverse image and video searching have become essential tools for verifying content authenticity. OSINT analysts, journalists, and fact-checkers rely on these methods to trace media back to their origins, detect manipulation, and debunk fake news. This subchapter explores the mechanics of reverse searching, outlines practical methodologies, and discusses real-world applications for investigating disinformation.

Understanding Reverse Image & Video Search

What is Reverse Image Search?

Reverse image search is a technique that allows users to upload or input the URL of an image to find its original source and other instances of the same or similar image online. This helps verify:

- The original context of an image.
- Whether the image has been altered or manipulated.
- If the image is being misused in a misleading narrative.

What is Reverse Video Search?

Reverse video search follows a similar principle but involves analyzing frames from a video to:

- Identify the original source of a video.
- Detect whether a video has been edited, cropped, or deepfaked.
- Cross-check instances where the same footage has been misrepresented in different contexts.

These methods are particularly useful in combating fake news, as misleading images and videos are often repurposed to fabricate events or exaggerate narratives.

Tools for Reverse Image & Video Searching

Several online tools and platforms enable reverse image and video searching. These can be categorized into search engines, AI-driven analysis tools, and OSINT-specific platforms.

- Reverse Image Search Tools
- Google Reverse Image Search
- Accessible via Google Images.
- Allows users to upload an image or paste an image URL to find related content.

TinEye

- A dedicated reverse image search engine that tracks where an image appears online.
- Useful for identifying stock images or checking for image modifications.

Yandex Image Search

- More advanced in facial recognition and object detection, often retrieving different results than Google.
- Particularly useful for tracking images from Russia and Eastern Europe.

Bing Visual Search

- Similar to Google but sometimes indexes different sources.
- Reverse Video Search Tools & Techniques

InVID & WeVerify

- A browser extension specifically designed for verifying videos.
- Extracts key frames from a video, allowing them to be reverse-searched using Google, Yandex, or TinEye.
- Provides metadata analysis to detect video tampering.

Google Lens

- Can be used for frame-by-frame analysis of video screenshots.
- YouTube DataViewer (Amnesty International)
- Retrieves metadata from YouTube videos, including upload dates and timestamps.

FFmpeg (For OSINT Experts)

- A command-line tool that allows analysts to extract frames from videos manually for reverse searching.

Step-by-Step Guide: Conducting Reverse Image & Video Search

Reverse Image Search Methodology

Obtain the Image:

Download the image or copy its URL.

Select a Reverse Search Tool:

Use Google Images, TinEye, or Yandex for best results.

Upload or Paste the URL:

Drag and drop the image into the search box or enter the image URL.

Analyze Search Results:

- Look at the earliest known instances of the image.
- Check for variations or edited versions.
- Identify if the image has been misused (e.g., an old war photo repurposed for a fake recent event).

Reverse Video Search Methodology

Extract Key Frames:

- Use InVID to break a video into individual frames.
- If unavailable, manually capture screenshots at different timestamps.

Perform a Reverse Image Search for Each Frame:

Upload frames to Google, Yandex, or TinEye.

Check Metadata (If Available):

Use YouTube DataViewer or FFmpeg to extract upload dates and descriptions.

Compare Findings:

Determine whether the video was repurposed or manipulated.

Real-World Applications of Reverse Image & Video Search

1. Debunking Misattributed Images in Fake News

Example: During a natural disaster, misleading social media posts often use old images from previous events to exaggerate the current situation. Reverse image search can trace these images back to their original publication, proving their inaccuracy.

2. Exposing Deepfake Videos

Example: Political disinformation campaigns sometimes use deepfake videos to spread false narratives. By reverse-searching extracted frames, analysts can find the original footage and detect manipulated content.

3. Verifying Eyewitness Reports

Example: A viral video claims to show an explosion in a war zone, but a reverse search reveals that the footage was originally uploaded years earlier from a different location. This method helps separate real-time events from fabricated news.

4. Tracking Propaganda and Influence Campaigns

Example: Governments and organizations use staged or misleading imagery to push political agendas. Reverse image search helps uncover patterns of repeated use of such media across various channels.

Challenges & Limitations of Reverse Searching

1. Image Manipulation & Editing

- Cropping, mirroring, or altering an image's colors can prevent accurate reverse searching.
- Advanced AI tools can detect modifications, but some manipulations may still evade detection.

2. Watermarks & Overlays

- Fake news creators often add watermarks or text overlays to obscure the original source.
- Tools like PhotoForensics can help detect image alterations.

3. Encrypted & Private Networks

- Some misleading images/videos circulate exclusively on private groups (e.g., Telegram, WhatsApp), making it difficult to reverse search.

4. Limited Video Reverse Search Tools

- While reverse image search is widely available, video search capabilities are still limited, requiring frame-by-frame extraction.

Future of Reverse Image & Video Verification in OSINT

With advances in AI-driven verification, the future of reverse searching looks promising. Emerging technologies such as machine learning algorithms for deepfake detection and blockchain-based image authentication will enhance the reliability of OSINT investigations.

Key Developments to Watch:

- AI-enhanced reverse search engines capable of detecting altered images with higher accuracy.
- Automated deepfake detection tools that analyze facial distortions and inconsistencies in video metadata.
- Decentralized verification systems that use blockchain to track image authenticity from its source.
- As misinformation tactics evolve, OSINT analysts must stay ahead by integrating new tools and methodologies into their verification processes.

Reverse image and video searching remain critical techniques in digital verification and OSINT investigations. By leveraging search engines, metadata analysis, and AI-driven tools, analysts can effectively trace media origins, debunk fake news, and combat disinformation campaigns. While challenges exist, continuous advancements in technology and collaborative efforts among fact-checkers and researchers will ensure that the fight against visual misinformation remains robust.

By mastering these techniques, OSINT professionals can strengthen media literacy, protect public discourse, and promote truth in an increasingly manipulated digital landscape.

2.4 Deepfake Technology: How It Works & How to Detect It

Deepfake technology has rapidly evolved, making it increasingly difficult to distinguish real from fake media. These AI-generated videos, images, and audio clips are often used to manipulate public opinion, create political disinformation, and spread fake news. For OSINT analysts, journalists, and cybersecurity professionals, understanding how deepfakes work and how to detect them is crucial in the fight against misinformation.

This subchapter explores the mechanics of deepfake technology, its real-world applications (both legitimate and malicious), and advanced detection methods used to verify authenticity.

Understanding Deepfake Technology

What is a Deepfake?

A deepfake is a synthetic media creation that uses deep learning algorithms to alter or replace visual and audio content. Unlike traditional media editing, deepfakes use

Generative Adversarial Networks (GANs) and autoencoders to create hyper-realistic manipulations.

How Deepfakes Are Created

Data Collection:

- AI systems require large datasets of images or audio from a target person.
- Publicly available content, such as social media posts and videos, is often used.

Face Mapping & Feature Extraction:

The AI identifies key facial features and expressions from source footage.

Training the AI (GANs & Autoencoders):

Generative Adversarial Networks (GANs): A deep learning model consisting of two networks:

- **Generator**: Creates fake images or videos.
- **Discriminator**: Evaluates authenticity and forces the generator to improve.
- **Autoencoders**: Compress and reconstruct images to match the target face seamlessly.

Face Swapping & Lip Synchronization:

- The AI aligns the target's face and expressions with the new content.
- Voice synthesis may be used to mimic speech patterns.

Post-Processing & Refinement:

- Developers use editing tools to remove inconsistencies, improving the realism of the final product.
- Deepfake technology continues to improve, with more sophisticated models reducing detection artifacts and making synthetic content nearly indistinguishable from reality.

Legitimate & Malicious Uses of Deepfakes

Legitimate Applications

- **Film & Entertainment**: Actors' faces can be digitally altered for movies or CGI effects.
- **Education & Accessibility**: AI-generated speech and visuals help create language translations and accessibility tools.
- **Corporate Training & AI Assistants**: Virtual AI avatars are used in training simulations and customer service.

Malicious Uses in Misinformation & Disinformation

- **Political Manipulation**: Deepfakes of politicians can be used to create false statements or fabricate scandals.
- **Reputation Damage**: Individuals have been falsely depicted in compromising situations, leading to blackmail or defamation.
- **Social Engineering & Fraud**: Cybercriminals use AI-generated voices and videos to impersonate CEOs or government officials in scams.
- **Fake News Amplification**: Deepfakes are used to strengthen false narratives, creating confusion in public discourse.

Given these risks, developing effective deepfake detection strategies is essential for OSINT investigations.

How to Detect Deepfakes: OSINT & AI-Driven Methods

Deepfake detection requires a combination of manual analysis, AI-assisted tools, and forensic techniques. Below are the most effective methods for identifying deepfake content.

1. Visual & Physical Inconsistencies

Manually analyzing deepfake videos and images can reveal subtle artifacts:

- **Unnatural Eye Movement & Blinking**: Many deepfakes struggle with realistic blinking patterns or fail to replicate natural eye motion.
- **Asymmetrical Facial Features**: Real faces are naturally asymmetrical, but deepfakes may exhibit inconsistent alignment.
- **Lip-Sync Errors**: Mouth movements may not align perfectly with spoken words, especially in voice-synthesized deepfakes.

- **Skin Texture & Lighting Issues**: AI-generated faces may have blurred skin textures, inconsistent lighting, or unnatural shadows.

2. Audio Forensics & Voice Analysis

Deepfake audio can be detected by examining speech patterns and voice inconsistencies:

- **Robotic or Metallic Tones**: AI-generated voices sometimes lack natural pitch variation.
- **Lack of Breathing Sounds**: Human speech naturally includes small pauses for breathing, which deepfakes may miss.
- **Overly Perfect Pronunciations**: AI-generated voices may sound "too perfect" compared to natural human speech.

Detection Tools:

- **Resemble.AI & ElevenLabs**: Can compare synthetic and real voices.
- **Adobe VoCo Detection Tools**: Help analyze manipulated voice recordings.

3. Metadata & File Analysis

Examining metadata (EXIF data) can help identify manipulated media:

- **Inconsistent Timestamps**: If metadata indicates multiple editing timestamps, the file may have been altered.
- **Camera & Software Mismatch**: Original media should have camera model details, while AI-generated images may lack this information.

Detection Tools:

- **FotoForensics**: Extracts metadata and highlights anomalies.
- **Forensic Scanner**: Identifies inconsistencies in video encoding.

4. Reverse Image & Frame-by-Frame Analysis

- **Reverse Image Search (Google, TinEye, Yandex):** Helps trace an image's origin to determine whether it was modified.
- **InVID & WeVerify**: Extracts key frames from videos and cross-references them with known sources.

Steps:

- Extract key frames from a video.
- Perform a reverse image search for each frame.
- Analyze inconsistencies in facial features and background details.

5. AI-Powered Deepfake Detection Tools

- **Microsoft Video Authenticator**: Uses AI to assign a "fake probability score" to videos.
- **Deepware Scanner**: Analyzes deepfake videos for facial inconsistencies.
- **Sensity AI**: Provides real-time deepfake detection services.

These tools use machine learning models trained to recognize deepfake artifacts that may not be visible to the human eye.

Real-World Examples of Deepfake Disinformation

Case 1: Political Deepfake Manipulation

In 2020, a deepfake video of a world leader surfaced online, depicting them making controversial statements they never actually said. OSINT analysts debunked the video using frame-by-frame analysis and lip-sync detection to prove it was AI-generated.

Case 2: Financial Fraud via AI Voice Cloning

A cybercriminal used deepfake voice cloning to impersonate a CEO and trick employees into transferring $35 million to a fraudulent account. Investigators analyzed audio inconsistencies and metadata to confirm the scam.

Case 3: Fake News Amplified with AI-Generated Video

A fake news network used AI-generated news anchors to spread propaganda. OSINT researchers exposed the operation by analyzing unnatural facial expressions and reverse-searching key frames.

Challenges in Deepfake Detection

Despite advancements in detection, deepfake technology continues to evolve. Key challenges include:

- **More Sophisticated AI Models**: Advanced deepfakes are reducing detectable artifacts.
- **Rapid Dissemination on Social Media**: Fake content spreads quickly, making real-time verification difficult.
- **Lack of Standardized Detection Methods**: While AI tools help, manual verification remains essential.

The ongoing development of blockchain-based authentication and deepfake-resistant AI models may help counteract these challenges.

Deepfake technology poses significant challenges in the fight against disinformation. While AI-generated videos and voices become increasingly convincing, OSINT analysts can stay ahead by leveraging AI detection tools, forensic analysis, and manual verification techniques. By integrating deepfake detection into investigative workflows, the risk of misinformation influencing public opinion can be minimized.

As technology evolves, a combination of technological solutions, media literacy, and policy regulations will be essential in combating deepfake-based disinformation in the digital age.

2.5 Analyzing AI-Generated Content & Synthetic Media

As artificial intelligence (AI) continues to advance, the ability to generate synthetic media—content created entirely by AI—has become increasingly sophisticated. AI-generated text, images, videos, and audio can be used for various purposes, both legitimate (such as creative applications and automation) and malicious (such as disinformation, deepfakes, and fake news). For OSINT analysts, understanding how to detect and analyze synthetic media is crucial in combating misinformation and verifying digital content.

This subchapter explores how AI-generated content works, common manipulation techniques, methods for detecting synthetic media, and real-world case studies where AI was used to create deceptive content.

Understanding AI-Generated Content & Synthetic Media

What is Synthetic Media?

Synthetic media refers to digital content created, modified, or enhanced using artificial intelligence. Unlike traditional media manipulation (e.g., Photoshop editing), synthetic media is generated through deep learning models that can create realistic human faces, voices, videos, and even full articles.

Types of AI-Generated Content

Type of Synthetic Media	Description	Examples
AI-Generated Text	AI models create human-like text.	Chatbots, fake news articles, AI-generated reviews.
AI-Generated Images	AI creates realistic or altered images.	Deepfake portraits, GAN-generated stock photos.
AI-Generated Videos	AI modifies or generates videos.	Deepfake political speeches, synthetic influencers.
AI-Generated Audio	AI mimics human speech.	AI-generated podcasts, fake voice recordings.

These AI-generated elements can be used to create convincing disinformation campaigns that are difficult to detect without proper forensic techniques.

How AI-Generated Content Works

Key Technologies Behind Synthetic Media

Generative Adversarial Networks (GANs)

A deep learning model with two AI components:

- Generator: Creates fake images, videos, or text.
- Discriminator: Evaluates the generated content and forces improvements.
- Used in fake profile pictures, deepfakes, and AI art.

Natural Language Processing (NLP) & Large Language Models (LLMs)

- AI models like ChatGPT, GPT-4, and Bard generate text that mimics human writing.
- Used in fake news generation, AI-written propaganda, and automated misinformation campaigns.

AI-Based Voice Synthesis & Cloning

- AI can generate synthetic voices that mimic real people.
- Used in voice phishing, CEO fraud, and fake political statements.

Diffusion Models & Neural Rendering

- AI generates high-quality images and videos from text prompts.
- Used in fake news graphics, propaganda posters, and AI-generated influencers.

With these technologies, AI can create hyper-realistic media that is difficult to distinguish from authentic content.

Detecting AI-Generated Content: OSINT Methods & Tools

1. Identifying AI-Generated Text

AI-generated text is becoming increasingly sophisticated, but there are still detectable patterns and anomalies:

- **Repetitive phrases & unnatural coherence**: AI text often lacks real-world context and may repeat phrases.
- **Overly formal or vague responses**: Some AI models produce factually correct but vague content.
- **Sudden topic shifts & logical inconsistencies**: AI-generated articles may lack a coherent argument.

Detection Tools for AI-Generated Text

- **GPTZero** – AI-generated text detection tool.
- **OpenAI AI Classifier** – Detects text written by large language models.
- **Copyleaks AI Detector** – Analyzes whether a document is AI-generated.

2. Identifying AI-Generated Images

AI-generated images, especially those created with GANs, often exhibit visual artifacts:

- **Asymmetrical facial features**: Eyes, ears, and earrings may be uneven.
- **Background distortions**: GAN-generated images may have warped backgrounds.
- **Unnatural reflections & lighting**: AI struggles to replicate real-world physics.

Detection Tools for AI-Generated Images

- **ThisPersonDoesNotExist.com** – Generates AI-created human faces.
- **Fake Profile Detector (PimEyes & FaceCheck)** – Detects GAN-generated faces.
- **GAN Detector (Mayachitra)** – Identifies AI-generated images.

3. Identifying AI-Generated Videos & Deepfakes

AI-generated videos (deepfakes) often include subtle inconsistencies:

- Blurry or unnatural facial movements.
- Mismatched lip sync.
- Lack of blinking or unnatural eye movement.

Detection Tools for AI-Generated Videos

- **InVID & WeVerify** – Extracts frames for reverse image searching.
- **Deepware Scanner** – Detects deepfake videos.
- **Microsoft Video Authenticator** – Assigns a probability score for deepfake detection.

4. Identifying AI-Generated Audio

AI-generated voice synthesis is increasingly difficult to detect, but some artifacts remain:

- Lack of breathing sounds.
- Unnatural pauses and emphasis.
- Metallic or robotic tones.

Detection Tools for AI-Generated Audio

- **Resemble.AI Voice Detector** – Identifies AI-generated voices.
- **Adobe VoCo Detection Tools** – Analyzes voice modifications.

Real-World Cases of AI-Generated Disinformation

Case 1: AI-Generated Fake News Articles

In 2023, AI-written news articles were used in a disinformation campaign to spread false political narratives. Analysts used GPTZero and metadata analysis to confirm AI authorship.

Case 2: AI-Generated Political Deepfake

A deepfake video of a world leader was circulated online, claiming they had made inflammatory statements. Fact-checkers used InVID and Microsoft Video Authenticator to debunk the fake.

Case 3: AI-Generated Social Media Bots

Thousands of AI-generated Twitter/X accounts used GAN-created profile pictures to push propaganda. OSINT researchers detected them using face asymmetry analysis and reverse image searches.

Challenges in Detecting AI-Generated Content

Despite progress in deepfake and AI-generated content detection, several challenges remain:

- **AI Continues to Improve** – New deepfake models are harder to detect.
- **Automated Content Flooding** – AI can generate massive amounts of disinformation rapidly.
- **Limited Public Awareness** – Many people cannot distinguish real from AI-generated content.
- **Lack of Standardized Verification Methods** – While AI tools help, manual verification remains essential.

Future Solutions

- **Blockchain-based verification** – Watermarking authentic content.
- **Advanced AI detection models** – AI that can detect its own fakes.
- **Stronger media literacy efforts** – Educating the public about synthetic media.

AI-generated content and synthetic media present both opportunities and threats in the digital landscape. While they have legitimate uses in entertainment, accessibility, and automation, they also enable disinformation, fraud, and political manipulation.

For OSINT analysts, mastering detection techniques—including text analysis, deepfake detection, reverse image searches, and metadata forensics—is essential to combat AI-driven disinformation. As synthetic media continues to evolve, a combination of advanced tools, AI detection models, and public awareness efforts will be necessary to preserve the integrity of digital information.

2.6 Case Study: Investigating a Viral Deepfake Video

In an era where artificial intelligence (AI) can generate hyper-realistic videos, deepfakes have emerged as a powerful tool for both legitimate applications and malicious disinformation campaigns. From manipulated political speeches to fabricated celebrity endorsements, deepfake videos have been used to mislead the public, spread propaganda, and even commit fraud. This case study delves into an OSINT (Open-Source Intelligence) investigation of a viral deepfake video, demonstrating the tools, techniques, and methodologies used to uncover its true origins and intentions.

Background: The Viral Deepfake Video

In early 2024, a video began circulating on social media featuring a prominent world leader seemingly making inflammatory statements about an ongoing geopolitical crisis. The video quickly gained traction, accumulating millions of views within hours. It was widely shared by both mainstream media outlets and anonymous social media accounts, leading to heightened political tensions.

However, skepticism arose among analysts and journalists who noticed slight irregularities in the video. Some viewers pointed out unnatural facial movements and audio mismatches, prompting OSINT investigators to begin verifying its authenticity.

Initial Clues Indicating a Possible Deepfake

- Slightly unnatural lip movements when compared to real footage of the leader.
- Inconsistent lighting and skin texture in certain frames.
- Lack of source attribution—no credible news agency reported the video's release.
- Anomalous metadata—file properties suggested it was created using AI-based software.

Step 1: Collecting & Preserving the Evidence

Before beginning the analysis, investigators followed OSINT best practices by preserving the evidence:

- Downloading the original video from multiple sources (Twitter/X, YouTube, Telegram).
- Extracting key frames using InVID & WeVerify, a tool designed for forensic analysis.
- Archiving the video using Wayback Machine and archive.is to ensure traceability.
- Checking video metadata to identify inconsistencies in timestamps and encoding software.

Step 2: Reverse Image & Frame Analysis

To verify if the video was manipulated from existing footage, investigators conducted a reverse image search on key frames:

- Using Google Reverse Image Search, TinEye, and Yandex, analysts uploaded stills from the video to check for earlier versions of the footage.
- The search results revealed that the video closely resembled an older speech given by the same leader three years prior, but with different wording.
- The mouth movements did not match the original speech, raising suspicion that AI had altered the lip-syncing.

Conclusion from Frame Analysis

The video was likely manipulated using deepfake lip-syncing AI to modify the leader's words.
It was based on authentic archival footage but altered to convey a different message.

Step 3: Audio Forensics & Voice Analysis

Next, the investigation focused on analyzing the voice and audio quality to detect deepfake-generated speech.

Spectrogram Analysis:

- Using forensic tools like Adobe VoCo Forensics and Resemble.AI, investigators analyzed the voice waveform for signs of AI synthesis.
- Results showed anomalies in pitch variation and unnatural pauses, which are common in AI-generated speech.

AI Speech Pattern Detection:

- Analysts compared the voice to the leader's authentic speeches using ElevenLabs voice synthesis detection.
- The software detected a 99% match with AI-generated voices, confirming it was artificially created.

Lack of Natural Breathing Sounds:

- In real speech, subtle breathing sounds occur between sentences.
- The deepfake audio lacked these natural inhalation patterns, further proving it was synthetic.

Conclusion from Audio Forensics

- The voice was AI-generated rather than genuine, reinforcing the theory that this was a deepfake.
- The speech did not match any real statements previously made by the leader.

Step 4: Deepfake Detection & Facial Analysis

To confirm whether the video was AI-generated, analysts conducted facial forensics using deepfake detection software.

Key Findings from Deepfake Analysis

Blinking Patterns:

- Human blinking follows a natural rhythm, typically 15–20 blinks per minute.
- The subject in the video blinked irregularly—often too little, which is common in deepfakes.

Facial Microexpressions & Artifacts:

- When analyzed with Microsoft Video Authenticator, the software flagged minor distortions around the mouth and eyes, indicating AI manipulation.
- Certain frames showed glitches in lighting consistency, a telltale sign of deepfake rendering.

Frame-by-Frame Analysis:

- Using Deepware Scanner, analysts noticed pixelation artifacts around the mouth, where the deepfake overlay was most likely applied.

Conclusion from Deepfake Detection

- The facial expressions and lip movements did not align perfectly with natural human speech.
- The video was confirmed to be a deepfake, generated using lip-sync deepfake AI.

Step 5: Tracing the Source & Disinformation Network

Once the deepfake was confirmed, OSINT analysts traced its origin to uncover the responsible parties.

Tracking Social Media Distribution:

- Using Hoaxy & TruthNest, analysts mapped how the video spread.
- They found that the first accounts to post the video were anonymous, bot-like accounts from a suspicious network.

Checking Network Coordination:

- Using Botometer, analysts identified that many accounts sharing the video exhibited bot-like behavior (e.g., high posting frequency, repetitive messaging).
- Several accounts were traced back to a disinformation operation linked to a foreign influence campaign.

Dark Web & Source Verification:

- Searching dark web forums and Telegram channels, OSINT specialists found discussions about creating and distributing the deepfake weeks before it went viral.
- This suggested a coordinated disinformation effort, likely aimed at political destabilization.

Key Takeaways from the Investigation

✅ The video was a deepfake, confirmed through frame analysis, AI voice detection, and forensic facial analysis.

✅ The voice was AI-generated, lacking natural speech patterns.

✅ The video originated from a past speech, proving the manipulation.

✅ A coordinated bot network amplified the deepfake, indicating an organized disinformation campaign.

✅ The campaign was traced to a foreign entity, showing geopolitical influence efforts.

Lessons for OSINT Analysts & Fact-Checkers

- Always archive and verify metadata before analyzing a viral video.
- Use reverse image searches & deepfake detection tools to spot AI manipulations.
- Monitor bot networks & social media amplification patterns to identify disinformation campaigns.
- Collaborate with journalists, cybersecurity experts, and AI researchers to strengthen verification methods.

Conclusion: The Power & Threat of Deepfakes

This case study highlights the growing threat of AI-generated disinformation and the critical role of OSINT in media verification. As deepfake technology advances, governments, fact-checkers, and intelligence analysts must stay ahead with better detection tools and collaborative efforts.

By applying forensic techniques, AI-assisted detection, and OSINT methodologies, investigators can expose digital deception and safeguard public trust in information.

3. Social Media Disinformation Tactics

Social media platforms have become the primary battleground for disinformation, with malicious actors exploiting their vast reach to influence public opinion and create chaos. This chapter delves into the tactics used to spread disinformation on social media, from the creation of fake accounts and bots to the manipulation of algorithms and echo chambers. We explore the strategies behind viral misinformation campaigns, including hashtag hijacking, coordinated inauthentic behavior, and targeted ad buys. By understanding these tactics, readers will learn how to use OSINT tools to track and expose disinformation campaigns, while also gaining insight into the digital behaviors that enable them to thrive.

3.1 How Fake News Spreads on Social Media

Fake news has become one of the most potent tools for manipulating public opinion, influencing elections, and shaping narratives in today's digital landscape. Social media platforms play a crucial role in amplifying disinformation, often making it difficult for users to differentiate between fact and fiction. Unlike traditional media, which has editorial oversight and fact-checking processes, social media allows anyone to publish, share, and promote information instantly, creating a fertile ground for fake news to spread.

This subchapter explores why and how fake news spreads on social media, examining key mechanisms, psychological drivers, platform algorithms, and real-world examples to illustrate how misinformation gains traction.

The Viral Nature of Fake News

Fake news spreads faster and wider than factual news due to several psychological and algorithmic factors:

1. Emotional Appeal & Confirmation Bias

- Fake news is often designed to evoke strong emotions—fear, anger, or excitement—prompting people to share it without verification.
- Confirmation bias leads users to believe and share content that aligns with their existing views, regardless of its accuracy.

2. Algorithmic Amplification & Engagement-Based Rankings

- Social media platforms use engagement-driven algorithms that prioritize content based on likes, shares, and comments.
- Fake news often gets higher engagement than factual content because it is sensational, polarizing, and emotionally charged.
- This creates an echo chamber effect, reinforcing false narratives within specific online communities.

3. Influence of Bots, Trolls & Coordinated Campaigns

- Automated bots and fake accounts help amplify fake news by generating artificial engagement.
- Troll farms and disinformation networks strategically push false stories to influence public discourse.

4. Lack of Immediate Fact-Checking

- False information spreads six times faster than true news, according to MIT research.
- Fact-checking organizations cannot keep up with the volume and speed of viral misinformation.

Key Mechanisms Behind Fake News Spread

1. Social Media Algorithms & Filter Bubbles

Social media feeds are personalized based on user behavior, creating filter bubbles where users are exposed only to content that reinforces their beliefs.

Example: If a user frequently engages with conspiracy theories, the platform will continue showing similar content, reinforcing their false beliefs.

2. The Role of Influencers & Echo Chambers

Influencers and online personalities with large followings can legitimize fake news by sharing it with their audiences.

Example: A celebrity tweets a misleading headline, and it instantly reaches millions of followers who trust their opinion without verifying the claim.

3. Bot Networks & Fake Accounts

Bots amplify fake news by mass-posting, commenting, and engaging with false content to increase its visibility.

Example: A fake news story about a political candidate is tweeted thousands of times by bot accounts, making it appear as a trending topic.

4. Clickbait & Sensationalism

Headlines designed to shock, outrage, or surprise attract more clicks, leading users to spread misinformation before reading or verifying it.

Example: "Breaking: Government Bans All Private Vehicles Starting Next Week!"—a false claim designed to provoke panic and engagement.

5. Deepfake Videos & AI-Generated Content

Advanced AI tools allow the creation of fake videos, images, and voice recordings that make disinformation even more convincing.

Example: A deepfake video surfaces showing a political leader "saying" something they never did, influencing voter opinions.

Case Study: The Infodemic During COVID-19

During the COVID-19 pandemic, misinformation spread rapidly through social media, influencing public behavior and policies.

Fake News Example:

- A viral WhatsApp message claimed that drinking hot water and lemon could cure COVID-19.
- The message was widely shared in multiple languages across different countries.
- Despite efforts by health organizations to debunk it, the false remedy continued circulating, delaying proper medical intervention for many.

How It Spread:

✓ Emotional Appeal: Played on fear and desperation.

☑ Viral Messaging Apps: Spread quickly through WhatsApp, making it harder to track.

☑ Influencer Endorsements: Some public figures unknowingly shared the misinformation.

This case highlights how misinformation can have real-world consequences, making the fight against fake news more urgent than ever.

Strategies to Identify & Counter Fake News

For Users & Researchers

🔍 **Check the Source**: Is it a credible news organization?
📷 **Reverse Image Search**: Verify if an image or video has been manipulated.
🖥 **Compare with Reputable Outlets**: Cross-check news with fact-checking websites.
🚫 **Avoid Sharing Before Verifying**: Even if it aligns with your beliefs.

For OSINT Analysts & Investigators

📊 **Use Social Media Analysis Tools**: Hoaxy, Botometer, and CrowdTangle help track disinformation patterns.
🔲 **Detect Bots & Coordinated Networks**: Look for unusual activity spikes, automated posting patterns, and AI-generated accounts.
🔗 **Analyze Metadata & Digital Fingerprints**: Verify the authenticity of viral content through forensic analysis.

Conclusion: The Future of Fake News on Social Media

Fake news is evolving alongside technology, with AI-generated content making it harder to detect. However, by combining critical thinking, OSINT methodologies, and fact-checking tools, users and analysts can combat digital deception.

As social media continues to shape public opinion, raising awareness, improving digital literacy, and holding platforms accountable will be essential in mitigating the harmful effects of misinformation.

3.2 The Role of Algorithms in Amplifying Misinformation

In the digital age, algorithms play a pivotal role in determining what content users see on social media platforms. While these algorithms are designed to enhance user experience by prioritizing engaging and relevant content, they also have unintended consequences— one of the most concerning being the amplification of misinformation and fake news.

This subchapter explores how social media algorithms contribute to the spread of misinformation, the mechanics behind their decision-making, and real-world examples illustrating their impact. Finally, we will discuss strategies for mitigating algorithm-driven misinformation using OSINT (Open-Source Intelligence) techniques and fact-checking tools.

How Algorithms Shape Information Consumption

Social media algorithms sort, rank, and recommend content based on user behavior, platform policies, and engagement patterns. These algorithms analyze:

✓ **User Interactions**: Likes, shares, comments, watch time, and clicks.
✓ **Content Type & Format**: Videos, images, memes, or text posts.
✓ **Virality & Engagement Metrics**: The number of people engaging with a post within a short time.
✓ **Network & Social Connections**: Content that is popular within a user's community.

While this system is efficient for delivering personalized content, it also creates an environment where misinformation spreads rapidly due to engagement-driven ranking mechanisms.

Why Do Algorithms Amplify Misinformation?

1. Engagement Over Accuracy

- Algorithms prioritize content that generates the most engagement, regardless of its accuracy.
- Fake news is often more sensational and emotionally charged, making it more likely to be shared.
- Studies have shown that false information spreads six times faster than real news on platforms like Twitter (now X).

★ **Example**: A fake tweet claiming a celebrity had died went viral within minutes, despite being false. The more people interacted with it, the more Twitter's algorithm promoted it.

2. The Filter Bubble Effect

- Social media platforms use personalization algorithms that show users content they are more likely to engage with.
- Over time, this traps users in echo chambers, reinforcing their existing beliefs while filtering out opposing views.
- This makes it easier for misinformation campaigns to target specific groups, as people see only content that aligns with their biases.

📌 **Example**: During the 2020 U.S. elections, Facebook's algorithm created ideological bubbles, where users who engaged with conspiracy theories continued to see more election-related misinformation.

3. Virality & The Snowball Effect

- Once misinformation gains initial traction, it gets boosted by recommendation algorithms, reaching a massive audience.
- Even after being debunked, the false information continues circulating, as algorithms keep suggesting similar content.
- Corrective content (fact-checks) rarely spreads as fast as the original misinformation.

📌 **Example**: A fake news article falsely claiming that "5G towers cause COVID-19" was heavily shared. YouTube and Facebook's recommendation systems kept suggesting related conspiracy videos, further spreading the false narrative.

4. Algorithmic Bias & Manipulation

- Some disinformation campaigns exploit algorithmic weaknesses to manipulate trends and search results.
- Coordinated bot networks artificially boost engagement, tricking algorithms into promoting misleading content.
- Certain keywords and hashtags are used strategically to ensure false information ranks higher in search results.

📌 **Example**: During the Russian disinformation campaigns of 2016, bot accounts flooded Twitter with fake news, manipulating trending topics to make false narratives appear credible.

5. Monetization of Misinformation

- Social media platforms profit from engagement, meaning viral misinformation often generates more ad revenue.
- Some fake news websites create clickbait content to maximize ad clicks and shares, exploiting algorithms for financial gain.
- Platforms have incentives to keep users engaged, even if that means recommending controversial or misleading content.

📌 **Example**: Fake health news websites spreading false COVID-19 cures made millions in ad revenue before being banned by Google and Facebook.

Real-World Cases of Algorithmic Misinformation Amplification

Case Study 1: Facebook's Role in Myanmar's Rohingya Crisis

- In 2018, Facebook's algorithm amplified hate speech targeting Myanmar's Rohingya Muslim population.
- Misinformation and incitement posts spread unchecked, fueling violence and ethnic cleansing.
- A UN report later blamed Facebook for failing to curb the spread of harmful misinformation, which contributed to real-world violence.

Case Study 2: YouTube's Radicalization Problem

- YouTube's autoplay and recommendation algorithm often pushes users toward increasingly extreme content.
- A study found that users watching mild conspiracy videos were quickly led to more extreme misinformation within a few recommendations.
- This "radicalization pipeline" has been exploited by extremist groups and conspiracy theorists to grow their influence.

How OSINT Analysts & Fact-Checkers Combat Algorithmic Misinformation

While algorithms amplify misinformation, OSINT techniques and digital forensics can help counteract it.

1. Identifying Algorithmic Manipulation

☐ Tools like Hoaxy and Botometer detect fake engagement and bot networks that artificially boost misinformation.

🔍 CrowdTangle (Meta-owned) helps track how false narratives spread across social platforms.

📊 Google Trends & Trendolizer analyze manipulated trending topics and keyword stuffing.

2. Fact-Checking & Debunking Virality Loops

✅ Use Reverse Image Search (Google, TinEye, Yandex) to debunk fake visuals spread by viral misinformation.

✅ Verify Sources using OSINT techniques to track the original source of a claim and compare it to reputable outlets.

✅ Amplify Corrective Information by using SEO tactics to ensure fact-checked content ranks higher than fake news.

3. Promoting Algorithmic Transparency & Regulation

⚖️ **Advocating for algorithm audits**—Social media companies must be held accountable for how their recommendation systems amplify misinformation.

🤖 **Pushing for AI-driven misinformation detection**—Developing AI models to identify and flag deepfakes, manipulated text, and synthetic media before they go viral.

🚫 **Demanding stronger content moderation policies**—Platforms should actively deprioritize debunked content instead of just labeling it.

Conclusion: The Future of Algorithmic Misinformation

Algorithms are not inherently bad, but their reliance on engagement-driven ranking systems makes misinformation a persistent problem. Unless social media platforms prioritize accuracy over virality, misinformation will continue to shape public perception, politics, and even real-world events.

However, with OSINT tools, fact-checking initiatives, and algorithmic transparency, researchers and analysts can counter the effects of algorithmic misinformation and protect the integrity of online information ecosystems.

3.3 Identifying Manipulated Hashtags & Trends

In the age of social media, hashtags and trending topics play a crucial role in shaping public conversations. They can mobilize social movements, spread information, and raise awareness—but they are also vulnerable to manipulation by disinformation campaigns, bot networks, and state-sponsored actors.

This subchapter explores how manipulated hashtags and trends are created, the tactics used by bad actors, and how OSINT (Open-Source Intelligence) analysts can detect and investigate these manipulations.

How Hashtag & Trend Manipulation Works

Social media platforms like Twitter (X), Facebook, Instagram, and TikTok use algorithm-driven trending lists that highlight the most discussed topics in real time. However, these trends can be artificially manipulated through coordinated efforts.

1. Artificial Amplification by Bot Networks

- Automated bot accounts flood platforms with posts using a specific hashtag, making it appear organically popular.
- Bots like, share, and reply to each other's posts, creating the illusion of engagement.
- **Example**: A network of fake accounts tweets a misleading political hashtag thousands of times within minutes, tricking Twitter's algorithm into promoting it as a top trend.

2. Astroturfing (Fake Grassroots Campaigns)

- Astroturfing creates a false impression of widespread public support by organizing coordinated posting campaigns.
- Real users (often paid influencers or trolls) post pre-written messages with the targeted hashtag.
- **Example**: A disinformation group pushes a hashtag like #ElectionFraud to falsely claim voter fraud, making it seem like a grassroots concern.

3. Hashtag Hijacking (Co-Opting Popular Trends)

- Bad actors hijack trending hashtags to insert disinformation into mainstream discussions.
- They use existing viral trends to spread propaganda, conspiracy theories, or divisive narratives.
- **Example**: During protests, misinformation groups hijack #BlackLivesMatter by posting fake riot videos to discredit the movement.

4. Fake Engagement & Paid Promotion

- Some groups buy fake likes, retweets, and comments to push a hashtag into the trending section.
- Platforms like Twitter and Instagram offer "boost" features, which can be misused to promote misinformation.
- **Example**: An anti-vaccine movement pays influencers to repeatedly tweet #VaccineDanger to drive engagement and manipulate discussions.

5. Coordinated Timing for Maximum Impact

- Disinformation actors often time their hashtag campaigns to coincide with major events (elections, crises, protests).
- They use time zone strategies to maintain global visibility over multiple hours.
- **Example**: A state-sponsored group starts pushing a false #TerrorAttack claim right before a presidential debate to distract from real issues.

OSINT Techniques to Detect Manipulated Hashtags & Trends

OSINT analysts and fact-checkers can use various digital forensic methods to investigate hashtag manipulation.

1. Analyzing Sudden Spikes in Hashtag Activity

🏛 Use Trend Analysis Tools:

- Trendolizer, Ritmotopic, and Google Trends can detect sudden, unnatural spikes in hashtag activity.
- Botometer helps analyze if a hashtag's engagement comes from real users or bots.

🔍 Check for Time-Based Anomalies:

- Legitimate trends build up gradually, but manipulated trends spike suddenly and then disappear.
- If a hashtag appears overnight without organic discussions, it might be manipulated.

📌 **Example**: A hashtag like #FakeScandal suddenly receives 50,000 tweets within 30 minutes, mostly from newly created accounts.

2. Identifying Bot Networks & Fake Accounts

☐ Use Bot Detection Tools:

- Hoaxy and BotSentinel analyze how hashtags spread and detect fake engagement patterns.
- Account Analysis: Many bot accounts share generic profile pictures, low follower counts, and high post frequencies.

📌 **Example**: If 80% of the tweets using #GovernmentCorrupt come from accounts created in the last 24 hours, it's likely a coordinated bot campaign.

3. Mapping the Origins of a Hashtag

🔎 Track the First Mentions:

- Using TweetDeck, Twint, and WhoPostedWhat, analysts can trace the earliest posts using a hashtag.
- Finding the first few users can reveal whether the trend started organically or through a coordinated push.

📌 **Example**: If #CrisisHoax originates from a cluster of anonymous accounts, it may be a manufactured trend rather than real public concern.

4. Reverse Image & Video Search for Hashtag Content

📷 Verify Viral Images & Videos:

- Google Reverse Image Search, Yandex, and InVID can confirm if images linked to a trending hashtag are old or doctored.

- **Example**: A viral photo claiming to show riots under #CityOnFire is actually from a protest years ago in a different country.

5. Geolocation & Language Analysis

🔎 Check Where the Hashtag is Trending:

- Trends should be geographically relevant, but manipulated hashtags often spike in unrelated regions.
- **Example**: A U.S.-focused hashtag like #ElectionFraud2024 suddenly trends in Russia and Serbia, indicating foreign interference.

🔤 Analyze Unusual Language Patterns:

- If multiple accounts tweet identical phrases, it suggests pre-scripted messaging.
- Using NLP (Natural Language Processing) tools, analysts can detect unnatural linguistic patterns that indicate bot activity.

Case Study: The 2016 U.S. Election & Hashtag Manipulation

During the 2016 U.S. elections, Russian disinformation campaigns:

- Created thousands of fake accounts to promote political hashtags.
- Used #MAGA, #ClintonEmails, and #TrumpWon to spread false claims.
- Paid influencers to legitimize misleading narratives.
- Hijacked neutral hashtags like #DebateNight to insert misinformation.

📌 **Impact**: Many of these manipulated trends shaped public opinion and increased political polarization, influencing election narratives.

How Social Media Platforms Are Responding

To combat manipulated trends, platforms have:

✅ Introduced bot detection and de-ranking of manipulated hashtags (Twitter & Facebook).

✅ Implemented fact-checking partnerships with organizations like Snopes & Reuters.

☑ Banned coordinated disinformation campaigns linked to state-sponsored actors (Meta's takedown of Russian troll farms).

➤ However, challenges remain—new AI-powered bot networks continue evolving, making detection harder than ever.

Conclusion: Fighting Hashtag Manipulation with OSINT

Manipulated hashtags and trends undermine trust in online discourse, influence elections, and spread disinformation at scale.

By using OSINT tools, AI detection models, and fact-checking techniques, investigators can track down disinformation networks, expose propaganda efforts, and protect digital information ecosystems.

Key Takeaways:

☑ Not all trends are organic—many are engineered through bot networks and paid campaigns.

☑ Hashtag manipulation relies on sudden spikes, bot engagement, and timing strategies.

☑ OSINT techniques like trend analysis, bot detection, and reverse searches are essential for debunking manipulated narratives.

As disinformation tactics evolve, continuous monitoring and investigative methodologies will be crucial in preserving truth in the digital age.

3.4 Sock Puppets, Troll Farms & Astroturfing

The manipulation of online discourse has become a strategic tool in disinformation campaigns, with bad actors using sock puppet accounts, troll farms, and astroturfing to spread false narratives, manipulate public opinion, and influence elections or social movements. These deceptive tactics exploit the illusion of grassroots engagement, creating an artificial sense of public consensus on controversial topics.

In this subchapter, we will explore:

- What sock puppets, troll farms, and astroturfing are.
- How they are used in disinformation campaigns.
- How OSINT (Open-Source Intelligence) analysts can detect and investigate these deceptive activities.

What Are Sock Puppets, Troll Farms & Astroturfing?

Sock Puppets: Fake Identities for Online Manipulation

A sock puppet is a fake online persona used to deceive audiences, amplify opinions, or manipulate discussions. Sock puppet accounts can be controlled by individuals or groups and are used to:

- Post fabricated opinions in online forums or social media.
- Defend, attack, or promote specific individuals, organizations, or governments.
- Spread disinformation while appearing to be a genuine user.

📌 **Example**: A single individual creates multiple fake Twitter accounts to support a conspiracy theory, making it appear more credible through fake engagement and replies.

Troll Farms: Organized Disinformation Squads

A troll farm is a coordinated group of individuals paid to post divisive, misleading, or inflammatory content to manipulate discussions. These groups are often:

- Hired by political groups, state actors, or corporations to influence narratives.
- Located in countries where cheap labor is used to manage thousands of accounts.
- Trained to pose as real users, engage in debates, and spread propaganda.

📌 **Example**: Russia's Internet Research Agency (IRA) was exposed for operating thousands of fake social media accounts, using them to push propaganda during the 2016 U.S. election.

Astroturfing: Fake Grassroots Movements

Astroturfing is the practice of disguising a coordinated campaign as a grassroots movement to create the illusion of widespread support. This is often done by:

- Paying influencers, activists, or regular users to post pre-scripted messages.

- Using bots and sock puppets to amplify false engagement.
- Manipulating public sentiment to influence political debates or brand perception.

📌 **Example**: A large oil company funds a "public movement" against climate change regulations, but in reality, it is backed by corporate interests rather than real activists.

How Sock Puppets, Troll Farms & Astroturfing Are Used in Disinformation Campaigns

1. Political Influence & Election Manipulation

- Disinformation groups create fake activist profiles to push political narratives.
- Trolls flood comment sections of political opponents, spreading false claims.
- Coordinated hashtag campaigns create fake public outrage.

📌 **Case Study**: In the 2020 U.S. election, foreign troll farms ran disinformation campaigns targeting both sides of the political spectrum to increase division and distrust in the voting system.

2. Undermining Opponents & Harassment Campaigns

- Sock puppets impersonate real people to attack critics or spread false allegations.
- Troll farms mass-report accounts to get opposing voices banned or censored.
- Astroturfing campaigns create fake petitions to pressure organizations.

📌 **Example**: A group of fake online activists started a hashtag calling for the boycott of a journalist, using bots and paid trolls to make it trend.

3. Spreading Conspiracies & Fake News

- Sock puppets "debunk" real news stories by introducing fake counter-narratives.
- Trolls push conspiracy theories through coordinated engagement.
- Astroturfing makes fringe ideas look mainstream, influencing real-world policy debates.

📌 **Example**: During the COVID-19 pandemic, fake medical experts on Twitter (sock puppets) spread false information about vaccines, while troll farms amplified their messages.

4. Corporate & Brand Warfare

- Companies use sock puppets to post fake reviews, boosting their brand or destroying competitors.
- Astroturfing campaigns manufacture public outrage against rival companies.

📌 **Example**: A company secretly funds an "independent consumer group" that promotes its own products while trashing competitors.

How OSINT Analysts Detect & Investigate Sock Puppets, Troll Farms & Astroturfing

1. Identifying Sock Puppet Accounts

🔍 **Check for Profile Inconsistencies**

- Reverse search profile pictures using Google Reverse Image Search or TinEye.
- Look for stock images, AI-generated faces, or stolen photos.

📌 **Example**: A supposed "activist" account has a profile photo that appears on multiple stock photo websites—a clear red flag.

🔎 **Analyze Posting Patterns**

- Sock puppet accounts often post at unrealistic frequencies or only engage with specific topics.
- They may copy-paste identical messages across multiple forums.

📌 **Example**: Multiple accounts posting the exact same message about a politician within seconds of each other.

2. Detecting Troll Farms

⬜⬜ **Look for Coordinated Behavior**

- Botometer detects automated troll accounts by analyzing activity patterns.
- Hoaxy maps how disinformation spreads, helping detect clusters of troll accounts.

📌 **Example**: A set of accounts repeatedly retweet each other's posts but rarely engage with real users.

3. Investigating Astroturfing Campaigns

▥ Trace the Origins of a Hashtag

- Use TweetDeck, Twint, or Meltwater to track how a hashtag started.
- Look for a sudden, unnatural spike in activity.

📌 **Example**: A hashtag promoting a fake social movement started with just five accounts, all created on the same day.

💰 Follow the Money

- Astroturfing groups leave financial trails, such as sponsored ads, donations, or funding from corporate/political entities.
- Investigative journalists use OSINT techniques to trace ownership of campaign websites.

📌 **Example**: A supposed "independent advocacy group" is actually registered under a major lobbying firm's name.

Case Study: Russia's Internet Research Agency (IRA) & Online Manipulation

Russia's Internet Research Agency (IRA) is one of the most well-documented troll farms. Their operations included:

- Creating thousands of fake social media profiles to impersonate real Americans.
- Running divisive ad campaigns on Facebook and Twitter.
- Organizing real-world protests by manipulating activists.

🔎 OSINT Investigations Uncovered:

- IRA accounts had AI-generated profile photos.
- Most IRA posts had coordinated publishing times based on U.S. political events.
- Their hashtags often spiked in engagement overnight, a classic astroturfing technique.

📌 **Impact**: These tactics deepened political divisions in the U.S. and influenced voter behavior.

Conclusion: Defending Against Online Manipulation

Sock puppets, troll farms, and astroturfing distort public discourse, manipulate elections, and spread false information. By using OSINT tools and investigative techniques, analysts can uncover fake accounts, expose coordinated campaigns, and prevent disinformation from shaping reality.

Key Takeaways:

✅ **Sock puppets** = Fake personas used for manipulation.

✅ **Troll farms** = Organized disinformation squads.

✅ **Astroturfing** = Fake grassroots movements for hidden agendas.

✅ OSINT tools like Hoaxy, Botometer & reverse image searches help track & expose these manipulations.

Fighting digital deception requires constant vigilance, advanced investigation techniques, and media literacy to ensure truth prevails in the information war.

3.5 Coordinated Social Media Attacks & Their Impact

Social media has become a battlefield for influence, where coordinated attacks are used to silence voices, spread disinformation, and manipulate public perception. These attacks are often organized by state actors, troll farms, extremist groups, or ideologically motivated individuals to achieve political, economic, or social objectives.

In this subchapter, we will explore:

- What coordinated social media attacks are and how they work.
- The tactics used in these digital assaults.
- The real-world impact of such attacks.
- How OSINT (Open-Source Intelligence) analysts can detect and counter these efforts.

What Are Coordinated Social Media Attacks?

A coordinated social media attack is a deliberate, organized effort to harass, discredit, or silence individuals, organizations, or narratives by overwhelming them with negative engagement, misinformation, or threats. These attacks can involve:

- Troll farms and bot networks amplifying harmful content.
- Sock puppet accounts spreading false accusations.
- Doxxing (leaking personal information) to intimidate targets.
- Mass reporting campaigns to trigger bans or shadowbanning.

📌 **Example**: A journalist exposing government corruption suddenly faces thousands of identical hate messages, fake accusations, and mass reporting of their social media accounts—indicating a coordinated attack.

Tactics Used in Coordinated Social Media Attacks

1. Dogpiling & Brigading

🔊 **How it Works:**

- Attackers flood a target's social media posts with negative comments, insults, and misinformation.
- They coordinate via private groups (Discord, Telegram, 4chan, etc.) to launch mass engagement.
- This creates the illusion that public opinion is turning against the target.

📌 **Example**: A scientist sharing pro-vaccine research is attacked with thousands of replies accusing them of lying, all from accounts created within days of each other.

2. Doxxing & Cyber Harassment

🔲 **How it Works:**

- Attackers search for and publicly share personal details (home address, phone number, family info).
- Doxxing often escalates to threats of violence or real-world harassment.
- It aims to intimidate and silence the victim.

📌 **Example**: A political activist is doxxed after a viral tweet, leading to death threats, unwanted deliveries, and calls to their workplace demanding their firing.

3. Mass Reporting & Deplatforming

🔒 **How it Works:**

- Attackers mass-report a target's social media accounts or posts for violating terms of service.
- Platforms automatically suspend or shadowban the target due to the sheer volume of reports.
- This tactic is often used to remove voices from online discussions.

📌 **Example**: A human rights organization's account is suspended after coordinated mass reports, even though they violated no rules.

4. Hashtag Poisoning & Narrative Hijacking

🎰 **How it Works:**

- Attackers spam a legitimate hashtag with irrelevant, offensive, or misleading content.
- This dilutes the real conversation and spreads disinformation.
- Hijacking allows bad actors to introduce alternative narratives that align with their goals.

📌 **Example**: A movement using #ClimateAction is derailed by climate denialists flooding the hashtag with fake data and conspiracy theories.

5. Impersonation & Fake Scandals

🎭 **How it Works:**

- Fake accounts impersonate public figures to post controversial content.
- AI-generated images or deepfake videos make fake scandals appear real.
- Attackers forge screenshots of offensive statements to trigger public backlash.

📌 **Example**: A deepfake video of a politician "saying" something racist goes viral before fact-checkers can debunk it.

Real-World Impact of Coordinated Social Media Attacks

Coordinated attacks don't just affect digital spaces—they have serious real-world consequences:

1. Silencing of Journalists, Activists & Experts

☐ **Impact**: Many victims of harassment quit social media or self-censor.

📌 **Example**: A female journalist covering extremism receives rape threats and death threats, forcing her to leave the profession.

2. Disinformation Becomes the Dominant Narrative

☐ **Impact**: If attacks successfully drown out real information, false narratives take hold.

📌 **Example**: Anti-vaccine groups attack doctors and scientists, reducing trust in public health.

3. Manipulated Elections & Political Destabilization

☐ **Impact**: Foreign and domestic actors use coordinated social media attacks to influence voter perception.

📌 **Example**: In 2016, Russian troll farms amplified divisive political content, influencing U.S. election discourse.

4. Economic & Corporate Warfare

☐ **Impact**: Competitors use coordinated attacks to damage brands and manipulate stock prices.

📌 **Example**: A company faces thousands of fake negative reviews after refusing to support a certain political stance.

- OSINT Techniques to Detect & Investigate Coordinated Social Media Attacks
- OSINT analysts can uncover, track, and attribute these attacks using specialized techniques.

1. Network Analysis of Attackers

🔍 **Use Tools Like:**

- Hoaxy & Botometer (detects coordinated bot activity).
- Graphika & Gephi (visualize networks of fake accounts).

📌 **Example**: A fake scandal's retweets come from accounts created in the past week, all following the same influencers.

2. Tracking Hashtag Manipulation

Use Tools Like:

- Twint, Meltwater, & TweetDeck (trace hashtag origins).
- Trendolizer & CrowdTangle (monitor viral content).

📌 **Example**: A political hashtag trends only in one country, despite pretending to be global.

3. Reverse Image & Deepfake Detection

📷 Use Tools Like:

- InVID, Yandex Reverse Image Search (trace fake images & deepfakes).
- AI-generated Face Detectors (analyze synthetic accounts).

📌 **Example**: An "activist" account using a stolen profile picture from a stock photo website.

4. Identifying Mass Reporting Campaigns

🚨 Use Tools Like:

- SNA (Social Network Analysis) to detect reporting patterns.
- Monitoring sudden spikes in reporting activity on Telegram & Discord channels.

📌 **Example**: A leaked chat reveals plans to mass-report a journalist to get them suspended.

Case Study: The 2021 Facebook Whistleblower Attack

When Frances Haugen leaked Facebook's internal files proving the company ignored harm caused by its platform:

- She faced thousands of harassing messages within hours.
- Bot networks flooded comment sections with discrediting narratives.
- Fake accounts spread false conspiracy theories about her motives.

🔎 **OSINT Findings:**

- Most attacks came from newly created accounts with no prior activity.
- Several attackers were linked to previous disinformation operations.
- Many used copy-paste messages, indicating a scripted, coordinated effort.

📌 **Impact**: The attack attempted to discredit a whistleblower and bury her findings, but OSINT investigations exposed it.

Conclusion: Defending Against Coordinated Attacks

Coordinated social media attacks distort public discourse, intimidate individuals, and manipulate truth. By leveraging OSINT tools and investigative techniques, analysts can uncover these campaigns, trace their origins, and expose digital deception.

Key Takeaways:

✓ Social media attacks use brigading, doxxing, bots, and fake news to manipulate narratives.

✓ OSINT tools like Hoaxy, Botometer & Twint help uncover attack networks.

✓ Understanding these tactics helps individuals and organizations defend against disinformation campaigns.

As digital warfare evolves, vigilance, digital literacy, and OSINT expertise are critical to preserving truth in the age of online manipulation.

3.6 Case Study: A Social Media Disinformation Operation Exposed

In this case study, we will examine a real-world disinformation operation that was uncovered through OSINT (Open-Source Intelligence) techniques. This example highlights the methods used by bad actors to spread falsehoods, the impact of the operation, and the investigative techniques used to expose it.

Background: The Disinformation Campaign

In early 2020, a coordinated disinformation campaign emerged on social media targeting a major political event. The operation aimed to:

- Discredit certain politicians and activists
- Spread false narratives about election fraud
- Amplify divisive social issues to polarize public opinion

The campaign was first detected when fact-checkers noticed a sudden surge of false claims originating from a network of Twitter and Facebook accounts. Many of these accounts used identical wording, images, and hashtags, suggesting a level of coordination beyond organic social media activity.

Phase 1: The Disinformation Playbook

1. Creating Fake Accounts & Personas

- The campaign used thousands of fake accounts, many of which were sock puppets (fake identities controlled by real users) and bot accounts (automated profiles).
- AI-generated profile pictures (created using ThisPersonDoesNotExist.com) made the fake accounts seem realistic.
- Some accounts impersonated journalists and influencers to lend credibility to the false claims.

📌 **Example**: A fake Twitter account using a deepfake profile picture posed as a "former election official" and spread fabricated reports of fraud.

2. Amplification Through Hashtags & Trends

- The campaign used bot networks to push specific hashtags into trending topics.
- Engagement pods (coordinated groups of real users) further amplified the content by liking, sharing, and commenting to make it appear organic.
- Troll farms, mainly operating from foreign locations, mass-posted identical messages across Facebook and Instagram.

📌 **Example**: The hashtag #StopTheSteal gained traction with thousands of retweets per minute, even though most engagement came from newly created accounts.

3. Spreading Fake News & Manipulated Media

- Fabricated news articles were published on pseudo-news websites designed to look legitimate.
- Fake screenshots and deepfake videos were circulated to support false claims.

- Misattributed images (e.g., old protest photos labeled as "current events") were used to mislead the public.

📌 **Example**: A deepfake video of a politician allegedly admitting to fraud went viral, but analysis later revealed inconsistencies in the audio sync and facial expressions.

4. Harassment & Deplatforming of Fact-Checkers

- Fact-checkers and journalists debunking the false claims became targets of harassment.
- Mass reporting campaigns led to temporary suspensions of credible accounts.
- Fake accounts impersonated fact-checkers and posted inflammatory statements to discredit them.

📌 **Example**: A well-known disinformation researcher was doxxed, leading to death threats and forced removal from social media.

Phase 2: OSINT Investigation & Exposure

1. Identifying the Bot Network

OSINT analysts used bot detection tools such as:

- **Botometer** (analyzes Twitter activity to detect bots).
- **Hoaxy** (traces how misinformation spreads).
- **Gephi** (visualizes networks of coordinated activity).

🔍 **Findings:**

- Many accounts in the network were created within days of each other.
- The majority followed only a handful of key influencers, indicating a top-down strategy.
- A sudden spike in engagement occurred at the exact same timestamps, a common sign of automation.

2. Reverse Image Searching for Fake Profiles

To detect fake personas, analysts performed reverse image searches on profile pictures using:

- Google Reverse Image Search
- Yandex Image Search
- TinEye

🔍 Findings:

- Several accounts used stock photos or AI-generated faces (which lacked normal facial asymmetry).
- Some images were stolen from real people's LinkedIn or Facebook profiles.

3. Metadata & Hashtag Analysis

Investigators examined the metadata of shared images and videos using tools like:

- **ExifTool** (extracts metadata from images).
- **Twint** (scrapes Twitter data for trends).
- **Trendolizer** (tracks viral content origins).

🔍 Findings:

- Many images originated from foreign sources but were presented as local events.
- Viral posts followed a coordinated pattern—all pushing the same hashtags within minutes of each other.

4. Unmasking the Organizers

Using WHOIS lookup and domain analysis, researchers traced fake news websites back to a PR firm with links to political actors.

🔍 Findings:

- Multiple websites shared the same IP address, linking them to a single operation.
- Some domains were registered just days before the disinformation campaign started.

Phase 3: The Fallout & Lessons Learned

Once OSINT analysts and journalists exposed the campaign:

✅ Social media platforms took action, suspending thousands of fake accounts.

✅ Fact-checkers debunked viral false claims, preventing further spread.

✅ Government agencies issued warnings about foreign influence operations.

📌 **Key Takeaways:**

- Disinformation operations rely on coordination across multiple platforms.
- Bot networks and fake personas can be unmasked through OSINT techniques.
- Reverse image searches and metadata analysis are crucial in verifying content.
- Public exposure is an effective countermeasure against disinformation campaigns.

By understanding these tactics and leveraging OSINT tools, analysts and researchers can detect, expose, and combat social media disinformation operations before they cause real-world harm.

4. Fact-Checking Tools & Methods

In the fight against disinformation, fact-checking is an essential skill for any OSINT analyst. This chapter introduces the various tools and methods available to verify the authenticity of information, images, and videos. From reverse image search engines to metadata analysis, we explore the practical techniques used by professionals to uncover the truth behind questionable claims. Additionally, we cover the importance of source credibility, cross-referencing multiple data points, and leveraging crowdsourced platforms to assess accuracy. By mastering these fact-checking methods, readers will be empowered to debunk falsehoods and ensure the reliability of the information they encounter in the digital realm.

4.1 The Science of Fact-Checking & Source Verification

In an era where misinformation spreads rapidly, fact-checking and source verification are critical to separating truth from falsehood. Whether dealing with breaking news, viral claims, or politically charged content, a systematic, evidence-based approach is necessary to evaluate the credibility of sources and claims.

This subchapter explores:

- The scientific principles behind fact-checking
- The importance of source verification
- Common methodologies used by fact-checkers

Key OSINT tools for verification

The Science Behind Fact-Checking

Fact-checking is not just about confirming or debunking a statement—it involves a structured approach based on logic, evidence, and investigative techniques. The scientific method provides a useful framework:

- **Observation**: Identify a claim, news article, image, or video that requires verification.
- **Hypothesis**: Formulate initial questions—Who is the source? Is this likely to be true? What evidence exists?
- **Investigation**: Collect and analyze data using fact-checking tools.

- **Testing**: Compare findings with reliable sources and historical data.
- **Conclusion**: Determine the truthfulness of the claim based on the weight of evidence.

🔍 **Example**: A viral claim states that a famous celebrity donated $1 million to a political campaign. A fact-checker investigates by examining campaign finance records, official statements, and news reports to verify or debunk the claim.

The Importance of Source Verification

Before fact-checking a specific claim, it is essential to verify the credibility of the source. The origin of a claim often determines its reliability. A three-tier approach helps assess a source's credibility:

1. Primary Sources (Most Reliable)

- Official government documents
- Scientific studies from peer-reviewed journals
- Eyewitness accounts with verifiable evidence
- Raw data from reputable organizations (e.g., WHO, UN, NASA)

📌 **Example**: A government census report provides direct demographic data, making it a primary source.

2. Secondary Sources (Moderately Reliable)

- News agencies with strong editorial standards (e.g., BBC, Reuters, AP)
- Academic institutions and think tanks
- Fact-checking organizations (e.g., Snopes, PolitiFact, FactCheck.org)

📌 **Example**: A Reuters article summarizing a scientific study is a secondary source because it interprets primary research.

3. Tertiary Sources (Least Reliable)

- Social media posts without citations
- Anonymous blogs or opinion pieces
- Partisan news sites with clear bias
- Content from known disinformation networks

📌 **Example**: A viral tweet claiming a political figure was arrested, with no supporting evidence, is unreliable.

Methodologies Used in Fact-Checking

Professional fact-checkers follow specific techniques to verify claims efficiently. Some of the most effective methods include:

1. The CRAAP Test

A widely used method in journalism and academia for evaluating sources based on five key factors:

- **Currency** – Is the information up to date?
- **Relevance** – Does it relate to the topic at hand?
- **Authority** – Who is the author/source, and are they credible?
- **Accuracy** – Is the information supported by evidence?
- **Purpose** – Is there bias or an agenda behind the claim?

📌 **Example**: A social media post about an "imminent food crisis" is evaluated using CRAAP. The post lacks credible sources (Authority), was written by an anonymous user (Purpose), and includes outdated statistics (Currency), making it questionable.

2. Lateral Reading (Cross-Checking Sources)

Instead of reading a single article, lateral reading involves opening multiple sources simultaneously to compare credibility.

✅ **Best Practices:**

- Check multiple reputable sources for consistency.
- Search for fact-checking reports from known verification platforms.
- Analyze who else is reporting the claim (independent confirmation).

📌 **Example**: A viral claim about a vaccine's side effects is checked against medical journals, WHO reports, and government health agencies to assess accuracy.

3. Reverse Image & Video Search

Images and videos are frequently manipulated, misattributed, or taken out of context. Verifying them requires tools like:

- **Google Reverse Image Search** – Checks for previous instances of an image online.
- **TinEye** – Finds older versions of an image to verify authenticity.
- **InVID** – A tool for analyzing video metadata and detecting deepfakes.

📌 **Example**: A supposed "war crime photo" from 2023 is traced back to a 2015 news report, proving it was falsely presented as new.

4. Evaluating Website Authenticity

Disinformation campaigns often use fake news websites that mimic real outlets. To verify a site's legitimacy:

✅ Check domain age using Whois Lookup (Newly registered sites are suspicious).

✅ Verify SSL security and professional web design.

✅ Search for the editorial team and contact details (Fake sites often lack transparency).

✅ Analyze writing style (Real news follows journalistic standards, fake sites use emotional language).

📌 **Example**: A website claiming a celebrity's death is registered just two weeks prior and contains no contact info or author details, raising red flags.

Key OSINT Tools for Fact-Checking

OSINT analysts and journalists use various verification tools to fact-check information efficiently:

For News & Article Verification

- **Snopes, PolitiFact, FactCheck.org** – Debunk viral misinformation.
- **Wayback Machine** – View archived versions of websites to check edits/deletions.
- **Google Advanced Search Operators** – Find past coverage of a claim.

For Social Media Analysis

- **Twint & TruthNest** – Analyze Twitter account authenticity.
- **Hoaxy & Botometer** – Detect bot-driven misinformation.
- **CrowdTangle** – Track content engagement trends.

For Image & Video Analysis

- **Google Reverse Image & TinEye** – Find original sources of images.
- **InVID** – Identify video manipulation and deepfake content.

For Website & Domain Verification

- **Whois Lookup** – Check domain registration details.
- **DNSlytics** – Investigate site ownership and connections.
- **ScamAdviser** – Assess a website's trustworthiness.

Case Study: Debunking a Viral Hoax

The Claim:

A widely shared Facebook post in 2022 claimed that a popular fast-food chain was using synthetic meat grown from human cells.

Fact-Checking Process:

- **Source Check**: The original post came from a blog known for false claims.
- **Cross-Checking**: No credible news agencies reported similar findings.
- **Reverse Image Search**: The attached image was from a 2014 art project, not a real food experiment.
- **Official Statements**: The fast-food chain denied the claim in an official press release.

✅ **Final Verdict**: False – The hoax was an example of fear-based disinformation targeting food safety concerns.

Conclusion: The Role of OSINT in Fact-Checking

Fact-checking is both a science and an investigative process, requiring logical reasoning, verification tools, and cross-referencing of information. By applying OSINT techniques, analysts can:

✓ Verify sources before trusting claims.

✓ Identify manipulated content using forensic tools.

✓ Expose disinformation networks spreading false narratives.

In an age where fake news influences public opinion and policy, mastering the science of fact-checking is essential for journalists, researchers, and digital citizens alike.

4.2 Open-Source Tools for Investigating Claims

As disinformation and fake news continue to evolve, open-source intelligence (OSINT) tools have become essential for verifying claims, tracking false narratives, and identifying deceptive content. These tools allow analysts, journalists, fact-checkers, and researchers to cross-check sources, analyze digital evidence, and uncover coordinated disinformation campaigns.

This subchapter explores:

Why OSINT tools matter in fact-checking

- Categories of OSINT tools for claim verification
- Practical techniques for using these tools effectively

Why OSINT Tools Are Essential for Fact-Checking

Traditional fact-checking relies on official records, journalist investigations, and expert opinions. However, disinformation spreads faster than corrections, making real-time verification crucial. OSINT tools help by:

✓ Tracking the origin of viral claims (Who first shared it? Where did it originate?)

✓ Verifying images, videos, and news reports (Is it manipulated? Is it taken out of context?)

✓ Analyzing social media activity (Are bots or troll farms amplifying it?)

✓ Identifying fake websites & fabricated sources (Is the site legitimate? Who owns it?)

By leveraging OSINT, investigators can uncover patterns of deception and counter false narratives more effectively.

Key Categories of OSINT Tools for Investigating Claims

There are six primary categories of OSINT tools used in claim verification:

- News & Fact-Checking Databases
- Reverse Image & Video Analysis Tools
- Social Media Analysis Tools
- Website & Domain Investigation Tools
- Metadata & File Forensics Tools
- Crowdsourced Verification Platforms

1. News & Fact-Checking Databases

These tools help verify whether a claim has already been debunked by professional fact-checkers:

◆ **Snopes (snopes.com)** – Investigates viral rumors, hoaxes, and misinformation.

◆ **PolitiFact (politifact.com)** – Verifies political claims using a truth-o-meter.

◆ **FactCheck.org (factcheck.org)** – Debunks misleading political and media statements.

◆ **AFP Fact Check (factcheck.afp.com)** – Provides global fact-checking reports.

◆ **Google Fact Check Explorer (toolbox.google.com/factcheck)** – A Google database aggregating fact-checks from multiple sources.

☐ **How to Use:**

- Copy and paste a claim or quote into Google Fact Check Explorer to see if it has been previously verified.
- Cross-check reports from multiple fact-checking organizations for consistency.

✦ **Example**: A viral claim that "5G networks cause COVID-19" is quickly debunked by PolitiFact, FactCheck.org, and Snopes.

2. Reverse Image & Video Analysis Tools

Images and videos are frequently manipulated, taken out of context, or completely fabricated. These tools help verify authenticity:

◆ **Google Reverse Image Search (images.google.com)** – Finds older versions of an image.

◆ **TinEye (tineye.com)** – Traces an image's origin and modifications.

◆ **Yandex Reverse Image Search (yandex.com/images)** – Detects similar images, often more effectively than Google.

◆ **InVID & WeVerify (invid-project.eu)** – Extracts video metadata, detects deepfakes, and helps verify visuals.

☐ **How to Use:**

- Upload an image into Google Reverse Image Search or TinEye to see its history.
- Use InVID to break a video into keyframes and check each frame for manipulation.

📌 **Example**: A viral photo of a flooded New York subway is revealed to be from Hurricane Sandy (2012), not a recent storm, by using reverse image search.

3. Social Media Analysis Tools

Disinformation spreads rapidly on social media. These tools help detect bot activity, fake profiles, and viral hoaxes:

◆ **Botometer (botometer.osome.iu.edu)** – Analyzes Twitter accounts for bot-like behavior.

◆ **Hoaxy (hoaxy.osome.iu.edu)** – Visualizes how misinformation spreads on Twitter.

◆ **CrowdTangle (crowdtangle.com)** – Tracks viral content on Facebook, Instagram, and Reddit.

◆ **TruthNest (truthnest.com)** – Provides in-depth analysis of Twitter accounts.

☐ **How to Use:**

- Input a Twitter username into Botometer to check if it behaves like a bot.
- Use CrowdTangle to track the spread of a meme or hashtag.

📌 **Example**: A trending anti-vaccine hashtag is found to be pushed by bot accounts, using Botometer and Hoaxy.

4. Website & Domain Investigation Tools

Fake news sites often appear legitimate but lack credibility. These tools help investigate them:

♦ **Whois Lookup (who.is)** – Finds domain registration details.
♦ **ScamAdviser (scamadviser.com)** – Checks if a website is trustworthy.
♦ **DNSlytics (dnslytics.com)** – Reveals a site's IP and hosting details.
♦ **Wayback Machine (archive.org)** – Allows access to historical versions of web pages.

☐ **How to Use:**

- Run a website's URL through Whois Lookup to see who owns it and when it was registered.
- Use the Wayback Machine to see if the site's content has changed over time.

✦ **Example**: A website spreading election fraud claims is traced back to a marketing company with no journalistic background using Whois Lookup.

5. Metadata & File Forensics Tools

Metadata can reveal when, where, and how a digital file was created. These tools help extract hidden details:

♦ **ExifTool (exiftool.org)** – Extracts metadata from images and videos.
♦ **FotoForensics (fotoforensics.com)** – Detects image manipulation.
♦ **Jeffrey's Image Metadata Viewer (exif.regex.info)** – Displays image metadata details.

☐ **How to Use:**

- Upload an image to ExifTool to see if it was edited, when it was taken, and what camera was used.

✦ **Example**: A viral photo of a warzone is analyzed in ExifTool, revealing it was actually taken in 2015, not 2023.

6. Crowdsourced Verification Platforms

Community-driven fact-checking adds an extra layer of verification:

- **Bellingcat (bellingcat.com)** – Open-source investigative journalism.
- **r/AskHistorians & r/AskScience (Reddit)** – Expert-led fact-checking communities.
- **Twitter Community Notes** – Crowdsourced context on misleading tweets.

Conclusion: The Power of OSINT in Claim Verification

OSINT tools empower investigators to quickly verify information by:

✓ Cross-checking sources & fact-checking claims

✓ Analyzing images & videos for manipulation

✓ Tracking disinformation trends on social media

✓ Exposing fake websites & misleading reports

By combining these tools, fact-checkers and OSINT analysts can combat disinformation and ensure the truth prevails in the digital age.

4.3 Using Metadata to Verify Digital Content

As digital disinformation continues to evolve, metadata analysis has become a crucial tool for verifying images, videos, and documents. Metadata—often referred to as data about data—contains valuable information such as timestamps, geolocation, device details, and editing history. By extracting and analyzing metadata, OSINT analysts, fact-checkers, and journalists can determine when, where, and how a digital file was created, helping to expose manipulation, misinformation, and deepfake content.

This subchapter will cover:

- What metadata is and why it matters
- Types of metadata in digital content
- Tools for extracting and analyzing metadata
- Practical case studies demonstrating metadata verification

What is Metadata, and Why Does It Matter?

Metadata is hidden information embedded in digital files that provides context about their origin, authorship, and modifications. It plays a crucial role in verifying content authenticity by:

✅ Identifying when and where an image or video was taken

✅ Detecting manipulated or edited media

✅ Uncovering inconsistencies in digital documents

✅ Tracing the source of misinformation campaigns

For example, a viral photo claiming to show a breaking news event might actually be years old—a fact that can be verified by analyzing its metadata.

Types of Metadata in Digital Content

Different types of digital files contain varying metadata fields. Below are the key metadata categories used in verification:

1. Image & Video Metadata (EXIF Data)

Most digital cameras and smartphones embed EXIF (Exchangeable Image File Format) metadata into images and videos. This metadata includes:

📷 **Camera Details** – Brand, model, lens type

🔎 **Geolocation Data** – GPS coordinates (if enabled)

☐ **Timestamps** – Date and time of capture

🎞 **Editing History** – Whether an image was modified in Photoshop or another tool

📌 **Example**: A viral protest photo claimed to be from 2024, but EXIF data revealed it was taken in 2015, debunking the misinformation.

2. Document Metadata (PDFs, Word Files, etc.)

Documents, especially PDFs and Word files, contain metadata fields that reveal:

🗓 **Creation & Modification Dates** – When the document was written and last edited

👤 **Author Details** – Username or organization behind the document

🖥 **Software Used** – The program used to create or modify the file

📌 **Example**: A leaked government report was suspected to be fake. Checking the metadata showed it was created using an anonymous username and a pirated software version, raising doubts about its authenticity.

3. Website & Social Media Metadata

Websites and social media platforms store metadata in the form of:

☐ **Domain Registration Data** – Who owns a website and when it was registered
☐☐ **Hidden HTML Tags** – Social media platforms embed metadata in posts to track engagement
📶 **User-Agent Strings** – Identifies the browser and device used to post content

📌 **Example**: A misleading news website spreading fake articles was investigated using WHOIS lookup, revealing it was created just a week before the "news" went viral—a common tactic in disinformation campaigns.

Tools for Extracting and Analyzing Metadata

There are several open-source and commercial tools for metadata extraction:

1. Image & Video Metadata Tools

◆ **ExifTool (exiftool.org)** – Extracts metadata from images and videos.
◆ **Jeffrey's Image Metadata Viewer (exif.regex.info)** – Easy-to-use metadata analysis tool.
◆ **FotoForensics (fotoforensics.com)** – Detects image manipulation and metadata inconsistencies.
◆ **InVID & WeVerify (invid-project.eu)** – Specialized in verifying social media videos.

☐ **How to Use:**

- Upload an image to ExifTool or Jeffrey's Image Metadata Viewer to see hidden details.
- Use InVID to extract metadata from a viral video and verify its origins.

2. Document Metadata Tools

◆ **FOCA (elevenpaths.com/lab/tools/foca)** – Extracts metadata from PDFs, Word, and PowerPoint files.
◆ **PDF-XChange Editor (tracker-software.com)** – Checks hidden metadata in PDFs.
◆ **Metagoofil** – Scrapes metadata from publicly available documents.

☐ **How to Use:**

- Open a suspicious PDF in PDF-XChange Editor and check its metadata.
- Use FOCA to extract metadata from multiple documents at once.

3. Website & Domain Investigation Tools

◆ **Whois Lookup (who.is)** – Checks domain registration details.
◆ **DNSlytics (dnslytics.com)** – Reveals website ownership and analytics.
◆ **Wayback Machine (archive.org)** – Shows past versions of websites.

☐ **How to Use:**

- Use Whois Lookup to check when a website was created.
- Use the Wayback Machine to see how a webpage has changed over time.

Case Studies: How Metadata Exposed Disinformation

1. Fake War Photos Debunked Using EXIF Data

A viral image claimed to show destruction in Ukraine (2023). However, ExifTool revealed it was taken in Syria in 2017. The metadata exposed the deception, proving the photo was reused from an unrelated conflict.

2. Leaked Government Document Proven Fake

A document allegedly leaked from a European intelligence agency claimed that a political party was involved in espionage. Metadata analysis using FOCA revealed:

- The author field contained the name of an activist, not an intelligence officer.
- The document was created using a home version of Microsoft Word, not a government-issued program.
- These inconsistencies confirmed the document was fabricated.

3. Tracking a Fake News Website with WHOIS Lookup

A website spreading false election fraud claims appeared legitimate. However, a Whois Lookup revealed:

- The domain was registered just two months before the election, a common red flag.
- The owner's details were hidden behind a privacy shield, making its origins suspicious.
- Further OSINT analysis confirmed the website was created specifically for disinformation purposes.

Best Practices for Metadata Verification

🔍 **Always cross-check metadata with other sources** – Metadata alone doesn't confirm a file's authenticity; it should be combined with reverse image search, fact-checking databases, and expert analysis.

🚫 **Beware of stripped or manipulated metadata** – Many social media platforms (e.g., Twitter, Facebook) remove EXIF data to protect user privacy, so additional verification methods are needed.

🔎 **Use metadata inconsistencies as red flags** – If a file claims to be from one date but metadata shows another, it may be manipulated.

✍️ **Keep records of metadata findings** – Screenshots and reports from metadata tools help build strong investigative cases.

Conclusion: Metadata as a Powerful OSINT Tool

Metadata analysis is an essential technique in digital verification. By using tools like ExifTool, FOCA, Whois Lookup, and InVID, OSINT analysts can:

✓ Verify the authenticity of images, videos, and documents

✓ Debunk misleading narratives and manipulated media

✓ Trace the origins of disinformation campaigns

As digital deception becomes more sophisticated, mastering metadata analysis is crucial for fighting fake news and maintaining truth in the information ecosystem.

4.4 Cross-Referencing Information with Trusted Sources

In an era where misinformation spreads rapidly, cross-referencing information with trusted sources is a fundamental practice for OSINT analysts, journalists, and fact-checkers. No single source should ever be considered completely reliable on its own; instead, verifying claims across multiple credible outlets strengthens the accuracy of an investigation. This subchapter explores effective strategies, tools, and best practices for cross-referencing information to combat disinformation and fake news.

Why Cross-Referencing is Crucial

Fake news and disinformation campaigns often rely on emotional manipulation, confirmation bias, and repetition to appear credible. If a false claim is repeated enough times across different platforms, people may accept it as truth. However, cross-referencing information with multiple independent and authoritative sources helps to:

✅ Distinguish facts from opinion or propaganda

✅ Identify biases and inconsistencies in reporting

✅ Verify the authenticity of images, videos, and documents

✅ Ensure that news is not manipulated or taken out of context

A well-verified claim should be supported by at least three independent sources before it is considered credible.

Key Methods for Cross-Referencing Information

1. Comparing Reports from Multiple Reputable News Outlets

One of the most effective ways to verify a claim is by checking if it is reported consistently by established and reputable news organizations.

Steps to follow:

- Search for the claim on major international and national news websites.
- Compare details—dates, locations, quotes, and key facts—across different reports.

- Identify contradictions or missing details, which may indicate unreliable reporting.

🔍 **Example**: If a breaking news report about an alleged terrorist attack is only covered by one obscure website and not by CNN, BBC, Reuters, or AP, it raises red flags.

📌 **Tip**: Use Google News Aggregator (news.google.com) to view coverage from multiple sources.

2. Checking Primary Sources (Official Documents, Statements & Data)

Many fake news stories rely on misrepresenting or distorting primary sources. Instead of trusting secondhand interpretations, OSINT analysts should always refer to official documents, government statements, and raw data.

Where to find primary sources:

- Government websites (gov.uk, usa.gov, europa.eu)
- Scientific journals (PubMed, Google Scholar)
- Official statistics databases (World Bank, UN Data)
- Election commissions & court documents

🔍 **Example**: A viral claim suggested that a politician proposed a controversial law, but the actual bill (available on a government website) contained no such provision.

📌 **Tip**: Use Wayback Machine (archive.org) to check if official sources have been altered over time.

3. Using Fact-Checking Platforms

Several independent fact-checking organizations investigate viral claims, political statements, and manipulated media. Before sharing or believing a claim, it's wise to check if it has already been debunked by a trusted fact-checking group.

🔍 **Trusted Fact-Checking Websites:**

- **Snopes (snopes.com)** – Debunks viral hoaxes and misinformation.
- **PolitiFact (politifact.com)** – Checks political claims for accuracy.
- **FactCheck.org (factcheck.org)** – Investigates US politics and policy claims.
- **Reuters Fact Check (reuters.com/fact-check)** – International fact-checking by professional journalists.

- **AFP Fact Check (factcheck.afp.com)** – Global fact-checking initiative.

📌 **Tip**: If multiple independent fact-checking organizations agree on the falsehood of a claim, it's highly likely to be misinformation.

4. Verifying Social Media Claims & User-Generated Content

Misinformation often spreads rapidly on social media platforms like Twitter, Facebook, and TikTok. To verify claims made on social media, OSINT analysts should:

- **Check the source** – Who posted the content? Are they reputable?
- **Look for media corroboration** – Is the claim being covered by independent journalists?
- **Use reverse image search** – Was the photo/video posted previously in a different context?
- **Analyze metadata** – Does the timestamp and location match the claim?

📌 **Tip**: Use CrowdTangle (Facebook-owned tool) to track the spread of misinformation on social media.

5. Analyzing Bias & Evaluating the Source's Credibility

Not all media sources have equal credibility. Some have strong political or ideological biases, while others are known for sensationalism or misinformation.

How to assess media bias & credibility:

✅ **Check the "About Us" section** – Is the publication transparent about its mission and funding?
✅ **Look at the author's credentials** – Are they an expert or anonymous?
✅ Use media bias rating tools:

Media Bias/Fact Check (mediabiasfactcheck.com)

Ad Fontes Media Bias Chart (adfontesmedia.com)

📌 **Tip**: If a news story only appears on extreme partisan sites and not in mainstream media, it may be unreliable.

Case Studies: How Cross-Referencing Exposed Misinformation

1. The Fake COVID-19 Cure Hoax

In 2020, a viral claim circulated that drinking hot lemon water could "kill" COVID-19. Many people shared this misinformation without verifying it. However, cross-referencing with:

- WHO and CDC websites
- Scientific journals like The Lancet
- Fact-checking sites like Snopes

showed that no scientific evidence supported the claim.

2. False Election Fraud Claims

During the 2020 US election, a viral video claimed to show "ballots being destroyed." However, cross-referencing with:

- Local election board statements
- News reports from multiple outlets
- Metadata analysis of the video

proved that the video actually showed ballots being legally discarded as part of routine election procedures.

Best Practices for Cross-Referencing Information

✔ Check at least three independent sources before considering information reliable.

✔ Use fact-checking databases to quickly verify viral claims.

✔ Prioritize primary sources like government records and scientific studies over secondhand reports.

✔ Be wary of sources with strong political or ideological bias.

✔ Verify timestamps, authorship, and context to prevent falling for outdated or misrepresented information.

Conclusion: The Power of Cross-Referencing in OSINT

Cross-referencing is an essential skill in OSINT and media verification. In a world flooded with fake news, propaganda, and manipulated content, systematically comparing sources ensures that truth prevails over misinformation. By leveraging fact-checking tools, primary sources, and reputable media outlets, OSINT analysts can build strong, evidence-based investigations that uncover the truth behind viral claims.

☞ **Final Tip**: Always ask yourself: "Who benefits if this claim is believed?" This question can often reveal the true motives behind disinformation.

4.5 Common Challenges in Fact-Checking Investigations

Fact-checking has become an essential practice in the fight against misinformation and disinformation. However, conducting thorough and accurate fact-checking investigations is not without its challenges. As disinformation tactics evolve, fact-checkers must navigate technological, psychological, and methodological obstacles that can complicate the verification process. This subchapter explores the most common challenges in fact-checking and provides strategies to overcome them.

1. The Rapid Spread of Misinformation

One of the biggest challenges fact-checkers face is the speed at which misinformation spreads, especially on social media. False information often spreads faster and wider than the truth due to its emotional appeal, sensationalism, and algorithmic amplification.

Example:

A fake news article about a celebrity's death can go viral in minutes, gaining millions of shares before any fact-checking organization can respond. Even after debunking, many people continue to believe the false claim.

How to Overcome This Challenge

✅ Use real-time monitoring tools like Crowdtangle, Hoaxy, and Google Trends to detect viral misinformation early.

✅ Prebunking: Instead of just debunking false claims after they spread, educate the public on common disinformation tactics before they encounter them.

✓ Speed vs. Accuracy: While it's important to act fast, fact-checking must remain rigorous and evidence-based to maintain credibility.

2. Evasion Tactics by Disinformation Campaigns

Disinformation actors frequently adapt their methods to evade detection. Some common tactics include:

- **"Death by a Thousand Lies"**: Overloading the public with numerous false claims to create confusion.
- **Mimicking trusted sources**: Fake news websites that imitate legitimate news outlets.
- **Changing keywords and phrasing**: To avoid being flagged by automated detection systems, misinformation actors alter spellings (e.g., "V@cc1ne hoax" instead of "Vaccine hoax").
- **Shifting narratives**: When one conspiracy theory is debunked, it quickly morphs into a slightly different version.

How to Overcome This Challenge

✓ Monitor historical patterns of disinformation actors to predict their next moves.

✓ Use OSINT tools to track website domain registrations and social media networks that spread false information.

✓ Collaborate with fact-checking organizations and journalists to stay ahead of evolving tactics.

3. Difficulty in Accessing Primary Sources

Fact-checking requires verifiable and authoritative sources to confirm or debunk claims. However, in some cases, obtaining primary sources is difficult due to:

- Lack of transparency from governments and organizations.
- Restricted access to official documents behind paywalls or firewalls.
- Language barriers when verifying information from international sources.

How to Overcome This Challenge

✓ Use Freedom of Information Act (FOIA) requests where applicable.

✓ Leverage open-source intelligence (OSINT) tools to find archived or alternative sources.

✓ Work with multilingual teams or use AI translation tools like Google Translate and DeepL to access foreign-language sources.

4. Deepfakes & AI-Generated Disinformation

With advances in artificial intelligence, deepfake videos, AI-generated articles, and synthetic images have made misinformation more sophisticated and harder to detect.

Example:

In 2023, a deepfake video of a political leader making controversial statements went viral before being debunked. The high-quality AI-generated footage fooled millions.

How to Overcome This Challenge

✓ Use AI detection tools like Deepware Scanner, Sensity.ai, and Reality Defender to identify deepfakes.

✓ Verify metadata and provenance of images and videos using tools like InVID, ExifTool, and Google Reverse Image Search.

✓ Cross-reference content with known, verified sources before accepting visual evidence as authentic.

5. The Persistence of False Narratives

Even after a false claim is debunked, people may continue to believe it. This is due to:

- **Confirmation bias**: People accept information that aligns with their beliefs and reject contradictory evidence.
- **The illusory truth effect**: Repetition makes false claims seem more believable over time.
- **Cognitive dissonance**: When faced with conflicting information, individuals may rationalize misinformation rather than change their views.

How to Overcome This Challenge

✅ Use clear, simple, and non-confrontational language when debunking claims to avoid reinforcing beliefs.

✅ Provide alternative explanations rather than just refuting misinformation.

✅ Leverage trusted messengers—people are more likely to believe fact-checks if they come from sources they already trust.

6. Algorithmic Bias & Platform Policies

Social media algorithms prioritize engagement over accuracy, often amplifying sensationalist and misleading content. Additionally, platforms have inconsistent content moderation policies, allowing some misinformation to persist.

How to Overcome This Challenge

✅ **Understand platform algorithms**: Awareness of how content spreads can help fact-checkers counter disinformation more effectively.

✅ Advocate for transparency and better content moderation policies from tech companies.

✅ Develop and promote independent fact-checking tools that integrate with social media platforms.

7. Risk of Harassment & Threats Against Fact-Checkers

Fact-checkers often become targets of harassment, doxxing, and online threats from individuals or groups who oppose their work.

How to Overcome This Challenge

✅ Use digital security best practices (e.g., two-factor authentication, VPNs, and secure messaging apps).

✓ Minimize personal exposure by keeping professional and personal online identities separate.

✓ Work within networks—collaborating with established organizations offers safety and support.

Conclusion: Strengthening Fact-Checking in the Digital Age

Despite the challenges, fact-checking remains a crucial defense against disinformation. By combining technological tools, strategic methodologies, and collaboration, fact-checkers can effectively counter misinformation and uphold the integrity of information.

◆ **Key Takeaways:**

- Speed is important, but accuracy is essential.
- Fact-checking must evolve to counter new disinformation tactics.
- Educating the public on misinformation patterns is just as important as debunking individual claims.

In the next section, we will explore open-source tools that can assist in fact-checking investigations and enhance the credibility of digital content verification.

4.6 Case Study: How OSINT Debunked a High-Profile Hoax

The rise of open-source intelligence (OSINT) has transformed how investigators, journalists, and fact-checkers expose false information. This case study examines a high-profile hoax that spread widely across social media, deceived mainstream audiences, and was ultimately debunked using OSINT techniques. By analyzing this case, we can understand the effectiveness of digital forensic methods, image verification, and network analysis in combating disinformation.

The Hoax: The "War Zone Attack" Video

In early 2023, a video allegedly showing a missile attack on a European city went viral across Twitter, TikTok, and Facebook. The footage, appearing to show explosions near a government building, spread panic and fueled conspiracy theories. The claim was that a foreign military operation had targeted the area, escalating geopolitical tensions.

Prominent influencers, some news outlets, and even politicians shared the footage, demanding immediate action. Within hours, hashtags like #CityUnderAttack and #WWIII trended worldwide. However, within 24 hours, OSINT investigators debunked the video using a combination of reverse image searches, geolocation, metadata analysis, and forensic techniques.

Step 1: Reverse Image & Video Search

The first step in analyzing any viral video is conducting a reverse image search on key frames extracted from the footage. Investigators used tools like:

🔎 Google Reverse Image Search
🔎 TinEye
🔎 Yandex Image Search

Findings:

- The explosion visuals matched a 2015 video game cinematic trailer.
- Some frames had appeared in an older news report about a different conflict zone from five years earlier.

📌 **Key Takeaway**: Fake videos often use recycled footage from unrelated events, making reverse image search an essential first step in verification.

Step 2: Metadata & Forensic Analysis

To further verify the video's authenticity, investigators analyzed its metadata using tools like:

☐ **ExifTool** – Extracted metadata from the video.
☐ **InVID-WeVerify** – Checked for video tampering and traced its source.

Findings:

- The file's metadata revealed that the video had been edited using Adobe After Effects, a common tool for CGI and video manipulation.
- The timestamps were inconsistent with the alleged attack time, showing it was created days before the supposed event.

📌 **Key Takeaway**: Authentic news footage should have metadata that aligns with the reported time, location, and source. Manipulated videos often lack this consistency.

Step 3: Geolocation & Weather Verification

To verify the geographical accuracy of the video, OSINT analysts:

☐ Compared landmarks in the footage with Google Earth & Google Street View.
☐ Checked the weather conditions in the video against historical weather data using Wolfram Alpha.

Findings:

- The video claimed to show an attack in Kyiv, Ukraine, but analysis showed that the skyline didn't match the actual city layout.
- The weather in the footage (clear skies) didn't match historical records, which reported rain on the alleged date of the attack.

📌 **Key Takeaway**: Even small inconsistencies in geography and weather conditions can reveal fabrications.

Step 4: Social Media Network Analysis

Once the video was exposed as fake, analysts investigated who spread the hoax and how it gained traction. Using tools like:

📶 **Hoaxy & Botometer** – Analyzed automated bot activity.
📶 **CrowdTangle** – Tracked viral spread on Facebook and Instagram.
📶 **TweetDeck & Twitter API** – Identified key influencers amplifying the claim.

Findings:

- The earliest shares came from newly created accounts with low follower counts, indicating a coordinated disinformation campaign.
- Some accounts boosting the video were linked to previous misinformation campaigns, showing a pattern of spreading false narratives.
- Bot analysis revealed that automated accounts were responsible for much of the viral engagement.

📌 **Key Takeaway**: Many viral hoaxes are intentionally amplified by bot networks, making social media forensics crucial in tracing disinformation origins.

Step 5: Fact-Checking & Expert Verification

Finally, professional fact-checkers from organizations like Bellingcat, Reuters Fact Check, and AFP Fact Check conducted independent verifications. They:

🔍 Consulted military analysts to confirm the explosions didn't match real-world missile strikes.
🔍 Contacted local journalists and eyewitnesses, who confirmed no such attack had occurred.
🔍 Published reports debunking the video with verified evidence.

The Impact of the Debunking

After OSINT investigators proved the video was fake, major social media platforms took action:

✕ Twitter, Facebook, and YouTube flagged the content as false and removed misleading posts.

✕ News agencies issued corrections and retracted their initial reports.

✕ The public narrative shifted, reducing panic and preventing escalation of tensions.

However, the false claim still persisted in conspiracy circles, proving that even when debunked, misinformation can linger.

📌 **Final Takeaway**: While OSINT is highly effective in debunking hoaxes, disinformation campaigns often rely on emotional engagement rather than facts—making public education on misinformation vital.

Conclusion: The Power of OSINT in Exposing Hoaxes

This case study highlights the importance of OSINT techniques in verifying digital content and countering disinformation campaigns. The viral hoax was dismantled using a structured, multi-step approach involving:

✓ Reverse image search to detect recycled footage.

✓ Metadata & forensic analysis to check for tampering.

✓ Geolocation & weather verification to expose location/time inconsistencies.

✓ Social media network analysis to trace the spread of misinformation.

✓ Expert verification & fact-checking to confirm findings.

In an era of deepfakes, AI-generated disinformation, and viral hoaxes, OSINT remains one of the most powerful tools in preserving truth and accountability in the digital age.

5. Tracking Bots & Coordinated Networks

Bots and coordinated networks are at the core of many disinformation campaigns, amplifying false narratives and spreading propaganda at an unprecedented scale. This chapter focuses on the techniques used to identify and track these automated systems and their human collaborators. We examine how bots manipulate social media trends, create fake engagement, and simulate organic interactions. Through OSINT tools and methodologies, we'll uncover how to detect bot-driven activity, analyze patterns of coordination, and trace the connections within these networks. By understanding the digital fingerprints of these malicious operations, readers will gain the expertise needed to dismantle the networks behind disinformation.

5.1 What Are Bots & How Are They Used in Disinformation?

The spread of disinformation is no longer just a human-driven activity—bots now play a central role in amplifying false narratives, manipulating public opinion, and distorting online conversations. These automated accounts, which can operate across social media platforms, forums, and comment sections, are designed to mimic human behavior while pushing specific agendas at scale. Understanding how bots function, the types of bots used in disinformation campaigns, and the techniques for detecting them is crucial for OSINT investigators and fact-checkers.

1. Understanding Bots: Definition & Functionality

A bot (short for "robot") is an automated software program that performs repetitive tasks on the internet. Bots can be simple scripts that post messages at set intervals, or advanced AI-driven entities capable of engaging in conversations and adapting to human responses.

While some bots serve legitimate purposes (e.g., customer service chatbots, weather updates, or financial alerts), others are designed specifically for manipulation and disinformation.

◆ **Key Features of Disinformation Bots:**

- Operate 24/7 without breaks.
- Generate mass content rapidly to flood platforms with a specific narrative.

- Amplify (like, share, retweet) certain posts to create false popularity.
- Attack opposing viewpoints with spam, trolling, or harassment.
- Pretend to be real users by stealing profile pictures and bios.

📌 **Example**: During major political events, Twitter bot networks can boost hashtags artificially, making them trend worldwide—even if real users aren't actually engaging with them in large numbers.

2. How Bots Are Used in Disinformation Campaigns

Bots can be deployed for various manipulative tactics to influence public perception and spread falsehoods. Below are some of the most common ways disinformation campaigns leverage bots:

A. Amplification of False Narratives

Bots can make fake news articles, conspiracy theories, or propaganda appear more popular than they actually are.

Example:

In 2020, researchers found that nearly half of the Twitter accounts spreading COVID-19 conspiracy theories were bots programmed to push misleading health information.

◆ **OSINT Tip**: Use tools like Hoaxy or Botometer to track suspicious amplification patterns.

B. Astroturfing: Fake Grassroots Movements

Astroturfing is the practice of creating fake public support for a political cause, product, or ideology using bot-driven engagement.

Example:

- Thousands of bots spam pro-government messages to create the illusion of widespread support.
- Fake accounts flood online petitions, polls, and comment sections to manipulate perceived public opinion.

◆ **OSINT Tip**: Check account creation dates—many bot networks are created in bulk on the same day.

C. Disrupting Conversations with Troll Bots

Some bots are designed to flood comment sections, Twitter threads, or Facebook discussions with disruptive or inflammatory remarks, making genuine discourse nearly impossible.

Example:

- During elections, bots post aggressive responses to critics of a candidate, making it appear as if a majority supports them.
- In news articles, bot comments attack journalists or spread contradictory claims to confuse readers.

◆ **OSINT Tip**: Look for accounts with very high activity levels—bots often post hundreds of times per day.

D. Fake Followers & Engagement Manipulation

Disinformation campaigns often inflate follower counts of influencers or political figures to artificially boost credibility.

Example:

- A politician's social media team purchases 100,000 bot followers to make them look more influential.
- A fake news outlet buys fake engagement (likes, shares, views) to trick algorithms into promoting its content.

◆ **OSINT Tip**: Analyze follower-to-engagement ratios—bots often have thousands of followers but very few real interactions.

E. Bot-Driven Hashtag Hijacking

Bots can take over trending hashtags by spamming unrelated or false content to distort discussions.

Example:

- A legitimate protest movement uses #JusticeForX, but disinformation bots flood the hashtag with fake news stories, memes, or off-topic posts to drown out real discussions.

◆ **OSINT Tip**: Use tools like TweetDeck and TrendsMap to analyze how a hashtag originated and evolved.

3. How to Identify & Investigate Bots with OSINT

Detecting bots is crucial in identifying coordinated disinformation campaigns. Here are some of the best OSINT techniques to spot and analyze bot activity:

A. Check for Unnatural Posting Patterns

🔍 **Tools to Use:**

- **Botometer (by Indiana University)** – Scores Twitter accounts based on bot-like behavior.
- **Hoaxy** – Visualizes how misinformation spreads on social media.

⚑ **Warning Signs:**

✓ Unrealistically high posting frequency (e.g., 500 tweets per day).

✓ Posts at perfectly regular intervals (bots operate on scheduled scripts).

✓ Retweets only, no original content (bots rarely create unique posts).

B. Analyze Account Creation Date & Profile Details

🔍 **Tools to Use:**

- **Twitter Advanced Search** – Filter accounts by creation date.
- **Whois Lookup** – Investigate suspicious websites linked to bot accounts.

⚑ **Warning Signs:**

✓ Multiple accounts created on the same date (common in bot farms).

✓ Default or stolen profile pictures (often AI-generated faces).

✓ Generic bios with vague political slogans (bots avoid personal details).

C. Investigate Network Connections

🔍 **Tools to Use:**

- **Graphika & Maltego** – Map bot networks and connections.
- **TweetDeck & Gephi** – Track patterns of coordinated behavior.

▶ **Warning Signs:**

✓ Multiple accounts posting the exact same message simultaneously.

✓ Accounts exclusively engaging with each other (bot networks often interact only within their group).

✓ Sudden spikes in engagement (bot networks activate in waves).

D. Reverse Image Search Profile Pictures

Many bots use stolen or AI-generated profile pictures. You can check authenticity by:

🔍 **Tools to Use:**

- Google Reverse Image Search
- Yandex Reverse Image Search
- PimEyes (for face recognition searches)

▶ **Warning Signs:**

✓ Profile pictures appearing on multiple unrelated accounts.

✓ AI-generated faces with unnatural symmetry or missing background details.

Conclusion: The Role of OSINT in Fighting Bot-Driven Disinformation

As bots become more sophisticated, so must our methods for detecting and countering their influence. OSINT provides powerful tools to:

✅ Track the origins of disinformation campaigns.

✅ Expose fake engagement tactics and bot networks.

✅ Identify bad actors behind manipulation efforts.

By understanding bot behavior and applying OSINT techniques, investigators, journalists, and analysts can disrupt coordinated disinformation campaigns before they shape public perception.

5.2 Identifying Bot Behavior & Automated Accounts

The widespread use of bots in disinformation campaigns has made it crucial for OSINT analysts, journalists, and researchers to develop techniques for detecting automated accounts. While some bots serve legitimate functions, malicious actors use them to spread propaganda, manipulate trends, and create artificial engagement. This chapter explores the key behavioral patterns of bot accounts, the most effective OSINT techniques for detecting them, and real-world examples of bot-driven disinformation campaigns.

1. Understanding Bot Behavior

Automated accounts exhibit predictable behaviors that distinguish them from real users. Bots range from simple scripts that post content on a schedule to AI-driven personas capable of holding conversations.

◆ **Common Characteristics of Bots:**

- **Unusual activity levels**: Posting hundreds or thousands of times per day.
- **Repetitive posting**: Sharing the same content repeatedly or copying other accounts.
- **Instantaneous engagement**: Retweeting or liking posts within seconds of publication.
- **Minimal personal interaction**: Rarely engaging in genuine conversations.
- **Coordinated behavior**: Multiple accounts posting identical messages at the same time.

📌 **Example:**

During major political events, bots amplify hashtags by posting thousands of tweets within minutes, making the topic trend artificially.

2. Types of Bots Used in Disinformation

Bots in disinformation campaigns can serve different purposes:

A. Amplification Bots

- **Primary function**: Boost content visibility by mass-sharing posts.
- **Used for**: Making fake news or propaganda appear more popular than it actually is.
- **Example**: A network of thousands of bots retweeting government propaganda to manipulate social media algorithms.

◆ **How to Detect:**

✓ **Check timestamp patterns** – Bots post at perfectly timed intervals.
✓ **Analyze network activity** – Use OSINT tools to see if the same accounts amplify content in an unnatural way.

B. Sock Puppet Accounts

- **Primary function**: Appear as real users to push narratives while hiding the true operator's identity.
- **Used for**: Influencing public opinion, harassing opponents, and spreading fake news.
- **Example**: A fake persona created to post fabricated reports about a political opponent.

◆ **How to Detect:**

✓ **Look for inconsistencies in profile details** – Fake accounts often lack personal photos or have vague biographies.
✓ **Perform a reverse image search** – Sock puppets frequently use stolen or AI-generated profile pictures.

C. Spam Bots

- **Primary function**: Overwhelm discussions with noise to drown out real conversations.
- **Used for**: Disrupting political discussions, pushing clickbait, or hiding criticism.
- **Example**: A sudden flood of irrelevant messages under a trending hashtag to distract from an important debate.

◆ **How to Detect:**

✅ Check for low follower counts with high posting rates.

✅ Identify repetition – If multiple accounts post identical messages within seconds, they are likely spam bots.

D. AI Chatbots & Deepfake Accounts

- **Primary function**: Engage in discussions and appear human-like.
- **Used for**: Mimicking real users, building fake credibility, or impersonating real people.
- **Example**: AI-generated profiles commenting on news articles to support a political agenda.

◆ **How to Detect:**

✅ **Use AI detection tools** – Some OSINT tools analyze writing styles to identify AI-generated text.
✅ **Check for emotional inconsistency** – AI chatbots often struggle with sarcasm or nuanced discussions.

3. OSINT Techniques for Identifying Bots

OSINT investigators use a variety of open-source tools and analytical methods to detect bots. Below are key approaches:

A. Monitoring Activity Patterns

🔍 **Tools to Use:**

- **Botometer (Indiana University)** – Analyzes Twitter accounts and scores them based on bot-like behavior.

- **Twitonomy** – Tracks posting frequency and engagement metrics.

▶ **Warning Signs:**

✓ Accounts posting at inhuman speeds (e.g., every few seconds).

✓ Highly repetitive content with no variation.

B. Investigating Account Metadata

🔍 **Tools to Use:**

- **Whois Lookup** – Checks the domain registration of websites linked to suspicious accounts.
- **ExifTool** – Extracts metadata from images and videos used by bot accounts.

▶ **Warning Signs:**

✓ Multiple accounts created on the same day (bot farms often register accounts in bulk).

✓ Missing metadata or anomalies in profile images.

C. Reverse Image Searching Profile Pictures

🔍 **Tools to Use:**

- **Google Reverse Image Search** – Detects stolen or AI-generated images.
- **Yandex Image Search** – Often more effective than Google for finding duplicates.
- **PimEyes** – A facial recognition search tool.

▶ **Warning Signs:**

✓ Profile pictures used by multiple accounts.

✓ AI-generated faces (symmetrical features, unnatural backgrounds).

📌 **Example:**

A group of bot accounts using AI-generated faces from ThisPersonDoesNotExist.com was uncovered during an election disinformation campaign.

D. Detecting Coordinated Bot Networks

🔍 Tools to Use:

- **Hoaxy** – Visualizes how misinformation spreads and identifies clusters of bot activity.
- **Gephi & Maltego** – Helps map relationships between accounts in bot networks.

⚑ Warning Signs:

✅ Accounts interacting only within a closed group.

✅ Identical messages posted simultaneously by multiple users.

📌 Example:

During a foreign interference operation, OSINT researchers used Gephi to uncover a network of 300+ accounts posting identical political messages within seconds of each other.

4. Case Study: Bot Network Manipulating an Election

In 2022, OSINT investigators exposed a bot network influencing an African election.

Key Findings:

- Thousands of fake accounts were promoting one candidate while attacking opponents.
- Bots amplified false reports of election fraud to undermine public trust.
- Reverse image searches revealed many accounts had stolen profile pictures.
- Network analysis showed that most accounts followed the same 10 influencers, indicating central coordination.

📌 Impact:

After being exposed, social media platforms removed thousands of fake accounts, and fact-checkers debunked false claims before they could influence the final vote.

Conclusion: The Importance of OSINT in Bot Detection

The increasing sophistication of bots in disinformation campaigns makes bot detection an essential skill for OSINT investigators, journalists, and researchers. By understanding bot behavior, leveraging OSINT tools, and applying analytical techniques, it is possible to unmask fake engagement, disrupt disinformation campaigns, and protect the integrity of online discussions.

Key Takeaways:

✓ Bots manipulate public opinion by amplifying false narratives and drowning out real conversations.

✓ Different types of bots serve different purposes, from spam to sophisticated AI-driven accounts.

✓ OSINT tools like Botometer, Hoaxy, and Gephi help uncover bot activity and coordinated networks.

✓ Analyzing metadata, network connections, and posting behavior is crucial in identifying automated accounts.

5.3 Network Analysis: Mapping Fake Engagement Campaigns

The spread of disinformation is rarely the work of a single account. Instead, it is orchestrated through coordinated networks that amplify false narratives, manipulate trends, and create artificial engagement. Fake engagement campaigns use botnets, sock puppets, and troll farms to deceive audiences into believing that certain ideas, political movements, or products have more public support than they actually do. In this chapter, we will explore how to map these networks, analyze connections, and expose coordinated disinformation operations using OSINT techniques.

1. Understanding Fake Engagement Campaigns

Fake engagement campaigns operate by leveraging a network of automated or coordinated accounts to artificially boost content. These campaigns can be designed to:

- ◆ **Increase visibility** – Make false or misleading content appear popular.
- ◆ **Distort public opinion** – Create the illusion of widespread support for a cause.
- ◆ **Suppress dissent** – Overwhelm opposing voices with harassment or spam.
- ◆ **Influence elections & policies** – Manipulate voters and policymakers.

📌 **Example:**

A government-backed bot network floods social media with supportive messages for a leader, making it seem like the majority of citizens approve of their policies—when, in reality, the engagement is entirely artificial.

2. Key Indicators of Coordinated Engagement Campaigns

Coordinated fake engagement campaigns can be identified through specific behavioral patterns:

✓ **Simultaneous Posting**: Multiple accounts post identical messages at the same time.
✓ **Repetitive Hashtag Usage**: Unusual hashtag surges, often with low original engagement.
✓ **Unusual Network Activity**: Many accounts interacting only with each other and not with genuine users.
✓ **Newly Created Accounts**: Large numbers of accounts registered in bulk on the same date.
✓ **Abnormal Like/Retweet Ratios**: A post receives thousands of likes/shares but few comments—indicating bot amplification.

📌 **Example:**

A disinformation campaign supporting a false narrative about a protest suddenly sees thousands of tweets with the same wording appearing in a short time frame, all from accounts created within the last three months.

3. OSINT Techniques for Mapping Fake Engagement Networks

To uncover coordinated engagement campaigns, OSINT investigators rely on a combination of social media analysis, network visualization, and metadata tracking.

A. Identifying Coordinated Posting Activity

🔍 Tools to Use:

- **TweetDeck & TrendsMap** – Track trending hashtags and how they originated.
- **Hoaxy (Indiana University)** – Visualize how misinformation spreads.

⚑ How to Spot Coordination:

✅ Multiple accounts tweeting the same message within seconds.

✅ Hashtags spiking unnaturally without organic discussion.

✅ Identical engagement patterns across multiple accounts.

B. Analyzing Bot Networks & Fake Followers

🔍 Tools to Use:

- **Botometer (Indiana University)** – Detects bot-like activity on Twitter.
- **AccountAnalysis** – Provides in-depth analysis of Twitter account activity.

⚑ How to Spot Fake Engagement:

✅ Suspicious follower-to-engagement ratios (e.g., 50,000 followers but only 3 likes per post).

✅ Retweets/likes coming from newly created or inactive accounts.

✅ Accounts exclusively interacting within a small circle.

📌 Example:

During an election campaign, researchers found that 40% of retweets for a candidate's viral post came from fake accounts created in the past two weeks, indicating an artificial popularity boost.

C. Mapping Connections Between Accounts

🔍 Tools to Use:

- **Gephi & Maltego** – Create network graphs to visualize how accounts interact.

- **Twint (Twitter Intelligence Tool)** – Scrape Twitter data for network analysis.

▶ **How to Identify Coordinated Networks:**

✅ Clusters of accounts frequently interacting with each other—but not with outsiders.

✅ Multiple accounts sharing the same URLs at the same time.

✅ Anomalous spikes in activity from a small group of users.

📌 **Example:**

An OSINT investigation into a coordinated troll campaign revealed a cluster of 200+ accounts retweeting each other's content exclusively, forming an isolated echo chamber to push a fabricated scandal.

D. Reverse Image Search for Fake Profile Pictures

🔍 **Tools to Use:**

- **Google Reverse Image Search** – Identify stolen images used for fake profiles.
- **PimEyes** – Perform facial recognition searches.
- **ThisPersonDoesNotExist.com** – Check for AI-generated profile pictures.

▶ **How to Detect Fake Profiles:**

✅ Profile pictures appearing on multiple unrelated accounts.

✅ AI-generated faces (often with minor distortions in the background).

✅ Stock images or celebrity photos used as profile pictures.

📌 **Example:**

A disinformation campaign pushing propaganda in Eastern Europe was found to have used dozens of fake accounts with AI-generated faces, making them appear as real activists supporting the cause.

4. Case Study: Exposing a Fake Engagement Campaign

Background:

In 2021, OSINT researchers exposed a bot network influencing COVID-19 vaccine discussions on Twitter.

🔎 Investigation Process:

1☐ **Hashtag Analysis**: Researchers noticed a surge in tweets using the hashtag #NoVaccineMandates within hours.

2☐ **Account Creation Dates**: 70% of the accounts promoting the hashtag were less than 6 months old.

3☐ **Coordinated Posting**: Hundreds of tweets contained identical phrasing, indicating automated posting.

4☐ **Network Mapping**: Visualization tools revealed that most interactions were happening within a small group of interconnected accounts, separate from real users.

📌 Outcome:

- Twitter suspended over 3,000 bot accounts linked to the campaign.
- Journalists debunked the narrative before it could spread further.
- OSINT investigators traced the network back to a foreign influence operation aiming to destabilize public trust in health policies.

5. Countering Fake Engagement Campaigns with OSINT

Once a fake engagement network is identified, OSINT analysts can take steps to disrupt and expose the campaign:

✅ Report coordinated activity to platforms like Twitter and Facebook.

✅ Publish investigative findings to inform the public and journalists.

✅ Work with fact-checking organizations to debunk the disinformation before it spreads.

✅ Educate users on recognizing fake engagement patterns.

📌 Example:

After OSINT researchers exposed a coordinated disinformation campaign about election fraud, media coverage helped neutralize the narrative, preventing widespread panic.

Conclusion: The Power of OSINT in Unmasking Fake Engagement

Mapping fake engagement campaigns requires a combination of network analysis, metadata research, and pattern detection. By leveraging OSINT tools, investigators can track coordinated disinformation efforts, expose hidden influence operations, and protect the integrity of online discussions.

Key Takeaways:

✓ Fake engagement campaigns use botnets, sock puppets, and troll farms to manipulate public opinion.

✓ Network analysis helps uncover coordinated activity patterns and identify bot clusters.

✓ OSINT tools like Gephi, Botometer, and Hoaxy are essential for mapping fake engagement campaigns.

✓ Reverse image searches can expose fake profiles used in disinformation networks.

✓ Public exposure of fake engagement campaigns is key to neutralizing their impact.

5.4 Tools for Detecting Coordinated Activity

The rapid spread of disinformation is often fueled by coordinated activity, where groups of accounts—sometimes bots, sock puppets, or paid operators—amplify narratives to manipulate public perception. Detecting these orchestrated efforts is a crucial step in OSINT investigations. In this chapter, we will explore specialized tools and techniques for identifying and analyzing these networks, helping investigators track their origins, behaviors, and impact.

1. Understanding Coordinated Activity

Coordinated activity refers to multiple accounts working together to amplify specific content in an organized manner. These networks can be fully automated (botnets), human-driven (troll farms, paid influencers), or a combination of both (hybrid campaigns).

Common Signs of Coordination:

◆ **Simultaneous Posting** – Multiple accounts post identical content at the same time.

◆ **Engagement Manipulation** – Unusual patterns of likes, shares, or retweets from the same group of accounts.

◆ **Hashtag Brigading** – A rapid and unnatural increase in the use of a specific hashtag.

◆ **Echo Chambers** – Accounts that mostly engage with each other rather than real users.

◆ **Unusual Account Behavior** – Many accounts created at the same time with similar bios and activity patterns.

📌 **Example:**

A bot network promoting false information about an election was detected when thousands of accounts posted identical messages within minutes, making it appear as a trending topic.

2. Tools for Detecting Coordinated Activity

OSINT professionals use various tools to identify, map, and analyze disinformation networks. Below are some of the most effective ones categorized by their functions.

A. Social Media Analysis & Visualization

🔍 **Hoaxy (hoaxy.iuni.iu.edu)**

✓ **Function**: Tracks how misinformation spreads across Twitter, mapping interactions between accounts.

✓ **Use Case**: Identify who is amplifying a false claim and whether the same group repeatedly pushes disinformation.

🔍 **Gephi (gephi.org)**

✓ **Function**: Open-source network visualization tool that maps connections between accounts.

✓ **Use Case**: Create network graphs to identify clusters of accounts engaging in coordinated behavior.

🔍 **TAGS (Twitter Archiving Google Sheet)**

✓ **Function**: Extracts Twitter data for trend analysis and detecting repeated narratives.

✓ **Use Case**: Investigate how hashtags evolve over time and identify anomalous activity spikes.

📌 **Example:**

During an election cycle, Gephi visualizations helped expose a bot-driven campaign where thousands of Twitter accounts repeatedly interacted with only a few key influencers.

B. Bot & Automation Detection

🔍 Botometer (botometer.osome.iu.edu)

✓ **Function**: Evaluates Twitter accounts and assigns a bot likelihood score.

✓ **Use Case**: Distinguish between human and automated engagement.

🔍 BotSentinel (botsentinel.com)

✓ **Function**: Identifies and tracks inauthentic behavior across social media.

✓ **Use Case**: Detect suspicious patterns that may indicate coordinated bot networks.

🔍 Twint (Twitter Intelligence Tool)

✓ **Function**: Scrapes Twitter data for analyzing bulk activity without using the Twitter API.

✓ **Use Case**: Identify synchronized posting patterns and interactions among suspected accounts.

📌 **Example:**

An OSINT analyst using Botometer found that 60% of the accounts pushing an anti-vaccine narrative exhibited bot-like behavior, revealing a likely disinformation campaign.

C. Hashtag & Trend Manipulation Detection

🔍 Trendsmap (trendsmap.com)

✔ **Function**: Provides real-time Twitter trend analysis, showing geographic origins and activity spikes.

✔ **Use Case**: Investigate whether a trend is organic or artificially boosted by bot activity.

🔍 Ritetag (ritetag.com)

✔ **Function**: Tracks hashtag usage trends over time.

✔ **Use Case**: Identify suspicious hashtag brigading, where a small number of accounts repeatedly push a narrative.

📌 Example:

During a geopolitical crisis, analysts discovered that a trending hashtag was initially pushed by a handful of bot accounts, artificially inflating its visibility.

D. Metadata & Content Verification

🔍 InVID & WeVerify (invid-project.eu)

✔ **Function**: Analyzes videos and images for manipulation, metadata, and provenance.

✔ **Use Case**: Detect fake engagement by identifying reused or doctored media.

🔍 ExifTool (exiftool.org)

✔ **Function**: Extracts metadata from images and videos.

✔ **Use Case**: Identify content that has been manipulated and its original source.

📌 Example:

An investigation into a viral protest video showed that its metadata indicated it was recorded years earlier, debunking the false claim.

3. Detecting Coordinated Narratives with OSINT

Beyond detecting bots and fake engagement, investigators must also analyze how disinformation narratives evolve.

Steps to Track a Coordinated Narrative:

1☐ **Identify the Core Message** – What is being pushed? Is it a repeated narrative?

2☐ **Analyze Early Adopters** – Which accounts started spreading it first?

3☐ **Track Amplification** – Are the same accounts repeatedly engaging with the content?

4☐ **Check for Cross-Platform Spread** – Does the content appear on Facebook, Telegram, or other platforms?

5☐ **Look for Patterned Behavior** – Does engagement appear organic or automated?

📌 **Example:**

During a cyberattack on a government, a narrative blaming a foreign state emerged on social media. Investigators used TAGS and Gephi to find that the narrative was initially pushed by a cluster of fake accounts, revealing a potential false-flag operation.

4. Case Study: Unmasking a Coordinated Influence Operation

🔎 **Scenario:**

In 2023, OSINT researchers uncovered a coordinated campaign aimed at discrediting Western journalists.

🔎 **Investigation Process:**

1☐ **Botometer & Twint Analysis** – Revealed that 80% of the accounts promoting anti-journalist content were likely bots.

2☐ **Gephi Visualization** – Showed that these accounts formed isolated clusters, amplifying each other's messages.

3☐ **Trendsmap Monitoring** – Detected that the hashtag promoting the disinformation narrative was artificially spiked.

📌 **Outcome:**

- The report led to mass account suspensions on Twitter.
- Media outlets debunked the false claims, preventing further spread.
- Researchers linked the campaign to a state-sponsored influence operation.

5. Countering Coordinated Disinformation Efforts

Once a coordinated activity is detected, OSINT analysts can take preventative actions:

✅ **Expose the network** – Publish findings to make the campaign ineffective.

✅ **Work with fact-checkers** – Verify false claims before they spread.

✅ **Report activity** – Alert platforms to potential ToS violations.

✅ **Educate the public** – Teach people to recognize coordinated disinformation.

📌 **Example:**

During an election, analysts exposed a bot-driven smear campaign, leading to media coverage that neutralized the disinformation before it influenced voters.

Conclusion: OSINT's Role in Detecting Coordinated Activity

Detecting coordinated disinformation efforts requires a combination of bot detection, network analysis, hashtag tracking, and content verification. By leveraging OSINT tools, investigators can unmask hidden influence campaigns, expose disinformation networks, and protect the integrity of online discourse.

5.5 How Governments & Organizations Use Bot Armies

The use of bot armies in digital influence campaigns has become a powerful tool for governments, political groups, and organizations to manipulate public opinion, amplify narratives, and distort online discourse. These bot networks—composed of automated accounts, sock puppets, and coordinated human operators—can shape perceptions of political events, social movements, and global conflicts. This chapter explores how different actors deploy bot armies, their tactics, objectives, and impact, and how OSINT investigators can track and expose them.

1. Understanding Bot Armies

A bot army is a large network of automated or semi-automated social media accounts that operate under a centralized command. These bots are programmed to engage in mass posting, retweeting, liking, and commenting to artificially amplify content and create the illusion of grassroots support for a particular cause.

Types of Bot Armies

◆ **Political Bots** – Used by governments and political groups to sway public opinion, attack opponents, or spread propaganda.

◆ **Commercial Bots** – Deployed by businesses to boost brand visibility or spread fake reviews.

◆ **Astroturfing Bots** – Fake grassroots movements designed to manipulate public perception.

◆ **Malicious Bots** – Used for cyberattacks, phishing, and spamming.

◆ **Hybrid Networks** – A combination of bots and human-run sock puppet accounts to make disinformation campaigns appear more authentic.

📌 **Example:**

A study found that over 20% of Twitter activity during a major election was driven by bot accounts, which systematically spread misleading narratives about candidates.

2. How Governments Use Bot Armies

Many governments use bot networks as part of information warfare and psychological operations (PSYOPS) to control narratives domestically and influence foreign affairs.

A. Political Propaganda & Election Interference

Governments deploy bots to amplify state-approved messaging while suppressing dissent. In election cycles, bot armies have been used to:

✓ Flood social media with positive messaging about a preferred candidate.

✓ Attack opposition leaders by spreading false scandals or conspiracy theories.

✓ Suppress negative news by overwhelming critics with pro-government posts.

📌 **Example:**

A Russian bot network was found to be manipulating online conversations during the 2016 U.S. election, spreading divisive narratives and misinformation on social media.

B. Censorship & Information Suppression

Authoritarian regimes use bots to:

✓ Bury dissenting voices by flooding social media with state-approved content.

✓ Disrupt activist movements by posting distracting or misleading information.

✓ Flag and report opposition posts to trigger bans or removals.

📌 Example:

During protests in Hong Kong, Chinese government-linked bot networks were caught spamming social media with anti-protester narratives, drowning out real grassroots discussions.

C. Psychological Warfare & Foreign Influence Operations

Governments also use bot armies to target foreign nations, influencing their domestic politics and destabilizing societies. These tactics include:

✓ Fueling divisions by amplifying both sides of a contentious issue.

✓ Spreading fake news to create distrust in democratic institutions.

✓ Interfering in conflicts by pushing narratives that favor their geopolitical interests.

📌 Example:

Iranian state-sponsored bot networks have been spreading anti-Western propaganda on social media platforms to shape Middle Eastern political narratives.

3. How Organizations & Private Groups Use Bot Armies

Bot networks are not just used by governments—corporations, activist groups, and cybercriminals also deploy them for their own agendas.

A. Corporate Disinformation & Marketing Manipulation

Businesses have been caught using bot armies to
:

✓ Generate fake reviews to promote or sabotage products.

✓ Artificially inflate social media engagement for brand recognition.

✓ Suppress competitors by flagging or spamming their content.

📌 **Example:**

Amazon has cracked down on thousands of fake bot accounts writing positive reviews for certain brands while posting negative reviews for competitors.

B. Activist Movements & Information Warfare

Activist groups and political organizations use bots to:

✓ Mobilize support for causes by artificially boosting hashtags.

✓ Disrupt political opponents by mass-reporting content.

✓ Manipulate online debates by controlling trending topics.

📌 **Example:**

During the 2020 U.S. protests, both left-wing and right-wing groups were accused of deploying bot networks to push false narratives about protest violence and law enforcement actions.

C. Cybercriminals & Financial Fraud

Cybercriminal networks use bots for:

✓ **Cryptocurrency scams** – Fake bot accounts endorse fraudulent investment schemes.

✓ **Phishing campaigns** – Bots send malicious links to steal personal data.

✓ **Pump-and-dump schemes** – Artificially inflating stock or crypto prices through fake hype.

A bot network was discovered pushing fake Elon Musk cryptocurrency giveaways, tricking users into sending funds to scammers.

4. OSINT Techniques for Detecting Bot Armies

OSINT investigators can track and expose bot networks using various analytical tools and investigative methods.

A. Identifying Bot-Like Behavior

✓ **Repetitive Posting Patterns** – Bots post at regular intervals, even at unnatural hours.

✓ **Copy-Paste Engagement** – Many bots reuse the same text or images in their posts.

✓ **Unusual Follower Ratios** – Bots often follow thousands of accounts but have few real followers.

✓ **Hashtag Brigading** – Bots flood specific hashtags within short timeframes.

📌 **Example:**

An OSINT researcher found that 80% of accounts pushing a false health claim were bots, all posting within a 10-minute window with identical phrasing.

B. Network Analysis to Map Bot Interactions

Investigators can use network mapping tools to visualize connections between suspected bot accounts.

🔍 **Gephi** – Maps relationships between accounts engaging in coordinated activity.
🔍 **TAGS** – Scrapes Twitter data to track engagement patterns.
🔍 **Botometer** – Analyzes accounts for bot-like activity scores.

📌 **Example:**

A bot-driven disinformation campaign about COVID-19 was exposed when Gephi revealed clusters of fake accounts all retweeting the same sources.

C. Detecting AI-Generated Bot Content

✓ **Using AI Detection Tools** – Check for GPT-generated content in bot posts.

✓ **Cross-Checking Profiles** – Identifying fake or stolen profile pictures using reverse image searches.

✓ **Metadata Analysis** – Extracting timestamps and geolocation to track bot origins.

📌 **Example:**

A network of fake "news" accounts spreading false stories was exposed when InVID revealed their profile pictures were AI-generated deepfakes.

5. Countering Bot Armies & Their Influence

Once identified, bot networks can be neutralized through strategic countermeasures:

✅ **Expose & Publicize** – Publish investigative findings to alert the public.
✅ **Report to Platforms** – Flag bot activity for social media takedowns.
✅ **Develop AI Filters** – Encourage platforms to improve bot detection.
✅ **Promote Digital Literacy** – Educate users on spotting bot-driven disinformation.

📌 **Example:**

After researchers exposed a Russian bot campaign amplifying anti-vaccine rhetoric, Twitter and Facebook removed thousands of fake accounts, disrupting the operation.

Conclusion: The Future of Bot Armies in Disinformation Warfare

Governments, organizations, and cybercriminals are increasingly using sophisticated bot networks to manipulate digital spaces. As AI improves, bot armies will become harder to detect, making OSINT investigations more critical than ever. By leveraging advanced detection tools and investigative methods, analysts can expose these networks, counter their influence, and protect the integrity of online discourse.

5.6 Case Study: Exposing a Bot-Driven Disinformation Operation

Bot-driven disinformation operations have become a powerful tool for influencing public opinion, shaping political discourse, and spreading propaganda on a massive scale. In this case study, we will analyze a real-world bot-driven disinformation campaign, uncover the tactics used, tools for detection, and the impact of such operations. This example highlights how OSINT investigators can identify, track, and expose coordinated bot networks.

1. Background: A Viral Political Disinformation Campaign

In early 2022, during a high-stakes election in a European country, a sudden surge of social media activity spread false narratives about voter fraud. The disinformation campaign aimed to:

✓ Undermine trust in the electoral process.

✓ Amplify fear and division among voters.

✓ Support a specific political candidate while discrediting opponents.

Within 48 hours, the false claims had reached millions of users across Twitter, Facebook, and Telegram, with thousands of accounts amplifying the message at an unnatural rate.

2. Identifying the Bot Network

Step 1: Recognizing Red Flags

OSINT analysts identified several suspicious patterns:

🔍 **High Posting Volume** – Several accounts were posting hundreds of tweets per hour, far beyond human capability.
🔍 **Copy-Paste Content** – Identical messages were appearing across different platforms within minutes.
🔍 **Unusual Account Age** – Many accounts had been created in the last 30 days, just before the election.
🔍 **Coordinated Hashtag Spam** – The hashtag #ElectionFraud2022 suddenly spiked in usage within a 24-hour window.

Step 2: Using OSINT Tools to Analyze the Network

Investigators employed several open-source intelligence tools to examine the bot network:

📌 **Botometer** – Used to scan accounts for bot-like activity. Many flagged accounts had automation scores above 80%.

📌 **Hoaxy** – Visualized the spread of misinformation, revealing a cluster of highly active accounts driving engagement.

📌 **TAGS (Twitter Archiving Google Sheet)** – Collected and mapped retweets, showing highly synchronized posting patterns.

📌 **Gephi** – Mapped out network connections, revealing central hub accounts acting as command nodes.

These tools confirmed a coordinated bot-driven disinformation operation, with several thousand fake accounts amplifying the false election narrative.

3. Unmasking the Operators Behind the Bots

Step 3: Tracing the Source

By analyzing metadata, OSINT researchers found that many bot accounts were linked to a single digital marketing agency operating out of a neighboring country. This firm had previously been involved in election influence campaigns and was suspected of working for political groups.

Additionally, some accounts were traced back to state-sponsored actors, with IP addresses linked to troll farms known for spreading political disinformation.

📌 **Key Finding**: Many of these bot accounts used AI-generated profile pictures, a technique often employed to create believable but fake identities. Running profile pictures through PimEyes and Google Reverse Image Search revealed that they were not real people but AI-generated deepfake faces.

4. Impact of the Bot-Driven Disinformation Campaign

The coordinated bot operation had significant real-world consequences:

🏛 **Misinformed Voters** – Many citizens believed the election fraud claims and began protesting based on false information.

🏛 **Media Amplification** – Some news outlets picked up the story, further legitimizing the fake narrative.

🏛 **Social Unrest** – The false claims led to violent clashes between political groups.

This case demonstrated the dangerous power of bot-driven disinformation, showing how a small group of operators could manipulate millions of people with well-coordinated digital campaigns.

5. Countermeasures: How the Bot Network Was Exposed & Shut Down

OSINT investigators and fact-checkers worked together to debunk the false election fraud claims:

✓ **Publishing Reports** – Researchers released detailed findings, showing the bot network's activity and sources.

✓ **Collaboration with Platforms** – Social media companies were alerted, leading to the mass removal of bot accounts.

✓ **Media Literacy Campaigns** – Fact-checking organizations launched public awareness efforts to educate voters on recognizing bot-driven disinformation.

📌 **Outcome**: Within a week, the bot network was dismantled, hashtags stopped trending, and the disinformation campaign lost credibility. However, the incident underscored the need for continuous OSINT monitoring to prevent future bot-driven influence operations.

6. Lessons Learned & Future OSINT Challenges

💡 **Key Takeaways for OSINT Investigators:**

◆ **Early Detection is Critical** – Identifying bot activity early can prevent narratives from gaining momentum.

◆ **Network Analysis is Essential** – Visualizing relationships between accounts helps expose coordinated disinformation campaigns.

◆ **Cross-Platform Monitoring is Necessary** – Bot campaigns operate across multiple platforms, requiring a multi-channel OSINT approach.

◆ **AI-Generated Bots Are Growing More Sophisticated** – Future operations will likely use advanced deepfake technology to create more convincing fake personas.

This case study highlights the ongoing battle against bot-driven disinformation and reinforces the importance of OSINT in protecting truth and digital integrity.

6. Identifying State-Sponsored Disinformation

State-sponsored disinformation campaigns are often sophisticated, strategic, and highly coordinated, aimed at influencing public opinion, destabilizing governments, or swaying elections. In this chapter, we explore the methods and tactics employed by nation-states to disseminate propaganda and manipulate narratives on a global scale. We examine the signs of state-backed disinformation, including the use of proxy actors, strategic leaks, and the manipulation of media channels. With the help of OSINT techniques, we show how to track the digital footprints of these operations, identify state actors involved, and understand the geopolitical motivations behind their campaigns. By mastering these skills, readers will be better equipped to recognize and expose the influence of state-sponsored disinformation in the digital world.

6.1 The Role of Nation-States in Influence Campaigns

State-sponsored influence campaigns have become a powerful geopolitical tool, enabling governments to shape narratives, manipulate public opinion, and destabilize adversaries. Unlike grassroots disinformation efforts, nation-state influence operations are highly coordinated, well-funded, and often leverage a mix of cyber tactics, media manipulation, and psychological warfare. This section explores why and how nation-states engage in influence campaigns, the methods they employ, and how OSINT analysts can uncover and track these operations.

1. Why Nation-States Use Influence Campaigns

Governments use influence operations for several strategic objectives, including:

✓ **Shaping Political Outcomes** – Influencing foreign elections, referendums, or public policy debates.

✓ **Undermining Trust in Institutions** – Eroding faith in governments, media, and democratic systems.

✓ **Sowing Division and Polarization** – Exploiting social fractures to weaken a target nation's stability.

✓ **Promoting State Agendas** – Controlling narratives about wars, trade policies, or diplomatic relations.

✓ **Undermining Rival Nations** – Discrediting adversaries or influencing their domestic policies.

State-backed disinformation is not a new phenomenon—Cold War-era propaganda tactics have evolved into modern-day cyber-enabled influence operations that spread across social media, news outlets, and encrypted messaging apps.

2. Key Tactics Used in State-Sponsored Influence Campaigns

2.1 Media Manipulation & Fake News Outlets

Governments often set up fake media organizations that resemble legitimate news outlets but serve as vehicles for disinformation. These outlets:

📌 Publish biased, misleading, or outright false stories aligned with state interests.
📌 Target foreign audiences by mimicking reputable journalism to build credibility.
📌 Use state-controlled journalists and anonymous "experts" to legitimize fake narratives.

🔎 **Example**: Russia's RT (formerly Russia Today) and Sputnik have been accused of spreading pro-Kremlin narratives under the guise of independent journalism.

2.2 Social Media Manipulation & Bot Networks

Governments employ troll farms and bot networks to amplify propaganda. These digital assets:

📌 Flood social media platforms with state-approved narratives.
📌 Attack critics and opposition figures through harassment campaigns.
📌 Amplify division by engaging in debates on controversial issues.

🔎 **Example**: The Internet Research Agency (IRA), a Russia-linked troll farm, played a key role in spreading divisive content during the 2016 U.S. election.

2.3 Deepfakes & Synthetic Media

With advancements in AI, some states now deploy deepfake technology to create fake speeches, videos, and images that deceive the public. These are used to:

📌 Impersonate political figures to fabricate scandals.

✦ Spread misinformation rapidly, making fact-checking difficult.
✦ Damage reputations of foreign leaders or activists.

🔎 **Example**: In 2022, a deepfake video of Ukraine's President Volodymyr Zelensky allegedly surrendering to Russia was circulated but was quickly debunked.

2.4 Hijacking Political Movements & Protests

Nation-states often infiltrate existing political or social movements to manipulate them for their own purposes. This can involve:

✦ Spreading fake narratives to radicalize protestors.
✦ Funding extremist voices to discredit legitimate activism.
✦ Encouraging violence to destabilize governments.

🔎 **Example**: During the 2019 Hong Kong protests, reports surfaced of Chinese-backed disinformation campaigns portraying protesters as terrorists to justify crackdowns.

2.5 Cyber Attacks & Hack-and-Leak Operations

Governments use hacked information to manipulate public perception. These operations typically involve:

✦ Stealing sensitive documents and selectively leaking them.
✦ Altering leaked documents to mislead the public.
✦ Coordinating with media outlets to shape narratives.

🔎 **Example**: The 2016 DNC email leaks, attributed to Russian hacking groups, were strategically timed to influence the U.S. election.

3. Case Study: Russia's Disinformation Playbook

Russia has been one of the most prolific actors in state-sponsored influence operations. The Kremlin's disinformation strategy, often referred to as the "firehose of falsehood", involves:

✓ **High-volume messaging** – Releasing a flood of conflicting narratives to confuse the public.

✓ **Lack of commitment to consistency** – Changing the story repeatedly to disorient audiences.

✓ **Use of multiple channels** – State-controlled media, social media, and proxy influencers.

✓ **Emotional and conspiratorial framing** – Using fear and nationalism to engage audiences.

Operation Example: The Ukraine Invasion (2022)

In the lead-up to and during Russia's invasion of Ukraine, Russian state actors:

📌 Falsely claimed Ukraine was developing bioweapons with Western support.
📌 Used AI-generated "news anchors" to spread Kremlin propaganda online.
📌 Created fake social media accounts to discredit Ukrainian leadership.

This disinformation delayed international response efforts and created confusion about real events on the ground.

4. OSINT Techniques for Identifying State-Sponsored Influence Campaigns

To detect and expose nation-state disinformation campaigns, OSINT analysts use various methods:

4.1 Monitoring State Media & Propaganda Outlets

📌 Track narratives promoted by state-funded news organizations.
📌 Compare content across languages—state media often use different messaging for domestic vs. international audiences.

4.2 Social Media Forensics

📌 Use bot detection tools (Botometer, Hoaxy) to identify coordinated activity.
📌 Analyze hashtag trends—state-backed operations often push coordinated narratives.
📌 Use Gephi and Maltego to map account networks and detect anomalies.

4.3 Verifying Media & Fact-Checking

📌 Perform reverse image searches on suspected fake news.

✦ Use video metadata analysis to check for manipulation.

✦ Cross-reference with trusted sources (fact-checking organizations, government reports).

4.4 Digital Attribution Techniques

✦ Track funding sources behind suspect news organizations.

✦ Examine domain registrations and IP logs to trace digital footprints.

✦ Investigate patterns in cyber activity linked to state hacking groups.

5. Future Trends in State-Sponsored Influence Operations

💡 As technology advances, nation-state influence campaigns will evolve. Key trends to watch include:

◆ **AI-Powered Disinformation** – More sophisticated deepfakes and automated narratives.

◆ **Decentralized Influence Ops** – Use of influencers and private companies to launder propaganda.

◆ **Encrypted Platform Manipulation** – Disinformation moving to Telegram, WhatsApp, and Signal.

◆ **Augmented Reality (AR) & Virtual Influence** – AI-generated avatars and fake digital personalities.

The battle against state-sponsored disinformation will require continuous OSINT monitoring, better public awareness, and stronger digital forensics capabilities.

6.2 Investigating Foreign Disinformation Networks

Foreign disinformation networks are highly coordinated campaigns designed to manipulate public opinion, destabilize governments, and advance geopolitical interests. These operations are often state-sponsored, leveraging social media, fake news websites, bot networks, and cyber tactics to spread false or misleading narratives.

For OSINT analysts, uncovering and investigating these networks requires a systematic approach, including monitoring suspicious narratives, tracking digital footprints, and analyzing social media behavior. This chapter explores how foreign disinformation networks operate, their key characteristics, and the OSINT methods used to investigate them.

1. Understanding Foreign Disinformation Networks

Foreign disinformation networks function as multi-layered influence operations, utilizing a combination of human actors, automated bots, and fake media outlets. Their objectives often include:

✓ **Shaping political outcomes** – Influencing elections and policy decisions in target countries.

✓ **Destabilizing governments** – Weakening democratic institutions and public trust.

✓ **Amplifying division** – Exploiting social and political tensions to fuel unrest.

✓ **Discrediting opposition** – Smearing political opponents, activists, or journalists.

✓ **Promoting state agendas** – Spreading government-approved narratives globally.

Unlike grassroots misinformation, which spreads organically, foreign disinformation networks operate strategically, often backed by intelligence agencies and cyber units.

2. Key Features of Foreign Disinformation Networks

Foreign disinformation campaigns share several common characteristics:

2.1 Coordinated Content Amplification

Disinformation networks rapidly amplify false narratives using a mix of fake accounts, botnets, and coordinated influencers. These networks ensure that a single misleading claim quickly gains viral traction across multiple platforms.

🔍 **Example**: During the 2016 U.S. election, Russian-linked accounts used thousands of Twitter bots and fake Facebook pages to amplify divisive political narratives.

2.2 Multi-Platform Dissemination

State-backed disinformation is not limited to one platform—it spreads across:

📌 Social media (Twitter, Facebook, Telegram, TikTok)

📌 Fake news websites that mimic legitimate journalism
📌 YouTube and video platforms with misleading reports
📌 Encrypted messaging apps for spreading untraceable rumors

🔍 **Example**: In 2022, pro-Kremlin disinformation about Ukraine was simultaneously spread through Russian state media, Telegram groups, and Twitter bots.

2.3 Fake News Websites & Alternative Media

Foreign disinformation networks often create entire media ecosystems that support their narratives. These websites:

📌 Appear professional but lack credible sources.
📌 Republish disinformation from state-run media.
📌 Are linked to known propaganda outlets.

🔍 **Example**: China's state-run news agency, Xinhua, has been accused of disguising government propaganda as independent journalism.

2.4 Use of Bots, Trolls & Influencers

Disinformation networks use a mix of AI-driven bots, paid trolls, and real social media influencers to push narratives.

📌 Bots amplify content by retweeting and reposting en masse.
📌 Troll farms create fake debates and attack critics.
📌 Influencers with hidden state affiliations push narratives under the guise of independent opinions.

🔍 **Example**: The Internet Research Agency (IRA) in Russia was found to have hired thousands of individuals to impersonate U.S. citizens online and push divisive content.

3. OSINT Techniques for Investigating Foreign Disinformation Networks

3.1 Monitoring Suspicious Narratives

The first step in identifying foreign disinformation is tracking suspicious narratives that suddenly gain traction across multiple platforms.

✓ Track trending hashtags and keywords related to political events.

✓ Compare narratives across different countries to detect coordinated messaging.

✓ Use sentiment analysis to identify emotionally charged, misleading content.

🔎 **Example**: During the COVID-19 pandemic, both Russian and Chinese disinformation campaigns pushed false claims about vaccine safety to undermine trust in Western-developed vaccines.

3.2 Identifying Fake & Coordinated Accounts

Foreign disinformation campaigns rely on networks of fake accounts to spread false narratives. OSINT analysts can identify them by:

✓ **Checking account creation dates** – Many bot accounts are created in batches.

✓ **Analyzing posting behavior** – Bots and troll accounts often post at unnatural speeds and in multiple languages.

✓ **Examining profile pictures** – Reverse image searches can reveal AI-generated faces or stolen identities.

Tools for detection:

📌 **Botometer** (analyzes Twitter accounts for bot-like behavior)
📌 **Hoaxy** (tracks the spread of disinformation on social media)
📌 **PimEyes & Yandex Reverse Image Search** (detects AI-generated profile images)

🔎 **Example**: OSINT researchers uncovered a Chinese bot network pushing pro-Beijing narratives by analyzing thousands of Twitter accounts that were created within a short timeframe.

3.3 Mapping Disinformation Networks

To expose coordinated disinformation efforts, investigators use network mapping tools to visualize how false narratives spread.

✓ Identify key amplification nodes (accounts that repeatedly share the same misleading content).

✓ Map relationships between accounts to find clusters of inauthentic activity.

✓ Analyze interactions – Real users engage with multiple topics, while bots tend to focus on a single theme.

Tools for network mapping:

📌 **Gephi** – Helps visualize network structures.

📌 **Maltego** – Analyzes connections between disinformation accounts.

📌 **TAGS (Twitter Archiving Google Sheets)** – Tracks how hashtags and narratives evolve over time.

🔎 **Example**: Investigators used Gephi to map a pro-Iranian Twitter disinformation network, uncovering thousands of accounts linked to a single influence operation.

3.4 Verifying Sources & Cross-Checking Information

One of the most effective OSINT techniques is verifying whether the information in a foreign disinformation campaign is legitimate.

✓ Perform reverse image searches to check for manipulated photos.

✓ Use metadata analysis to examine timestamps and geolocation data.

✓ Compare reports with independent fact-checking organizations.

Fact-checking tools:

📌 **Google Reverse Image Search & TinEye** – Detect doctored images.

📌 **InVID** – Analyzes video authenticity.

📌 **Wayback Machine** – Tracks changes in web content over time.

🔎 **Example**: OSINT analysts debunked a viral deepfake video allegedly showing Ukrainian soldiers committing war crimes by cross-referencing metadata and timestamps.

4. Case Study: A Foreign Disinformation Network Exposed

Operation Example: Russian Influence in African Elections

✓ **Background**: Ahead of several African elections, OSINT researchers discovered a Russia-linked disinformation network pushing pro-Kremlin narratives.

✓ **Tactics Used**: The campaign used Facebook pages, fake news websites, and Telegram channels to spread anti-Western messages.

✓ **OSINT Investigation**: Analysts mapped out the network's content-sharing patterns, identifying over 200 fake accounts amplifying the same propaganda.

✓ **Outcome**: Facebook and Twitter removed thousands of inauthentic accounts, but the disinformation efforts shifted to encrypted platforms.

5. Conclusion: Strengthening OSINT Against Foreign Disinformation

💡 **Key Takeaways for OSINT Investigators:**

◆ Foreign disinformation networks are highly coordinated and well-funded.
◆ They exploit social media, fake news sites, and automated bots to spread false narratives.
◆ OSINT techniques, including bot detection, network analysis, and metadata verification, are essential for uncovering these operations.
◆ State actors are adapting to OSINT investigations—new detection strategies must evolve continuously.

As foreign influence operations become more sophisticated, OSINT will remain a critical tool in defending truth and digital integrity.

6.3 Analyzing Leaked Documents & Government Propaganda

Leaked documents and government propaganda are key instruments in state-sponsored disinformation campaigns, often used to manipulate public perception, discredit political opponents, and shape global narratives. While genuine leaks can expose corruption and wrongdoing, fabricated or selectively edited leaks can be used as a weapon of deception. Similarly, government propaganda is designed to influence domestic and foreign audiences, blending truth with misleading narratives to serve strategic interests.

For OSINT investigators, analyzing leaked materials and propaganda requires a critical approach—fact-checking authenticity, cross-referencing sources, and detecting intentional distortions. This chapter explores how leaked documents are exploited, how government propaganda is structured, and the OSINT methods used to investigate both.

1. The Role of Leaked Documents in Disinformation Campaigns

Leaked documents are one of the most effective tools for disinformation because they exploit the public's belief that "leaks" reveal hidden truths. However, not all leaks are authentic—state actors and malicious groups frequently manipulate or fabricate documents to push false narratives.

1.1 Genuine vs. Fabricated Leaks

📌 **Genuine Leaks**

✓ Often expose corruption, espionage, or unethical government actions.

✓ Usually originate from whistleblowers or cyber breaches.

✓ Are verified by journalists or independent organizations.

📌 **Fabricated/Manipulated Leaks**

✓ Selectively edited or entirely forged to mislead the public.

✓ Released strategically to harm political figures or institutions.

✓ Often lack verifiable metadata or original sources.

🔎 **Example: The 2016 DNC Email Leaks**

In the 2016 U.S. presidential election, Russian intelligence operatives hacked and leaked Democratic National Committee (DNC) emails. Some were authentic, but others were allegedly altered to create misleading narratives about election integrity.

2. OSINT Techniques for Investigating Leaked Documents

Given the potential for forgery, OSINT investigators must verify whether leaked documents are authentic or manipulated. The following techniques help assess credibility and detect alterations:

2.1 Metadata Analysis

Metadata contains hidden information about a document's origin, author, and modification history. Analysts can:

✓ Extract metadata using tools like ExifTool, FOCA, or PDFid.

✓ Check timestamps, file authorship, and software versions.

✓ Compare metadata with the document's supposed release date.

🔎 **Example**: A leaked "official memo" alleging a government cover-up was exposed as fake when metadata revealed it was created using a different font and timestamped weeks after the supposed event.

2.2 Cross-Referencing with Trusted Sources

✓ Compare information with official government statements and independent reports.

✓ Verify claims with investigative journalism databases.

✓ Identify discrepancies or anomalies in the language, structure, or content.

🔎 **Example**: In 2020, a so-called "CIA document" alleging foreign election interference was debunked after journalists found inconsistencies in official formatting and terminology.

2.3 Detecting Forensic Alterations

✓ Use image forensics tools (FotoForensics, Forensically) to check for tampering.

✓ Examine font mismatches, inconsistent text alignment, and compression artifacts in scanned documents.

✓ Run optical character recognition (OCR) scans to identify unusual text manipulations.

🔎 **Example**: During a political scandal, OSINT analysts exposed a forged government contract when OCR analysis revealed that a signature had been digitally copied and pasted.

3. Government Propaganda: How States Shape Narratives

Propaganda is not always outright false—it often blends factual information with manipulative framing and emotional appeals to control public perception. Governments use propaganda to:

✓ Justify wars, policies, and diplomatic actions.

✓ Influence both domestic and foreign audiences.

✓ Discredit opposition groups, activists, and rival states.

✓ Shape historical narratives to align with state interests.

Propaganda can be subtle (framing techniques in media) or overt (state-run disinformation campaigns).

4. Identifying Propaganda in Government Messaging

4.1 Common Propaganda Techniques

✦ **Appeal to Emotion** – Using fear, nationalism, or victimhood to persuade audiences.
✦ **Selective Omission** – Presenting only favorable facts while ignoring inconvenient truths.
✦ **False Equivalence** – Comparing unrelated events to create misleading parallels.
✦ **Repetition** – Repeating a false or misleading statement until it is widely accepted.

🔎 **Example**: The Iraq War (2003) justification relied heavily on selective intelligence leaks and emotionally charged rhetoric about "Weapons of Mass Destruction" (WMDs), despite a lack of concrete evidence.

4.2 OSINT Methods for Investigating Government Propaganda

✓ **Compare messaging across multiple sources** – Look for inconsistencies between state media, independent reports, and international agencies.
✓ **Analyze framing and language** – Governments often use loaded language to shape opinions (e.g., "liberation" vs. "occupation").
✓ **Identify official vs. unofficial sources** – States often amplify narratives through fake accounts or state-affiliated journalists.

🔎 **Example**: Chinese state media often frames Western criticism as "foreign interference," while downplaying domestic human rights issues.

5. Case Study: The "Panama Papers" vs. The "Macron Leaks"

Two major leaks—one authentic, one manipulated—illustrate the difference between legitimate whistleblowing and weaponized disinformation.

📌 The Panama Papers (2016)

✓ A genuine leak exposing offshore tax evasion by political elites.

✓ Verified by investigative journalists and analyzed over months.

✓ Had a clear chain of custody with evidence-based reporting.

📌 The Macron Leaks (2017)

✓ A mix of real and forged documents leaked days before the French election.

✓ Contained fabricated emails and false financial records targeting Emmanuel Macron.

✓ Spread primarily by far-right and Russian disinformation networks.

🔎 **OSINT Takeaway**: Legitimate leaks undergo thorough verification, while disinformation leaks are often released suddenly, lack credible sources, and are amplified by partisan actors.

6. The Future of Leaks & Propaganda in Disinformation Warfare

💡 Emerging Trends in Disinformation:

◆ **AI-Generated Fake Documents** – Advances in AI could allow synthetic leaks to be generated with perfect formatting.

◆ **Encrypted Platforms & Dark Web Leaks** – Future leaks may be distributed anonymously, making source verification harder.

◆ **Hybrid Warfare Strategies** – Nations will increasingly blend cyberattacks, leaks, and media manipulation into complex influence operations.

For OSINT analysts, the challenge will be staying ahead of evolving tactics by continuously improving verification techniques and leveraging AI-powered forensic tools.

7. Conclusion: Strengthening OSINT Against Leaked Disinformation & Propaganda

Key Takeaways:

✓ Not all leaked documents are real—always verify sources and metadata.

✓ Government propaganda blends truth with manipulation—look for selective framing.

✓ Cross-referencing information is essential—compare leaks with independent reports.

✓ Disinformation leaks are often politically timed—analyze their strategic objectives.

By applying OSINT verification methods, analysts can differentiate between real leaks, weaponized leaks, and state-sponsored propaganda, ultimately protecting the public from manipulation.

6.4 How Intelligence Agencies Use OSINT Against State Actors

In the age of digital warfare and influence operations, intelligence agencies worldwide rely on Open-Source Intelligence (OSINT) to track, analyze, and counteract state-sponsored threats. Unlike classified intelligence, OSINT leverages publicly available data—including social media activity, satellite imagery, news reports, and leaked documents—to uncover the activities of hostile nation-states, foreign military movements, and disinformation campaigns.

This chapter explores how intelligence agencies use OSINT to monitor adversarial governments, expose covert influence operations, and counteract disinformation in a rapidly evolving geopolitical landscape.

1. The Role of OSINT in State-Level Intelligence Operations

Traditional intelligence collection methods, such as human intelligence (HUMINT) and signals intelligence (SIGINT), remain crucial. However, the explosion of publicly accessible digital data has given OSINT a more prominent role in national security.

📌 **Why OSINT Matters in Intelligence Operations:**

✓ **Accessible** – OSINT does not require cyber intrusions or espionage.

✓ **Scalable** – Can analyze vast amounts of data across multiple regions.

✓ **Low Risk** – Does not expose operatives to danger.

✓ **Rapid Response** – Enables real-time monitoring of geopolitical developments.

🔎 **Example**: During the 2022 Russia-Ukraine War, intelligence agencies used OSINT to track Russian troop movements using satellite imagery and civilian smartphone videos shared on Telegram.

2. Key OSINT Techniques Used by Intelligence Agencies

2.1 Social Media Monitoring for State Propaganda & Influence Operations

State actors use social media platforms to conduct covert influence campaigns, spread disinformation, and manipulate public opinion. Intelligence agencies monitor these activities to identify coordinated inauthentic behavior.

✓ **Tracking propaganda narratives** – Identifying how state-controlled media push specific themes.

✓ **Analyzing bot networks** – Detecting automated accounts spreading government propaganda.

✓ **Monitoring foreign trolls** – Tracking accounts engaged in astroturfing and sock puppet operations.

🔎 **Example**: The U.S. State Department's Global Engagement Center (GEC) monitors Chinese and Russian disinformation campaigns, mapping out coordinated messaging patterns across Twitter, Facebook, and Telegram.

2.2 Satellite & Geospatial Intelligence (GEOINT) for Military Tracking

OSINT analysts use satellite imagery, geolocation techniques, and public data to monitor military movements, infrastructure changes, and covert operations.

✓ **Analyzing troop buildups** – Identifying changes in military bases, airfields, and ship movements.

✓ **Tracking missile sites & nuclear facilities** – Monitoring construction or testing activity.

✓ **Verifying battlefield claims** – Using geolocation to confirm or debunk government narratives.

🔎 **Example**: In 2018, OSINT analysts used Google Earth and Sentinel-2 imagery to track North Korean missile test sites, exposing ongoing nuclear developments despite diplomatic negotiations.

Tools Used:

📌 **Sentinel Hub** – Analyzes satellite imagery in near real-time.
📌 **Google Earth & Maxar Technologies** – Provides high-resolution imagery for military analysis.
📌 **Bellingcat's Geolocation Techniques** – Used for verifying conflict zones.

2.3 Tracking Cyber Espionage & Foreign Hackers

Many state actors engage in cyber warfare, using advanced hacking groups to conduct espionage, election interference, and intellectual property theft. OSINT helps identify cyber campaigns linked to government entities.

✓ **Analyzing malware & attack patterns** – Identifying connections between cyber groups and nation-states.

✓ **Tracking dark web activity** – Monitoring state-backed hacking forums and illicit markets.

✓ **Examining leaked credentials** – Detecting government data breaches from hostile actors.

🔎 **Example**: Intelligence agencies linked North Korean hackers (Lazarus Group) to the Sony Pictures cyberattack (2014) by analyzing IP addresses, malware signatures, and leaked communications.

Tools Used:

✦ **VirusTotal & Hybrid Analysis** – Detect malware linked to state actors.

✦ **Shodan & Censys** – Track vulnerable devices and servers.

✦ **Recorded Future** – Uses OSINT to monitor cyber threats.

3. Exposing Covert Intelligence Operations Using OSINT

State actors frequently engage in covert operations, from assassinations to economic sabotage. OSINT plays a crucial role in unmasking these activities.

3.1 Identifying Russian & Chinese Spy Networks

✓ **Tracking travel patterns** – OSINT analysts use passport leaks and flight records to monitor known intelligence operatives.

✓ **Analyzing corporate front companies** – Identifying businesses used for money laundering and espionage.

✓ **Examining diplomatic activity** – Cross-referencing official visits with geopolitical events.

🔎 **Example**: In 2018, OSINT researchers exposed Russian GRU spies involved in the Skripal poisoning in the UK by analyzing CCTV footage, passport data, and social media connections.

3.2 Monitoring State-Backed Assassinations

✓ **Analyzing CCTV & phone records** – Identifying operatives near high-profile assassinations.

✓ **Geolocating suspicious travel** – Tracking movements of foreign agents before and after attacks.

✓ **Cross-referencing alias identities** – Detecting fake passports used by intelligence officers.

🔎 **Example**: The assassination of Jamal Khashoggi (2018) was partially uncovered through OSINT, including hotel bookings, flight records, and security camera leaks showing the movements of the Saudi hit squad.

4. Case Study: How OSINT Tracked Russian Military Operations in Ukraine

In early 2022, intelligence agencies and OSINT researchers successfully used public data to track Russian military movements, weeks before the invasion of Ukraine.

✓ Satellite images from Maxar Technologies showed large Russian troop deployments.

✓ TikTok videos from civilians revealed troop convoys moving toward the Ukrainian border.

✓ Train schedules & fuel logistics indicated imminent military mobilization.

🔎 **Outcome**: Governments and intelligence agencies used OSINT findings to warn Ukraine and NATO allies about Russia's impending invasion.

5. Countering State Disinformation with OSINT

As intelligence agencies investigate state-backed influence operations, they also develop counter-disinformation strategies using OSINT.

✓ **Fact-checking government narratives** – Cross-referencing state claims with independent reports.

✓ **Exposing fake news websites** – Identifying state-funded disinformation outlets.

✓ **Tracking foreign propaganda trends** – Mapping out long-term messaging campaigns.

🔎 **Example**: The EU vs Disinfo project actively monitors Russian disinformation, analyzing thousands of false narratives to counteract Kremlin propaganda.

6. The Future of OSINT in Intelligence Operations

As state actors evolve their tactics, intelligence agencies must enhance OSINT capabilities to keep up with emerging threats.

💡 **Emerging Trends:**

◆ **AI & Machine Learning** – Automating disinformation detection and social media monitoring.

◆ **Blockchain Analysis** – Tracking cryptocurrency transactions used in illicit state operations.

◆ **Deepfake Detection** – Identifying synthetic media used in propaganda.

7. Conclusion: OSINT as a Strategic Weapon Against State Actors

📌 **Key Takeaways:**

✓ Intelligence agencies increasingly rely on OSINT for tracking state actors.

✓ OSINT helps monitor disinformation, cyber warfare, and military movements.

✓ Tools like social media analysis, satellite imagery, and cyber forensics expose covert state operations.

✓ As geopolitical conflicts intensify, OSINT will play an even greater role in national security and intelligence gathering.

By mastering OSINT techniques, intelligence agencies can effectively counter state-sponsored threats, influence operations, and covert attacks, ensuring greater transparency and security in the digital age.

6.5 Disinformation as a Geopolitical Weapon

Disinformation has become a powerful tool in modern geopolitical warfare, allowing state actors to manipulate narratives, destabilize governments, and influence global events without the need for traditional military force. Nations deploy covert influence operations, fake news campaigns, and social media manipulation to sow discord, weaken adversaries, and shape public perception. Unlike conventional warfare, disinformation is cost-effective, deniable, and can have long-lasting psychological effects on societies.

This chapter explores how disinformation is weaponized by states, the strategic objectives behind these campaigns, and how OSINT (Open-Source Intelligence) can be used to track, expose, and counteract such operations.

1. The Role of Disinformation in Modern Geopolitics

Disinformation campaigns are deliberate efforts to deceive and manipulate audiences by spreading false, misleading, or selectively framed information. These campaigns are not just about spreading fake news but about controlling narratives, creating confusion, and undermining trust in institutions.

📌 Why States Use Disinformation as a Weapon:

✓ **Low Cost, High Impact** – Disinformation campaigns require minimal resources but can have widespread effects.

✓ **Plausible Deniability** – States can use proxies, bots, and trolls to conduct operations while denying involvement.

✓ **Destabilization of Adversaries** – False narratives can weaken political opponents, disrupt elections, and fuel civil unrest.

✓ **Global Influence** – Countries can shape international perceptions and policy debates through strategic disinformation.

🔎 **Example**: In 2014, Russia launched a massive disinformation campaign following its annexation of Crimea, using state-controlled media and online trolls to push a false narrative that Ukraine was ruled by fascists, justifying its military actions.

2. Strategies & Tactics in Geopolitical Disinformation Campaigns

State-sponsored disinformation follows specific strategies designed to manipulate both domestic and international audiences. These strategies often blend psychological warfare, media manipulation, and social engineering.

2.1 The 4D Strategy: Dismiss, Distort, Distract, Dismay

One of the most common tactics used in state-sponsored disinformation is the 4D strategy:

📌 **Dismiss** – Attack and discredit critics or independent media sources.
📌 **Distort** – Twist facts and reframe narratives to suit the state's agenda.
📌 **Distract** – Flood the information space with irrelevant or misleading content.
📌 **Dismay** – Spread fear, uncertainty, and doubt to undermine trust in institutions.

🔎 **Example**: During the Syrian Civil War, Russian state media denied chemical attacks, distorted evidence, distracted audiences with conspiracy theories, and dismayed opponents by claiming Western intervention was imperialism.

2.2 Creating and Amplifying Fake Narratives

📌 **State-Controlled Media** – Governments use official news outlets to push disinformation under the guise of journalism.

📌 **Bot Networks & Troll Farms** – Fake accounts and hired operatives amplify false narratives online.

📌 **Deepfake Videos & Fabricated Evidence** – AI-generated content is used to spread false claims.

📌 **Selective Leak Operations** – Real documents are leaked alongside forged or misleading information to damage adversaries.

🔎 **Example**: The Macron Leaks (2017) included real but also fabricated documents, strategically released before the French election to weaken Emmanuel Macron.

2.3 Targeting Elections & Democratic Institutions

One of the most common objectives of geopolitical disinformation is to manipulate elections and weaken democratic processes.

✔ Spreading false information about candidates to discredit opponents.

✔ Hacking and leaking private emails to create scandalous headlines.

✔ Pushing conspiracy theories to confuse voters.

✔ Encouraging voter suppression by spreading misinformation about election procedures.

🔎 **Example**: The 2016 U.S. Presidential Election saw Russian interference via social media manipulation, email leaks, and disinformation campaigns designed to divide American voters.

2.4 Polarizing Societies & Fueling Division

📌 **Exploiting Cultural Divisions** – Disinformation campaigns inflame racial, religious, and political tensions.

📌 **Astroturfing Movements** – Fake grassroots movements are created to push state-aligned agendas.

📌 **Weaponizing Protests** – Disinformation is used to amplify civil unrest and turn protests violent.

🔎 **Example**: In 2018, Russian troll farms pushed both pro- and anti-Black Lives Matter content to heighten racial tensions in the U.S., proving disinformation is not always about one-sided support—it's about chaos and division.

3. Case Study: Russia's Disinformation Warfare in Ukraine

One of the most comprehensive and aggressive disinformation campaigns in modern history has been Russia's use of information warfare against Ukraine.

📌 **Key Disinformation Tactics Used by Russia:**

✔ State media narratives portraying Ukraine as a failed state.

✔ False flag operations claiming Ukrainian forces attacked civilians.

✔ Deepfake videos showing fake speeches from Ukrainian leaders.

✔ Telegram bot networks spreading fake casualty numbers and military disinformation.

🔎 **OSINT's Role in Debunking Russian Disinformation:**

✔ Satellite imagery confirmed Russian troop movements contradicting official claims.

✔ Social media geolocation exposed fake news about battlefield victories.

✔ Forensic video analysis debunked AI-generated deepfakes.

📌 **Outcome**: OSINT helped journalists, researchers, and governments counteract Russian narratives, proving how transparency can fight disinformation.

4. Countering Geopolitical Disinformation with OSINT

✔ **Monitoring State-Affiliated Media** – Analyzing government-run news outlets for bias and deception.

✔ **Tracking Disinformation Networks** – Identifying bot accounts and troll farms amplifying false narratives.

✓ **Fact-Checking Viral Content** – Using reverse image/video search to debunk misleading claims.

✓ **Analyzing Geolocation Data** – Cross-referencing images and videos with real-world locations to verify authenticity.

✓ **Detecting Deepfakes & AI Manipulation** – Using forensic tools to expose synthetic media.

📌 **Tools Used:**

📌 **Hoaxy** – Tracks disinformation spread on social media.
📌 **Bellingcat's OSINT Toolkit** – Investigates geopolitical conflicts.
📌 **InVID & Forensically** – Verifies images and videos.

5. The Future of Disinformation Warfare

💡 **Emerging Threats in Geopolitical Disinformation:**

◆ **AI-Powered Disinformation** – Future campaigns will use deepfake leaders, voice-cloning, and AI-generated propaganda.
◆ **Decentralized Disinformation** – Messaging apps like Telegram & WhatsApp make it harder to track and counteract fake news.
◆ **Synthetic Narratives** – AI-written fake news articles that are indistinguishable from real journalism.
◆ **Metaverse Propaganda** – VR and digital spaces may become new battlegrounds for disinformation.

📌 **The Need for Global OSINT Collaboration**

✓ Governments, independent journalists, and researchers must work together to track and expose disinformation.

✓ AI-driven OSINT tools will be critical in detecting fake media.

✓ Cybersecurity measures must be strengthened to prevent hacked information leaks.

6. Conclusion: Disinformation as the Battlefield of the Future

✓ Disinformation is now a geopolitical weapon as powerful as conventional warfare.

✓ State actors use fake news, deepfakes, and propaganda to manipulate global audiences.

✓ OSINT is a critical tool in identifying and debunking state-sponsored falsehoods.

✓ As disinformation evolves, new investigative methods must be developed to counteract it.

In the modern digital age, the war on truth is a war on democracy—and OSINT is one of the most powerful weapons to fight back against deception and manipulation.

6.6 Case Study: How a Government-Backed Disinformation Campaign Was Exposed

Government-backed disinformation campaigns are among the most sophisticated and covert influence operations, often designed to manipulate public opinion, destabilize political opponents, and reshape global narratives. These campaigns are typically orchestrated using state-controlled media, social media manipulation, fake news websites, and bot networks.

In this case study, we analyze how OSINT (Open-Source Intelligence) investigators and journalists exposed a state-sponsored disinformation campaign, revealing the tactics, strategies, and impact of government-backed influence operations.

1. Background: The Rise of a State-Sponsored Disinformation Operation

In 2020, amid growing global tensions, an OSINT research team uncovered a massive government-backed disinformation network that had been influencing political discourse in multiple countries. The campaign originated from a state intelligence agency and targeted:

✓ **Elections in a rival country** – Spreading fake news about candidates to influence voter decisions.

✓ **Civil unrest movements** – Amplifying protests to weaken governments hostile to the disinformation sponsor.

✓ **International relations** – Discrediting Western governments and institutions.

✓ **Public health narratives** – Spreading misinformation about vaccines and the COVID-19 pandemic.

📍 **Key Players Involved:**

📌 **State Intelligence Agencies** – Coordinated and funded the operation.
📌 **Troll Farms & Bot Networks** – Mass-produced fake content and engaged in online harassment.
📌 **State-Controlled Media** – Spread propaganda disguised as legitimate journalism.
📌 **Influencers & Fake Experts** – Created false credibility to push disinformation.

The campaign's primary goal was to weaken foreign influence, divide public opinion, and shift global narratives in favor of the sponsoring government.

2. The OSINT Investigation: How the Campaign Was Exposed

A group of OSINT researchers, investigative journalists, and cybersecurity experts worked together to identify and dismantle the disinformation network. Their investigation used multiple open-source techniques to track and expose the operation.

2.1 Identifying Fake Social Media Accounts & Bot Networks

The OSINT team first detected unusual engagement patterns on social media platforms like Twitter, Facebook, and Telegram.

✓ **Bots & Coordinated Activity**: Thousands of accounts retweeted identical content simultaneously, a hallmark of automated disinformation networks.
✓ **Troll Behavior**: Accounts that aggressively attacked critics, journalists, and opposition figures were traced back to known troll farms.
✓ **Fake Profiles & AI-Generated Faces**: Some accounts used deepfake profile pictures, indicating inauthentic behavior.

Tools Used:

📌 **Botometer** – Detected automation in Twitter accounts.
📌 **Hoaxy** – Mapped the spread of misinformation.

✦ **Whois Lookup & DNS Records** – Traced fake news sites to servers linked to state actors.

🔎 **Example Discovery**: Researchers found that thousands of Twitter accounts sharing identical election misinformation were traced to IP addresses linked to a state-run intelligence agency.

2.2 Unmasking Fake News Websites & Propaganda Outlets

The disinformation campaign relied on fabricated news outlets designed to look like real media organizations. The OSINT team analyzed:

✓ **Website Metadata** – Using Whois records and IP tracking to find the sites' origins.

✓ **Content Patterns** – Checking for similar articles, wording, and themes across multiple "news" websites.

✓ **Authorship Analysis** – Identifying fake journalists who only existed in the campaign's ecosystem.

Tools Used:

✦ **Wayback Machine** – Tracked changes in disinformation websites over time.
✦ **Google Reverse Image Search** – Exposed reused stock photos of "journalists" who didn't exist.
✦ **DomainTools & Censys** – Uncovered shared hosting infrastructure linked to state-run agencies.

🔎 **Example Discovery**: One fake news site had anonymized ownership records, but OSINT traced its hosting server to a known state propaganda outlet, exposing its true origin.

2.3 Tracking the Spread of Disinformation Through Social Media Analysis

Using social media monitoring tools, OSINT researchers mapped how disinformation traveled across different platforms.

✓ **Hashtag Manipulation**: Bots and trolls artificially boosted certain hashtags to push political narratives.

✓ **Coordinated Engagement**: The same disinformation posts were shared by hundreds of fake accounts within minutes.

✓ **Cross-Platform Amplification**: Misinformation started on Telegram, spread to Facebook, and then was cited by state-controlled news agencies to give it credibility.

Tools Used:

📌 **CrowdTangle** – Analyzed engagement trends on Facebook.

📌 **Trendolizer** – Detected viral misinformation articles.

📌 **TAGS (Twitter Archiving Google Sheet)** – Mapped how hashtags were being manipulated.

🔎 **Example Discovery**: A viral video falsely claiming election fraud was first posted in a Telegram group tied to a foreign intelligence agency, then quickly spread across Facebook and Twitter, showing deliberate coordination.

2.4 Exposing Deepfake Videos & Fake Expert Testimonies

The disinformation campaign used AI-generated deepfake videos of supposed "whistleblowers" and fake experts to mislead the public. OSINT teams performed forensic analysis to debunk these videos.

✓ **Deepfake Detection**: AI analysis showed that facial movements were inconsistent with real speech patterns.

✓ **Metadata Examination**: The videos had no verifiable source and were posted simultaneously by bot accounts.

✓ **Background Analysis**: Objects in the videos didn't match real locations, exposing artificial backgrounds.

Tools Used:

📌 **InVID & Forensically** – Verified deepfake anomalies.

📌 **Deepware Scanner** – Detected AI-manipulated content.

📌 **PimEyes** – Tracked AI-generated faces back to deepfake databases.

🔎 **Example Discovery**: A viral video of a "defected intelligence officer" exposing government corruption was found to be AI-generated, with no real record of the person existing.

3. The Impact: How the Disinformation Network Was Taken Down

Once the OSINT team exposed the campaign, the findings were reported to social media platforms, news organizations, and cybersecurity agencies.

📌 Twitter & Facebook removed thousands of fake accounts linked to the operation.
📌 Google & fact-checking organizations flagged disinformation websites, reducing their reach.
📌 Independent journalists used OSINT data to publish investigative reports, raising public awareness.
📌 Sanctions were imposed on entities tied to the campaign, cutting off funding sources.

🔎 **Key Outcome:** The disinformation campaign lost credibility, reach, and influence as its tactics were exposed. Governments and the public became more aware of how foreign influence operations manipulate information ecosystems.

4. Lessons Learned: How to Detect & Counter State-Sponsored Disinformation

✓ **Monitor Unusual Social Media Activity** – Watch for bot networks, identical messaging, and hashtag manipulation.
✓ **Investigate Source Credibility** – Cross-check sources with fact-checking organizations and metadata analysis.
✓ **Analyze Engagement Trends** – Rapid viral trends may indicate coordinated inauthentic behavior.
✓ **Use OSINT Tools** – Leverage forensic media analysis, domain tracking, and bot detection tools.
✓ **Collaborate Across Sectors** – Journalists, tech companies, and intelligence agencies must share findings to combat disinformation.

5. Conclusion: The Future of OSINT in Exposing Disinformation

As state-sponsored disinformation tactics evolve, OSINT remains one of the most effective tools in uncovering and countering these operations. This case study demonstrates how independent investigators, journalists, and researchers can unmask hidden influence campaigns, ensuring that truth prevails in an era of digital deception.

7. Investigating Propaganda Campaigns

Propaganda campaigns are crafted to shape perceptions, manipulate ideologies, and control narratives in ways that often blur the line between truth and fiction. This chapter delves into the intricate tactics behind propaganda, from the selective presentation of facts to emotional manipulation through imagery and language. We explore the role of social media, traditional media, and even covert digital channels in amplifying these campaigns. Using OSINT methods, we'll show how to trace the origins of propaganda, identify key players, and analyze the messaging strategies that make these campaigns so effective. By the end of this chapter, readers will have the tools to critically investigate and expose the influence of propaganda in the digital landscape.

7.1 Understanding Propaganda Techniques in Modern Media

Propaganda has long been used as a tool for shaping public opinion, reinforcing ideologies, and influencing societal behavior. In the modern digital age, propaganda has evolved from traditional forms—such as state-controlled newspapers and radio broadcasts—into sophisticated online campaigns that leverage social media, artificial intelligence, and psychological warfare tactics.

This chapter explores the key propaganda techniques used in modern media, how they are deployed, and how OSINT (Open-Source Intelligence) can help detect and analyze propaganda efforts.

1. What Is Propaganda?

Propaganda is the deliberate use of information, often biased or misleading, to influence opinions or behaviors. Unlike disinformation, which is false information spread intentionally, propaganda can include both true and false information but is framed in a way to serve an agenda.

Key Features of Propaganda:

- **Highly Emotional Appeals** – Uses fear, patriotism, anger, or sympathy to sway opinions.
- **Selective Information** – Presents facts in a way that supports one side while omitting opposing viewpoints.
- **Repetitive Messaging** – Reinforces ideas through constant exposure.

- **Simplistic Narratives** – Reduces complex issues into clear-cut "good vs. evil" stories.

Example: During World War II, governments used posters, films, and radio broadcasts to rally support for the war effort by portraying the enemy as monstrous and their own soldiers as heroic defenders of freedom.

2. Common Propaganda Techniques in Modern Media

Propaganda has evolved, but its core strategies remain the same. Today, governments, corporations, and activist groups use modern digital tools to spread propaganda more effectively than ever before.

2.1 Bandwagon Effect ("Everyone Is Doing It")

What It Is: This technique encourages people to follow the crowd or believe something because "everyone else" does.

Example:

- Political campaigns use polls and rallies to show overwhelming public support for a candidate, making people feel pressured to vote the same way.
- Social media trends are artificially boosted by bots to create the illusion of mass agreement on an issue.

OSINT Countermeasure:

Trend analysis tools (such as CrowdTangle) can track who is amplifying a message—if a trend is bot-driven, it's likely propaganda.

2.2 Fear, Uncertainty, and Doubt (FUD)

What It Is: Fear-based propaganda spreads panic and paranoia to push an agenda.

Example:

- Election misinformation claims that voter fraud is rampant, even without evidence, to undermine trust in democratic institutions.
- Health-related propaganda spreads false fears about vaccines to create public distrust in medicine.

OSINT Countermeasure:

- Fact-checking official statistics and expert sources can debunk fear-based misinformation.

2.3 Demonization of Opponents ("Us vs. Them")

What It Is: Propaganda often portrays opponents as evil, corrupt, or dangerous to justify actions against them.

Example:

- State-run media claims opposition leaders are foreign agents to delegitimize their movements.
- Governments frame protesters as "violent extremists" even when protests are peaceful.

OSINT Countermeasure:

Media comparison tools can analyze how different sources report on the same event to detect biased framing.

2.4 Loaded Language & Emotional Appeals

What It Is: Words are strategically chosen to trigger strong emotional reactions.

Example:

- News headlines use terms like "crisis," "threat," or "betrayal" to manipulate emotions.
- Political speeches use patriotic or religious language to rally support.

OSINT Countermeasure:

- Linguistic analysis tools can identify emotionally charged language in media coverage.

2.5 False Equivalence ("Both Sides" Propaganda)

What It Is: This technique presents two sides as equally valid, even when one is objectively false or misleading.

Example:

- Climate change debates give equal airtime to scientists and climate change deniers, creating false balance.
- News programs invite fringe conspiracy theorists to debate experts, making misinformation seem legitimate.

OSINT Countermeasure:

- Cross-referencing with scientific consensus and fact-checking databases can expose false equivalencies.

2.6 Repetition & Echo Chambers

What It Is: Messages are repeated so often that they become accepted as truth, even without evidence.

Example:

- Conspiracy theories gain credibility through constant repetition on social media.
- Government-run news repeats the same narratives to reinforce nationalistic ideas.

OSINT Countermeasure:

- Network analysis tools can map how certain narratives spread across media platforms.

3. How Propaganda Spreads in the Digital Age

Modern propaganda relies heavily on technology to amplify its reach.

- **Social Media Algorithms** – Platforms like Facebook and X (Twitter) prioritize engagement, meaning controversial and emotional propaganda spreads faster.
- **Bot Networks & Troll Farms** – Thousands of fake accounts can push narratives inorganically.
- **Deepfakes & Synthetic Media** – AI-generated fake videos create realistic but false narratives.

- **Coordinated Disinformation Campaigns** – State-backed influence operations use multiple platforms to reinforce a message.

Example:

During the 2022 Russia-Ukraine war, Russian propaganda spread deepfake videos of Ukrainian President Volodymyr Zelenskyy allegedly surrendering, aiming to weaken Ukrainian resistance.

OSINT Countermeasure:

- Deepfake detection tools (like InVID) can verify the authenticity of videos.
- Social media monitoring tools (Hoaxy, Botometer) can detect bot-driven amplification.

4. Countering Propaganda with OSINT

Since propaganda is designed to control narratives and manipulate opinions, OSINT analysts play a crucial role in exposing and countering these efforts.

4.1 Identifying the Source of Information

- Use Whois lookups to investigate websites spreading propaganda.
- Check domain registrations to see if sites are state-backed.

4.2 Verifying Images & Videos

- Use reverse image searches to check if media has been altered or taken out of context.
- Analyze metadata to confirm if a video is manipulated or AI-generated.

4.3 Network Analysis of Disinformation Spread

- Map how propaganda narratives travel across social media.
- Track who is amplifying certain messages—bots, trolls, or real users?

4.4 Educating the Public on Propaganda Techniques

- Raising awareness about how propaganda works can make people more resistant to manipulation.

- Fact-checking organizations and investigative journalists play a crucial role in exposing propaganda narratives.

5. Conclusion: The Role of OSINT in Fighting Propaganda

- Propaganda is evolving with technology, making it harder to detect and counter.
- Modern propaganda relies on emotional manipulation, repetition, and algorithmic amplification.
- OSINT provides essential tools to investigate, verify, and expose propaganda campaigns.
- Public awareness and media literacy are key defenses against manipulation.

As propaganda becomes more sophisticated, the role of OSINT analysts, fact-checkers, and investigative journalists becomes more crucial than ever. By uncovering hidden agendas, verifying media content, and exposing manipulation tactics, we can help defend the integrity of information in the digital age.

7.2 Analyzing Bias in News Coverage & Information Sources

In today's media landscape, bias is an unavoidable reality. While some sources strive for objectivity, others intentionally or unintentionally shape narratives to reflect political, ideological, or financial interests. Understanding media bias is crucial for OSINT analysts, journalists, and researchers who seek to uncover truth amid misinformation and propaganda.

This chapter explores the different types of media bias, techniques for detecting them, and how OSINT methods can be used to analyze news coverage objectively.

1. What Is Media Bias?

Bias in news reporting occurs when information is presented in a way that favors a particular perspective, group, or agenda. Bias doesn't always involve false information— sometimes, the issue lies in how the facts are framed, what details are omitted, or how stories are prioritized.

Key Features of Media Bias:

- **Selective Reporting** – Emphasizing certain facts while ignoring others.
- **Framing & Language** – Using emotionally charged words to influence perception.

- **Source Selection** – Relying on experts or data that support one viewpoint.
- **Story Placement** – Highlighting or burying stories based on agenda.
- **False Balance** – Treating both sides as equal even when evidence favors one side.

Example: A politically biased news outlet might cover the same event differently:

- Left-leaning media might emphasize social justice concerns.
- Right-leaning media might highlight law and order issues.

Even though both reports may be factually accurate, the framing shapes public perception differently.

2. Types of Bias in News Coverage

Different types of bias influence how stories are told and interpreted. Recognizing these biases helps identify when narratives are being manipulated.

2.1 Political & Ideological Bias

What It Is: Favoring one political party, ideology, or leader over another.

Example:

- A conservative news outlet might portray environmental regulations as harmful to businesses.
- A liberal news outlet might emphasize the environmental crisis and corporate responsibility.

☐ OSINT Countermeasure:

Compare how multiple outlets (from different political spectrums) report on the same event.

2.2 Sensationalism & Clickbait

What It Is: Exaggerating or dramatizing news to attract attention.

Example:

A headline like "New Study Reveals Coffee Causes Cancer!" (when the study only found a minor correlation).

OSINT Countermeasure:

Fact-check the original study or source before sharing dramatic claims.

2.3 Omission & Censorship

What It Is: Leaving out critical information that changes the context of a story.

Example:

Reporting on a violent protest but failing to mention police brutality that triggered it.

OSINT Countermeasure:

Check independent reports and primary sources to see if important details are missing.

2.4 False Balance ("Both Sides" Journalism)

What It Is: Presenting two opposing views as equally valid, even when one lacks credibility.

Example:

Giving equal airtime to scientists and climate change deniers, even when 97% of scientists agree on climate change.

OSINT Countermeasure:

Assess the credibility of sources before accepting a debate as balanced.

2.5 Corporate & Financial Bias

What It Is: News coverage influenced by advertisers or corporate ownership.

Example:

A media outlet owned by a pharmaceutical company may avoid reporting on drug price scandals.

OSINT Countermeasure:

Investigate who owns the media company and what financial interests they have.

3. OSINT Techniques for Detecting Media Bias

OSINT can help detect bias by analyzing sources, tracking narrative shifts, and cross-referencing information.

3.1 Comparing Multiple News Sources

- Use websites like AllSides or Ground News to see how different outlets report the same story.
- Track bias patterns in left-leaning, right-leaning, and centrist news sources.

Example:

If three left-wing sources and three right-wing sources frame a political scandal differently, the truth may lie somewhere in the middle.

3.2 Checking Source Credibility & Ownership

- Use Whois lookups to investigate who owns a media website.
- Search for editorial policies and conflicts of interest.
- Use Media Bias/Fact Check to see historical bias ratings.

Example:

If a "neutral news site" is funded by a political think tank, its neutrality is questionable.

3.3 Analyzing Language & Framing

- **Identify emotionally charged words** (e.g., "radical," "corrupt," "heroic").
- **Look for leading questions** (e.g., "Why is the government hiding the truth?").
- **Use linguistic analysis tools like LIWC** (Linguistic Inquiry and Word Count) to detect word sentiment bias.

Example:

A report that describes a protest as "a violent mob" vs. "a passionate demonstration" reveals editorial bias.

3.4 Fact-Checking & Verifying Claims

- Use tools like FactCheck.org, Snopes, and PolitiFact to verify claims.
- Cross-check with official data sources (e.g., government reports, scientific studies).

Example:

If a news outlet claims "crime rates are skyrocketing," but official crime statistics show a decline, there is bias in the reporting.

3.5 Tracking Media Narratives Over Time

- Use the Wayback Machine to see how media changes stories over time.
- Monitor headline changes (e.g., did a headline start with a strong claim but later become more neutral?).
- Analyze how different outlets shift coverage depending on political or financial interests.

Example:

During political scandals, some outlets may initially downplay the issue, only to shift tone when public pressure increases.

4. Why Media Bias Matters in OSINT Investigations

- **Misinformation thrives in biased environments** – Biased reporting can reinforce false narratives.
- **Disinformation campaigns exploit bias** – Foreign influence operations target existing media divides.
- **Critical thinking is essential for analysts** – OSINT investigations require understanding how media manipulation works.

5. Conclusion: Developing a Critical Approach to News Sources

- No news source is 100% objective, but by using OSINT techniques, we can identify patterns of bias.
- Comparing multiple sources, verifying claims, and analyzing language helps detect hidden agendas.
- Bias detection is a core skill for OSINT analysts, journalists, and fact-checkers in the fight against disinformation and propaganda.

By developing a structured, analytical approach to news consumption, we can separate fact from spin and make informed decisions in an era of digital manipulation.

7.3 Identifying State-Controlled & Fake News Websites

The rise of state-controlled media and fake news websites has significantly impacted public perception, shaping narratives for political, economic, and ideological gain. These websites often disguise themselves as legitimate news outlets while serving government interests, spreading propaganda, or promoting disinformation campaigns.

In this chapter, we explore how to identify state-controlled and fake news websites, the tactics they use, and OSINT techniques for verifying their credibility.

1. What Are State-Controlled & Fake News Websites?

1.1 State-Controlled Media

State-controlled media refers to news organizations that are owned, funded, or heavily influenced by governments. While some state-funded outlets provide credible journalism, others act as propaganda arms to manipulate public perception.

📌 **Examples of State-Controlled Media:**

✓ **RT (Russia Today)** – Funded by the Russian government, known for pro-Kremlin narratives.

✓ **CGTN (China Global Television Network)** – A Chinese state-run media outlet promoting CCP perspectives.

✓ **Press TV (Iran)** – Iranian state-run news with anti-Western narratives.

🔎 **Characteristics of State-Controlled Media:**

✓ Echoing official government statements without criticism

✓ Dismissing opposition voices or independent perspectives

✓ Framing events to align with state interests

✓ Ignoring government corruption or wrongdoing

1.2 Fake News Websites

Fake news websites differ from state-controlled media in that they are often run by independent actors, political groups, or financially motivated individuals who create false or misleading content.

📌 Examples of Fake News Sites:

✓ **Before It's News** – Publishes conspiracy theories and unverifiable claims.

✓ **YourNewsWire (now NewsPunch)** – Known for spreading hoaxes and disinformation.

✓ **Natural News** – Promotes anti-science and medical misinformation.

🔎 Characteristics of Fake News Websites:

✓ Sensationalist headlines (e.g., "SHOCKING: Government Hiding the Truth!")

✓ No clear author or editorial oversight

✓ Heavily biased content with little or no sourcing

✓ Plagiarized or manipulated images and videos

2. Tactics Used by State-Controlled & Fake News Websites

State-run and fake news sites use various tactics to spread propaganda, disinformation, and conspiracy theories.

2.1 Domain Spoofing & Impersonation

✓ Fake news sites sometimes mimic legitimate news organizations by using similar URLs.

✓ Example: "BBCNews.co" instead of the official "BBC.com".

☐ OSINT Countermeasure:

✓ Use Whois lookups (who.is, DomainTools) to check domain registration details.

✓ Check for recently registered domains—many fake news sites are created just before major events.

2.2 Anonymous Ownership & Lack of Transparency

✓ State-controlled and fake news sites often hide their ownership or use shell organizations to mask affiliations.

✓ Example: Many Russian disinformation sites use "independent think tanks" as fronts.

☐ OSINT Countermeasure:

✓ Check ownership records using ICANN or Whois databases.

✓ Search business registries for links to governments or political groups.

2.3 Use of Coordinated Amplification (Bots & Trolls)

✓ Fake news websites rely on social media bot networks and troll farms to spread their articles.

✓ Example: During the 2016 U.S. elections, Russian bots amplified fake news stories to influence voters.

☐ OSINT Countermeasure:

✓ Use Botometer or Hoaxy to detect bot-driven content sharing.

✓ Conduct network analysis to see who is amplifying stories and where they originate.

2.4 Manipulated Images & Videos

✔ Fake news sites frequently use altered images, misleading captions, or AI-generated videos.

✔ Example: A deepfake video of a politician appearing to say something inflammatory.

☐ **OSINT Countermeasure:**

✔ Use reverse image search tools (Google Reverse Image, TinEye, InVID) to check image origins.

✔ Analyze video metadata to see if it has been altered.

2.5 Fabricated Experts & Unverifiable Sources

✔ Fake news sites often invent "experts" or cite anonymous sources.

✔ Example: An article claims, "A top scientist warns of a secret government experiment!" but provides no source.

☐ **OSINT Countermeasure:**

✔ Search for the expert's credentials and verify if they are affiliated with recognized institutions.

✔ Use Google Scholar, LinkedIn, and ORCID to verify academic backgrounds.

3. OSINT Techniques for Detecting State-Controlled & Fake News Websites

To determine whether a news source is legitimate, state-controlled, or fake, OSINT analysts use various verification techniques.

3.1 Checking Domain & Website Ownership

✔ Use Whois lookup tools (who.is, DomainTools) to check registration details.

✔ Investigate who owns the website and whether it has links to a state or political entity.

🔎 **Example:**

✔ Checking RT's Whois data reveals its connection to the Russian government.

3.2 Verifying Source Credibility

✔ Search for the news outlet on Media Bias/Fact Check, AllSides, or Ad Fontes Media.

✔ Cross-check the outlet's history of accuracy and fact-checking reliability.

🔎 Example:

✔ A website claiming to be "independent news" but consistently pushing pro-government narratives may be state-controlled.

3.3 Analyzing Website & Content Patterns

✔ **Look for hallmarks of fake news:**

- Overuse of ALL CAPS headlines
- Emotional, clickbait-style language
- Lack of verifiable sources

✔ Use Wayback Machine to check if the website's content has changed over time.

🔎 Example:

✔ A website that only started covering politics before an election may be part of an influence campaign.

3.4 Investigating Social Media Amplification

✔ Use Hoaxy to track how a news story spreads across social media.

✔ Check for bot-driven activity using Botometer or Twitter Audit.

🔎 Example:

✓ A news website with no real audience but thousands of bot shares is likely part of a disinformation campaign.

3.5 Cross-Referencing With Trusted Sources

✓ Compare reports with BBC, Reuters, AP, or major fact-checking organizations.

✓ If a shocking claim appears only on one website, it is likely fabricated.

🔎 Example:

✓ A "leaked government report" only appearing on fringe websites is likely a hoax.

4. Conclusion: Strengthening OSINT Against Fake News & Propaganda

✓ State-controlled and fake news websites manipulate public perception for political or financial gain.

✓ They use domain spoofing, fake experts, manipulated media, and coordinated amplification to spread misinformation.

✓ OSINT techniques—domain analysis, source verification, metadata analysis, and network tracking—can expose fake news sites.

By staying vigilant and applying OSINT methods, analysts, journalists, and researchers can identify and combat digital misinformation campaigns, ensuring that the public has access to credible and factual information in an era of growing information warfare.

7.4 How Propaganda Influences Elections & Public Policy

Propaganda is a powerful tool that has been used for centuries to manipulate public opinion, sway elections, and shape government policies. In the digital age, propaganda campaigns have become more sophisticated, leveraging social media, state-controlled media, and coordinated influence operations to spread misleading narratives, suppress dissent, and reinforce ideological divides.

This chapter explores how propaganda influences elections and public policy, the tactics used to manipulate voters, and how OSINT can help detect and counter such campaigns.

1. The Role of Propaganda in Elections

Political propaganda is designed to influence voter behavior, perceptions of candidates, and public trust in democratic institutions. It can be used to:

✓ Promote a candidate or political party through biased narratives.

✓ Discredit opponents with false or misleading information.

✓ Suppress voter turnout by creating confusion or apathy.

✓ Undermine trust in election systems to delegitimize results.

✦ **Example**: During the 2016 U.S. election, Russian-backed propaganda campaigns spread disinformation about candidates on social media, state-controlled news sites, and troll forums, leading to polarization and confusion among voters.

1.1 Types of Election Propaganda

Propaganda in elections can take many forms, including:

✓ **Fake News & Disinformation** – Spreading false stories to manipulate public opinion.

✓ **Misinformation** – Misleading but unintentional errors that distort reality.

✓ **Deepfake Videos & AI-Generated Content** – Creating realistic but fake media to mislead voters.

✓ **Astroturfing** – Fabricated grassroots movements pushing political narratives.

✓ **Fearmongering & Scaremongering** – Using fear to control voter sentiment.

🔎 **Case Study**: In 2020, doctored videos of U.S. politicians were circulated on social media, making it appear as if they said things they never did. This was a form of deepfake propaganda designed to undermine their credibility.

2. How Propaganda Shapes Public Policy

Beyond elections, propaganda is used to influence government policies, public attitudes, and legislative decisions. Governments, corporations, and advocacy groups all engage in narrative control to push specific agendas.

📌 **Examples of Propaganda in Public Policy:**

✓ **War & Military Actions**: Governments use war propaganda to gain public support for conflicts (e.g., Iraq War's "Weapons of Mass Destruction" narrative).

✓ **Economic Policies**: Media outlets with financial interests can promote biased economic policies to benefit corporations.

✓ **Public Health & Science**: Anti-vaccine propaganda, climate change denial, or false medical claims can shape public opinion against scientific consensus.

🔎 **Case Study**: In 2020, state-sponsored propaganda campaigns spread misinformation about COVID-19 vaccines, leading to public distrust in health policies.

3. Propaganda Tactics in Elections & Public Policy

Understanding how propaganda operates is essential for detecting and countering its influence.

3.1 Controlled Media & State-Sponsored Narratives

✓ Governments own or control media outlets to push nationalistic, political, or ideological narratives.

✓ **Example**: In Russia, China, and Iran, state-run media actively promotes pro-government messaging while censoring opposition voices.

☐ **OSINT Countermeasure:**

✓ Analyze media ownership and funding sources to detect state influence.

✓ Compare news coverage across multiple sources to identify biases.

3.2 Social Media Manipulation & Fake Engagement

✔ Bots and troll farms create fake engagement on social media to make certain political narratives appear more popular.

✔ **Example**: Russian bot networks amplified divisive political content during U.S. elections.

☐ **OSINT Countermeasure:**

✔ Use Botometer, Hoaxy, and network analysis tools to detect fake social media activity.

✔ Track how hashtags and narratives spread across different accounts.

3.3 Fake News & Misinformation Campaigns

✔ Political operatives create misleading news articles and conspiracy theories to shape public perception.

✔ Example: False claims of widespread voter fraud were used to undermine trust in the 2020 U.S. election results.

☐ **OSINT Countermeasure:**

✔ Cross-check news stories with fact-checking sites like Snopes, PolitiFact, and FactCheck.org.

✔ Use metadata analysis and reverse image search to verify digital content.

3.4 Deepfakes & Synthetic Media in Political Campaigns

✔ AI-generated videos and audio clips fabricate political speeches or actions to deceive voters.

✔ Example: In 2024, a deepfake video of a political candidate went viral before an election, falsely showing them making racist comments.

☐ **OSINT Countermeasure:**

✓ Use deepfake detection tools like InVID and Microsoft's Video Authenticator.

✓ Analyze video inconsistencies, lighting, and unnatural facial movements.

3.5 Voter Suppression & Psychological Manipulation

✓ Propaganda can be used to discourage certain groups from voting by spreading false information.

✓ Example: Fake messages claiming "Election Day was postponed" were sent to minority communities.

☐ OSINT Countermeasure:

✓ Track disinformation campaigns targeting voter groups.

✓ Verify official election announcements from government websites.

4. OSINT Techniques for Detecting & Countering Political Propaganda

Political propaganda is often coordinated, well-funded, and difficult to detect without OSINT techniques.

4.1 Investigating Media Sources

✓ Use Whois lookup tools to investigate ownership of media websites.

✓ Check funding sources, affiliations, and editorial biases of news organizations.

🔎 Example:

✓ A "neutral" news site turns out to be funded by a political think tank with vested interests.

4.2 Network Analysis of Propaganda Campaigns

✓ Map how disinformation spreads across social media networks.

✓ Identify key amplifiers (bots, influencers, and news sites) behind propaganda campaigns.

🔎 **Example:**

✓ A hashtag pushing a political narrative is traced back to a coordinated bot network.

4.3 Reverse Image & Video Verification

✓ Use reverse image search (Google, TinEye) to check if viral political images are real or manipulated.
✓ Verify metadata of videos to detect edited or AI-generated content.

🔎 **Example:**

✓ A viral image of ballot boxes being burned was actually from a different country years ago.

4.4 Identifying Foreign Influence Campaigns

✓ Track state-sponsored disinformation campaigns using OSINT tools like:
◆ EUvsDisinfo (for Russian propaganda)
◆ Hamilton 2.0 (for tracking foreign influence in U.S. politics)

🔎 **Example:**

✓ Chinese state-run media spreads narratives about Western democracies failing to influence public perception.

5. Conclusion: Protecting Democracy from Propaganda

✓ Propaganda is a powerful tool used to manipulate elections and shape public policy.

✓ Social media, fake news, and AI-generated content have made election propaganda more effective than ever.

✓ OSINT techniques—network analysis, fact-checking, and media verification—are crucial for detecting and countering disinformation.

By staying informed and applying OSINT methods, analysts, journalists, and voters can identify propaganda tactics and protect democratic processes from manipulation.

7.5 Tracking Media Manipulation Across Multiple Platforms

In the digital age, media manipulation is no longer confined to a single platform. Disinformation campaigns strategically spread across multiple online ecosystems, including social media, news websites, forums, and encrypted messaging apps. This multi-platform approach allows propagandists to amplify false narratives, evade content moderation, and create the illusion of widespread support.

This chapter explores how media manipulation operates across different platforms, the tactics used by disinformation actors, and how OSINT techniques can be leveraged to track and expose these operations.

1. How Media Manipulation Works Across Platforms

Disinformation campaigns are often multi-layered and strategically coordinated across multiple platforms. They typically follow this pattern:

✓ **Seeding the Narrative**: False or misleading information is introduced on fringe websites, anonymous forums, or encrypted messaging apps.

✓ **Amplification by Social Media**: Bots, troll farms, and influencers share the content on mainstream platforms (Twitter, Facebook, Instagram, etc.).

✓ **Reinforcement by Alternative News Sources**: Partisan news sites or propaganda outlets cite the misinformation, giving it an appearance of credibility.

✓ **Mainstream Adoption**: If successful, the false narrative trickles into mainstream media or is picked up by prominent figures.

📌 **Example:**

During the COVID-19 pandemic, false claims about vaccine side effects originated on Telegram groups, spread to Twitter via bot accounts, and were later amplified by alternative news sites, eventually reaching mainstream audiences.

2. Key Platforms Used for Media Manipulation

Disinformation actors use different platforms for different purposes, depending on their target audience and objectives.

2.1 Social Media Networks (Facebook, Twitter, Instagram, TikTok)

✓ Used for mass amplification of narratives.

✓ Relies on bots, influencers, and viral memes.

✓ Algorithms help spread engagement-driven misinformation.

☐ **OSINT Countermeasures:**

✓ Use Hoaxy and Botometer to detect bot-driven trends.

✓ Analyze hashtag campaigns and viral spread patterns.

2.2 Encrypted Messaging Apps (Telegram, WhatsApp, Signal)

✓ Used for covert coordination and spreading unmoderated content.

✓ Harder to monitor due to end-to-end encryption.

✓ Often used by extremist groups and conspiracy theorists.

☐ **OSINT Countermeasures:**

✓ Join open Telegram or WhatsApp groups to monitor disinformation trends.

✓ Use channel tracking tools like Tgstat or Telemetr to analyze message spread.

2.3 Anonymous Forums & Imageboards (4chan, 8kun, Reddit, Discord)

✓ Serve as launchpads for disinformation campaigns.

✓ Used for coordinated trolling, doxxing, and narrative seeding.

✓ Memes and conspiracies originate here before spreading to mainstream platforms.

☐ **OSINT Countermeasures:**

✓ Monitor 4chan's /pol/ board and Reddit disinformation subreddits.

✓ Archive and analyze trending discussions on disinfo-heavy forums.

2.4 State-Controlled & Alternative News Websites

✓ State-backed outlets spread official propaganda and disinformation.

✓ Partisan or extremist sites amplify unverified claims.

✓ Some use domain spoofing to impersonate real news sites.

☐ **OSINT Countermeasures:**

✓ Use Whois lookups and domain analysis to verify ownership.

✓ Cross-check news claims against trusted fact-checkers (Snopes, PolitiFact, BBC Reality Check, etc.).

2.5 Video Platforms (YouTube, Rumble, Odysee, Bitchute)

✓ Used to create compelling narratives using video content.

✓ Deepfake technology is increasingly used for visual disinformation.

✓ Algorithm-driven recommendations can promote extremist or conspiratorial content.

☐ **OSINT Countermeasures:**

✓ Use InVID and reverse image search to verify video authenticity.

✓ Track YouTube channel metadata and history for suspicious patterns.

3. Techniques for Tracking Cross-Platform Media Manipulation

To effectively track media manipulation, OSINT analysts must connect data points across multiple platforms.

3.1 Hashtag & Trend Analysis

✓ Disinformation campaigns often use coordinated hashtags to boost visibility.

✓ **Example**: "#ElectionFraud" was artificially amplified by bot accounts during the 2020 U.S. election.

☐ **OSINT Tools:**

✓ **Hoaxy** – Visualizes how disinformation spreads on Twitter.

✓ **Trendsmap** – Analyzes trending hashtags worldwide.

3.2 Network Analysis of Disinformation Actors

✓ Identify key influencers, bot networks, and troll farms spreading misinformation.

✓ **Example**: A single Telegram group might seed false claims that later appear in multiple news articles.

☐ **OSINT Tools:**

✓ Graphika and Maltego – Map connections between disinfo actors.

✓ Botometer – Detects automated Twitter accounts.

3.3 Reverse Image & Video Verification

✓ Disinformation campaigns frequently reuse old images or AI-generated media.

✓ Example: A viral image claiming to show Ukrainian soldiers in 2023 was actually from 2014.

☐ **OSINT Tools:**

✓ **Google Reverse Image Search & TinEye** – Find original image sources.

✓ **InVID** – Analyze video metadata and detect AI-generated manipulation.

3.4 Website & Domain Analysis

✓ Fake news sites often use misleading domains to appear credible.

✓ **Example**: "BBCNews.co" was used to impersonate the real BBC website.

☐ **OSINT Tools:**

✓ **Whois Lookup & DomainTools** – Check website ownership and registration details.

✓ **Wayback Machine** – View past versions of suspicious websites.

3.5 Timeline Analysis of Narrative Evolution

✓ Track how a false claim evolves from its origin to mainstream adoption.

✓ **Example**: A fabricated story about voter fraud started on 4chan, spread to Twitter, and was later cited by partisan news outlets.

☐ **OSINT Tools:**

✓ **Timeline JS** – Create a visual timeline of disinformation spread.

✓ **CrowdTangle** – Monitor how false news spreads on Facebook and Instagram.

4. Case Study: Coordinated Disinformation in the 2022 French Election

In 2022, a disinformation campaign aimed at undermining the French presidential election used multiple platforms to spread false claims about electoral fraud.

✓ **Step 1 (Seeding):** The narrative originated on Telegram and 4chan, claiming ballot tampering.

✓ **Step 2 (Amplification):** Bot networks on Twitter and Facebook artificially inflated the hashtag #RiggedElection.

✓ **Step 3 (Legitimization):** Russian state media outlets RT and Sputnik cited the claims as "concerns raised by voters."

✓ **Step 4 (Mainstreaming):** Right-wing political figures referenced the claims in TV interviews, giving them wider credibility.

☐ **OSINT Tools Used:**

✓ Botometer detected high bot activity around the hashtag.

✓ Hoaxy mapped the spread of false narratives across Twitter.

✓ Wayback Machine showed how misleading articles evolved over time.

5. Conclusion: Strengthening OSINT Against Multi-Platform Disinformation

✓ Disinformation campaigns strategically operate across multiple platforms, making them harder to detect.

✓ Social media, encrypted apps, anonymous forums, and state-run media work together to spread false narratives.

✓ OSINT techniques—network analysis, hashtag tracking, metadata verification, and domain analysis—are critical for exposing media manipulation.

By applying multi-platform monitoring and OSINT methodologies, analysts can identify, track, and counteract digital propaganda campaigns, ensuring the public has access to accurate and verifiable information in an increasingly manipulated media landscape.

7.6 Case Study: OSINT Unveiling a State-Run Propaganda Machine

State-run propaganda is one of the most sophisticated and well-funded forms of disinformation, often backed by governments, intelligence agencies, and state-controlled media networks. These operations aim to influence public perception, destabilize foreign governments, and control domestic narratives.

This case study demonstrates how OSINT techniques were used to uncover a state-run propaganda machine, exposing its methods, key players, and the platforms it leveraged to manipulate public opinion.

1. Background: The Rise of State-Sponsored Disinformation

Governments worldwide have invested heavily in digital propaganda operations, using tactics such as:

✓ **Controlled Media Networks** – State-run TV channels and websites that publish biased or false information.

✓ **Social Media Manipulation** – Fake accounts, bots, and troll farms that amplify propaganda.

✓ **Influence Operations** – Targeting foreign audiences to weaken trust in democratic institutions.

✓ **Fake News Websites** – Websites posing as independent news outlets but pushing government narratives.

The Case: The "Global Truth Network" Disinformation Operation

In 2023, OSINT researchers uncovered a large-scale, state-sponsored propaganda network dubbed the Global Truth Network (GTN). The operation was linked to a nation-state intelligence agency and was designed to spread disinformation about Western governments while boosting the image of its own country.

📌 **Objective:**

GTN aimed to:

✓ Undermine trust in Western media and democratic institutions.

✓ Promote pro-government narratives worldwide.

✓ Spread false information about geopolitical events to shift public opinion.

2. Step 1: Identifying Suspicious Media Outlets

Tracking Suspicious Domains & Websites

✓ OSINT analysts first noticed a rise in anti-Western narratives from unknown media sites.

✓ Many of these sites had professional layouts but lacked transparency on funding and editorial staff.

✓ Researchers used Whois lookup and domain analysis tools to investigate ownership.

☐ OSINT Tools Used:

✓ **Whois Lookup & DomainTools** – Traced ownership to a shell company registered in a state-aligned country.

✓ **Wayback Machine** – Showed that the sites suddenly appeared in early 2022, coinciding with geopolitical tensions.

✓ **DNS Analysis** – Revealed that multiple sites shared the same hosting infrastructure, suggesting coordination.

🔎 Key Finding:

✓ Over 50 news websites were connected through shared hosting, indicating a centralized network of disinformation sites.

3. Step 2: Investigating Social Media Amplification

Bot Networks & Fake Engagement

Once articles from the GTN websites were published, they were immediately amplified on social media.

✓ Thousands of Twitter accounts shared the links within minutes of publication.

✓ Many accounts displayed bot-like behavior (posting at regular intervals, no profile pictures, repetitive messages).

✓ The same hashtags were used across multiple platforms, suggesting coordinated activity.

☐ **OSINT Tools Used:**

✓ **Botometer** – Detected high levels of automation among accounts sharing GTN content.

✓ **Hoaxy** – Mapped how disinformation spread across Twitter.

✓ **CrowdTangle** – Tracked Facebook and Instagram pages sharing identical narratives.

🔎 **Key Finding:**

✓ Over 5,000 social media accounts were linked to this campaign, many created within the same time frame.

✓ Some of these accounts also posed as journalists or experts to add credibility.

4. Step 3: Exposing the Influence of State-Controlled Media

How GTN Content Reached Mainstream News

Once GTN articles gained traction, they were cited by state-controlled media outlets, including:

✓ **Government-backed TV channels** – Framing GTN stories as legitimate news.

✓ **Anonymous Telegram channels** – Spreading GTN content among private groups.

✓ **Influencer Partnerships** – Paying pro-government influencers to promote GTN narratives.

☐ **OSINT Tools Used:**

✓ **Media Bias Fact Check** – Identified known pro-government outlets sharing GTN stories.

✓ **Google Reverse Image Search** – Showed how the same images were used across different GTN sites, proving a coordinated effort.

✓ **Tgstat & Telemetr** – Monitored how GTN stories spread in Telegram disinformation groups.

🔎 Key Finding:

✓ Mainstream state-controlled TV channels cited GTN articles to make them appear credible.

✓ The same misleading stories were translated into multiple languages, targeting foreign audiences.

5. Step 4: Unmasking the Coordinators & Financial Ties

Following the Money & Identifying Key Players

✓ Researchers traced financial records and sponsorships linking GTN websites to a government-affiliated PR firm.

✓ A leaked database revealed that many of the "journalists" on GTN's payroll were actually government employees.

✓ Some of these sites were registered using fake identities, but OSINT analysts cross-referenced LinkedIn profiles to connect individuals to state-run institutions.

☐ OSINT Tools Used:

✓ **LinkedIn & People Search Engines** – Identified fake journalists linked to GTN.

✓ **Company Registration Databases** – Traced funding to government-backed media organizations.

✓ **Leak Monitoring (Distributed Denial of Secrets, Wikileaks, etc.)** – Found leaked documents revealing internal communication from GTN operatives.

🔎 Key Finding:

✓ GTN was not an independent media network, but a covert propaganda arm of a government's intelligence agency.

6. Outcome & Impact of the Investigation

✓ GTN's operations were exposed in international media, leading to widespread condemnation.

✓ Social media platforms suspended bot accounts and flagged GTN-related content as misleading.

✓ Some governments sanctioned organizations involved in GTN's funding.

🔎 **Key Takeaway:**

✓ This case demonstrated how OSINT can systematically uncover state-run propaganda machines, proving how disinformation is coordinated, financed, and disseminated.

7. Lessons Learned: Using OSINT to Combat State Propaganda

✓ **Media Manipulation is Multi-Layered** – Fake news websites, bots, social media influencers, and state-controlled TV work together in a propaganda ecosystem.

✓ **Disinformation Spreads in Waves** – It starts on fringe platforms, moves to social media, and gets legitimized by larger media outlets.

✓ **Tracking Funding & Domain Registration is Critical** – Many propaganda networks can be traced to their financial backers.

✓ **OSINT is Essential for Exposing State Propaganda** – By combining network analysis, media tracking, and financial investigation, disinformation networks can be uncovered and neutralized.

8. Conclusion: The Role of OSINT in Fighting State Disinformation

State-run propaganda operations pose a significant threat to global information integrity. As these campaigns grow more sophisticated, OSINT analysts play a crucial role in exposing manipulation, verifying sources, and disrupting digital influence operations.

By leveraging domain analysis, social media tracking, metadata verification, and financial forensics, OSINT investigators can unmask hidden propaganda networks and help protect the integrity of public discourse in an increasingly manipulated media landscape.

8. Analyzing Memes & Viral Trends

In the digital age, memes and viral trends have become potent vehicles for spreading disinformation, manipulating emotions, and influencing public opinion. This chapter explores how memes are created, shared, and weaponized in disinformation campaigns to quickly capture attention and shift narratives. We'll examine the subtle ways in which these seemingly innocent, humorous images or videos can carry embedded messages, stereotypes, or political agendas. By utilizing OSINT techniques, readers will learn how to trace the origins of viral trends, assess their impact, and uncover the hidden agendas behind them. Understanding the anatomy of memes and viral content is crucial in identifying when they are being used as tools for manipulation, allowing analysts to respond with insight and accuracy.

8.1 The Power of Memes in Influence Campaigns

In today's digital landscape, memes are far more than just internet humor—they have become powerful tools for influence campaigns, political messaging, and disinformation operations. Their ability to condense complex narratives into easily shareable images, videos, and slogans makes them ideal for psychological manipulation and social engineering.

This chapter explores how memes are weaponized in influence campaigns, their effectiveness in shaping public opinion, and how OSINT techniques can be used to track and analyze their spread.

1. Why Memes Are Effective in Influence Campaigns

Memes are particularly effective in disinformation and propaganda because they:

✓ **Bypass Critical Thinking** – People engage with memes emotionally rather than analytically, making them effective for spreading disinformation.

✓ **Spread Rapidly & Virally** – Memes can reach millions of users within hours, thanks to social media algorithms.

✓ **Exploit Visual Persuasion** – Images trigger faster and stronger cognitive reactions compared to text-based content.

✔ **Anonymity & Plausible Deniability** – Governments and actors behind disinformation can claim they are "just jokes" to avoid accountability.

📌 **Example:**

During the 2016 U.S. presidential election, political meme campaigns on 4chan and Facebook spread misleading narratives to influence voter perceptions. Some memes falsely claimed that people could vote via text message, leading to actual voter suppression.

2. How Memes Are Used in Influence Campaigns

Memes are strategically crafted to promote ideologies, manipulate emotions, and reinforce echo chambers.

2.1 Political & Ideological Manipulation

✔ Used to promote political candidates or attack opponents.

✔ Often contain misleading statistics or out-of-context quotes.

✔ Encourages polarization by reinforcing "us vs. them" narratives.

📌 **Example:**

✔ During Brexit, memes circulated online claiming that leaving the EU would result in an extra £350 million per week for the NHS, a false claim that shaped public opinion.

2.2 Disinformation & Fake News Distribution

✔ Memes can spread conspiracy theories in an easily digestible format.

✔ Fake screenshots of news articles, tweets, or official statements make disinformation appear credible.

✔ AI-generated or manipulated images enhance false narratives.

📌 **Example:**

✓ The "Plandemic" meme campaign used visual content to spread COVID-19 conspiracy theories, misleading millions about vaccine safety.

☐ **OSINT Tools to Detect This:**

✓ **Google Reverse Image Search** – Check if a meme's image has been manipulated or taken out of context.
✓ **TinEye** – Identify the first known use of an image.

2.3 Meme Warfare & Psychological Operations (PsyOps)

✓ Memes are used in military and intelligence operations to demoralize opponents or influence enemy populations.
✓ Troll farms and bot networks mass-produce propaganda memes targeting adversaries.
✓ Used in geopolitical conflicts to manipulate public perception.

📌 **Example:**

✓ Russian disinformation campaigns during the Ukraine conflict used memes to mock Ukraine's leadership and spread anti-Western narratives.

☐ **OSINT Tools to Track This:**

✓ **Hoaxy** – Tracks how disinformation spreads through social networks.
✓ **CrowdTangle** – Identifies how memes circulate on Facebook and Instagram.

2.4 Memes as Engagement Traps for Algorithm Manipulation

✓ Disinformation campaigns use memes to trigger outrage, increasing engagement and visibility.
✓ Social media algorithms boost highly engaged content, regardless of accuracy.

✓ Some groups intentionally create offensive memes to provoke reactions and game the algorithm.

📌 **Example:**

✓ A study found that far-right groups on Facebook used memes to increase engagement, which led to algorithmic amplification of their content.

☐ **OSINT Tools to Monitor This:**

✓ **Trend Analysis (Twitter Trends, Google Trends)** – Detect spikes in meme-driven engagement.
✓ **Botometer** – Identify automated accounts spreading memes artificially.

3. Tracking & Investigating Meme-Based Disinformation with OSINT

To counter meme-driven disinformation, OSINT analysts use various investigative techniques to track their origins, spread, and impact.

3.1 Reverse Image Search & Metadata Analysis

✓ Identify whether a meme's image has been altered, misused, or repurposed from older content.
✓ Check embedded metadata (EXIF data) for information about the meme's origin.

☐ **Tools:**

✓ InVID & FotoForensics – Analyze image metadata and digital manipulation.

✓ Google Reverse Image Search & TinEye – Find original versions of images.

3.2 Hashtag & Network Analysis

✓ Memes often trend alongside hashtags, making it possible to track their spread.
✓ Network analysis can identify coordinated accounts pushing memes simultaneously.

☐ **Tools:**

✓ **Hoaxy** – Maps how meme-based disinformation spreads.

✓ **Trendsmap & Hashtagify** – Analyze which hashtags are amplifying memes.

3.3 Identifying Bot-Driven Meme Campaigns

✓ Many memes are artificially amplified by bot networks and troll farms.

✓ Identifying high-volume, low-engagement accounts can reveal bot-driven campaigns.

☐ **Tools:**

✓ **Botometer** – Detects bot-like behavior in meme-sharing accounts.

✓ **Graphika & Maltego** – Perform network analysis on meme-sharing clusters.

4. Case Study: Memes in the 2020 U.S. Election Disinformation Campaign

Background

✓ Ahead of the 2020 U.S. election, disinformation groups used memes to suppress votes and spread conspiracy theories.

✓ Memes falsely claimed that mail-in ballots would be discarded and that people could vote via text message.

How OSINT Exposed the Operation

1☐ Reverse Image Search revealed that some memes used old images with misleading captions.

2☐ Network Analysis showed that Russian-controlled bot accounts amplified the memes.

3☐ CrowdTangle Data exposed Facebook groups coordinating meme sharing to maximize visibility.

🔎 Key Takeaway:

✓ Memes played a significant role in spreading disinformation, proving that they are not just harmless jokes but strategic psychological tools.

5. Countermeasures: How to Combat Meme-Based Disinformation

✓ **Fact-Checking & OSINT Investigations** – Debunk memes with verifiable sources and visual analysis.

✓ **Algorithmic Interventions** – Social media platforms should detect and limit meme-based disinformation.

✓ **Public Awareness & Digital Literacy** – Educate users about how memes manipulate emotions and opinions.

6. Conclusion: The Future of Memes in Influence Campaigns

Memes will continue to be a major weapon in digital influence operations. As AI-generated content becomes more sophisticated, memes will become harder to trace and debunk.

✓ **AI & Deepfake Memes** – Future propaganda will likely use AI-generated images and videos for even more realistic and deceptive memes.

✓ **Decentralized Meme Networks** – Disinformation actors may move to encrypted or decentralized platforms to avoid detection.

✓ **Advanced OSINT Techniques** – Analysts will need to develop stronger tools to track, analyze, and verify meme-based influence campaigns.

Memes are no longer just entertainment; they are a powerful force in shaping beliefs, spreading disinformation, and manipulating political discourse. OSINT investigators play a critical role in ensuring that these digital weapons are exposed and neutralized.

8.2 Tracking the Origin of Viral Memes

Memes have become a powerful tool for propaganda, disinformation, and psychological manipulation in the digital age. Their ability to go viral quickly and reach millions makes them ideal for influence campaigns. However, tracking their origin is challenging due to their rapid spread, remixing, and reposting across multiple platforms.

This chapter explores OSINT techniques for tracing the origins of viral memes, including image forensics, metadata analysis, network tracking, and bot detection.

1. Why Tracking Meme Origins Matters

✓ **Disinformation Detection** – Many viral memes spread false or misleading narratives to influence public opinion.

✓ **Attribution & Accountability** – Identifying who started a meme can reveal if it was state-sponsored, bot-driven, or grassroots.

✓ **Exposing Covert Influence Campaigns** – Some memes appear organic but are actually part of coordinated propaganda efforts.

✓ **Combating Misinformation** – Debunking a meme's original context can prevent the spread of fake news.

📌 **Example:**

✓ In 2022, OSINT researchers traced a viral anti-Ukraine meme back to a Russian troll farm, proving that it was part of a coordinated disinformation campaign.

2. Methods for Tracking the Origin of Memes

Tracking a meme's origin requires a combination of image analysis, metadata examination, social media tracking, and network forensics.

2.1 Reverse Image Search: Finding the First Appearance

Reverse image search is the first step in identifying a meme's origin. It helps to:

✓ Find the earliest known version of an image.

✓ Identify if the meme's image has been repurposed or altered.

✓ Track which websites and social media pages shared it first.

☐ **OSINT Tools:**

✔ **Google Reverse Image Search** – Find where an image has appeared before.

✔ **TinEye** – Tracks the first known version of an image.

✔ **Yandex Reverse Image Search** – Useful for tracking images on Russian and Eastern European websites.

📌 **Case Example:**

✔ A meme falsely claiming a political leader made an inflammatory statement was traced back to a photoshopped image from a satirical news site using TinEye.

2.2 Metadata Analysis: Extracting Hidden Image Data

Many memes contain hidden metadata (EXIF data) that reveals:

✔ When & where the image was created.

✔ The camera or software used to edit it.

✔ Whether the image has been altered.

☐ **OSINT Tools:**

✔ **InVID & FotoForensics** – Extracts metadata and analyzes digital manipulation.

✔ **ExifTool** – Reads hidden metadata from images and videos.

📌 **Example**:

✔ A viral meme appearing to be a leaked government document was debunked after EXIF analysis revealed it was edited in Photoshop on a private laptop.

2.3 Social Media Forensics: Identifying the First Post

Memes often spread across multiple platforms, making it crucial to find the first post or earliest shares.

✓ **Check time stamps** – Find the earliest known share of a meme.

✓ **Analyze engagement patterns** – Identify bot-driven amplification.

✓ **Search by keyword & hashtag** – Look for posts that match the meme's content.

☐ **OSINT Tools:**

✓ **Hoaxy** – Maps how a meme-based disinformation campaign spreads across social media.

✓ **CrowdTangle** – Tracks meme virality across Facebook, Instagram, and Reddit.

✓ **TweetDeck & Twitter Advanced Search** – Finds the earliest Twitter post sharing the meme.

📌 **Example:**

✓ A misleading meme about a political scandal was traced back to a 4chan post, proving it was not from a legitimate news source.

2.4 Hashtag & Trend Analysis: Tracking Meme Amplification

Memes often trend alongside hashtags, which helps OSINT analysts:

✓ Identify coordinated disinformation campaigns.

✓ Detect bot networks boosting a meme.

✓ Find alternative versions of a meme that evolved over time.

☐ **OSINT Tools:**

✓ **Trendsmap & Hashtagify** – Track which hashtags are amplifying memes.

✓ **Botometer** – Detect bot-driven meme sharing.

✓ **Maltego & Gephi** – Map networks of accounts pushing a meme.

📌 **Example:**

✓ A meme promoting anti-vaccine misinformation was found to be amplified by thousands of bot accounts, showing it was part of a coordinated campaign.

3. Case Study: Tracking the Origin of a Viral Political Meme

Step 1: Reverse Image Search

✓ OSINT researchers found the meme had been circulating for months, but the earliest known image was posted on a fringe political forum.

Step 2: Metadata Analysis

✓ EXIF data revealed that the meme's original image was taken in 2019, but the meme only appeared online in 2023.

✓ The image had been digitally altered to add a misleading caption.

Step 3: Social Media Tracking

✓ Using Twitter Advanced Search, the earliest share of the meme was traced to a bot network promoting disinformation.

✓ The same accounts had previously spread similar political memes.

Step 4: Hashtag & Trend Analysis

✓ Researchers found that dozens of fake accounts shared the meme simultaneously, indicating a coordinated effort.

✓ The hashtag #FakeScandal2023 was artificially trending due to automated engagement.

🔍 **Key Takeaway:**

✓ The meme was not an organic viral trend, but part of a disinformation campaign designed to mislead voters before an election.

4. Countering Meme-Based Disinformation

✓ **Public Awareness Campaigns** – Educate people on how memes can be manipulated for propaganda.

✓ **Platform Interventions** – Social media sites should flag or remove memes spreading disinformation.

✓ **OSINT Investigations** – Analysts must continuously track meme origins and debunk false narratives.

5. Conclusion: The Importance of OSINT in Meme Tracking

Memes are a powerful weapon in influence campaigns, often originating from coordinated disinformation networks. OSINT techniques like reverse image search, metadata analysis, social media tracking, and network forensics are essential for:

✓ Tracing the origins of viral memes.

✓ Exposing hidden propaganda efforts.

✓ Preventing false narratives from spreading unchecked.

As AI-generated content and deepfake memes become more sophisticated, OSINT investigators must stay ahead by developing new strategies to track, analyze, and counter digital disinformation.

8.3 Decoding Hidden Messages & Symbolism in Memes

Memes are more than just humorous images with captions—they often contain hidden messages, coded symbolism, and ideological signals meant to influence, radicalize, or manipulate public perception. In the context of disinformation and influence campaigns, memes serve as covert tools for propaganda, psychological operations (PsyOps), and extremist recruitment.

This chapter explores how OSINT analysts can decode hidden messages in memes, identify symbolic references, and track how these coded communications spread within online communities.

1. Why Symbolism in Memes Matters

Memes with hidden messages are used for:

✔ **Covert Communication** – Extremist groups, conspiracy theorists, and disinformation actors embed hidden symbols and references that their audience understands but outsiders overlook.

✔ **Psychological Manipulation** – Symbolism in memes can trigger emotional reactions, reinforce cognitive biases, and deepen ideological divides.

✔ **Radicalization & Recruitment** – Hate groups and extremist movements use coded memes to signal in-group membership and indoctrinate new followers.

✔ **Misinformation & Disinformation** – Memes use subtle visual or linguistic cues to manipulate narratives, distort reality, or spread falsehoods.

📌 **Example**:

✔ The "OK" hand gesture meme was co-opted by white nationalist groups and later added to hate symbol databases—yet, many people still view it as a harmless sign.

2. Types of Hidden Messages in Memes

2.1 Symbolism in Visuals & Colors

Many memes use specific images, colors, and symbols to convey hidden meanings:

✔ **Colors** – Certain colors are associated with political movements, ideologies, or conspiracy theories (e.g., black-and-red color schemes in extremist propaganda).

✔ **Animals & Mythological Figures** – Some memes use wolves, eagles, or lions as symbols of power, nationalism, or racial superiority.

✔ **Historical & Esoteric Symbols** – Many extremist memes reinterpret historical symbols to push hidden agendas.

□ **OSINT Analysis Tools:**

✓ **Google Reverse Image Search** – Identifies the earliest appearance of a meme.

✓ **Symbolism Databases (ADL Hate Symbols, FBI Reports)** – Cross-references visual symbols with known extremist or propaganda materials.

📌 **Example:**

✓ The "Pepe the Frog" meme was originally an innocent cartoon but was later rebranded by extremist groups as a hate symbol.

2.2 Linguistic Codes & Double Meanings

Memes often use coded language, abbreviations, or alternative spellings to evade detection:

✓ **Numeric Codes** – Some numbers have hidden meanings (e.g., "88" for "Heil Hitler" in far-right memes).

✓ **Misspelled or Reversed Words** – Used to avoid automated content moderation on social media.

✓ **Dog Whistles** – Words or phrases that appear harmless but carry deeper meanings for in-group members.

□ **OSINT Analysis Tools:**

✓ **Urban Dictionary & Extremist Lexicons** – Help decode slang, abbreviations, and coded language.

✓ **CrowdTangle & Twitter Advanced Search** – Track how linguistic codes spread across platforms.

📌 **Example:**

✓ The phrase "honk honk" was used in seemingly harmless clown memes but was later co-opted as a coded far-right slogan.

2.3 Meme Format as a Message

The template or format of a meme itself can indicate a hidden message:

✓ **Classic Meme Templates** – Some formats become associated with specific ideologies (e.g., Wojak memes used in far-right propaganda).

✓ **Deepfake & AI-Generated Memes** – Increasingly used to manipulate reality and create false narratives.

✓ **Fake Screenshots & Quotes** – Altered memes that fabricate statements to smear public figures.

☐ **OSINT Analysis Tools:**

✓ **InVID & FotoForensics** – Detect manipulated images and fake screenshots.

✓ **KnowYourMeme** – Provides historical context on how a meme has evolved.

📌 **Example**:

✓ The NPC (Non-Player Character) meme started as a joke about conformity but was later used to dehumanize political opponents.

3. Case Study: How Extremist Groups Use Symbolic Memes

Background

In 2021, OSINT researchers discovered a viral meme campaign on Telegram where far-right groups used symbolic memes to recruit new members.

Step 1: Reverse Image Search

✓ Analysts traced the meme back to a fringe forum where extremist propaganda is shared.

Step 2: Symbolism Analysis

✓ The meme contained hidden numerical codes referencing a well-known extremist manifesto.

Step 3: Social Media Tracking

✓ The meme was being spread by newly created bot accounts, indicating a coordinated influence campaign.

🔎 **Key Takeaway:**

✓ Memes are not always innocent jokes—some are deliberate propaganda tools designed to recruit and radicalize users.

4. OSINT Techniques for Decoding Meme Symbolism

✓ **Reverse Image Search** – Identify where a meme first appeared and how it evolved.

✓ **Metadata & Image Forensics** – Check if a meme was altered or AI-generated.

✓ **Hashtag & Trend Analysis** – Track which groups are spreading a meme.

✓ **Text Analysis & Lexicon Lookup** – Decode hidden meanings in meme captions and comments.

✓ **Network Analysis** – Identify whether a meme is part of a coordinated disinformation campaign.

5. Countering Symbolic & Coded Memes

✓ **Public Awareness & Digital Literacy** – Educate people about hidden messages in memes.

✓ **Social Media Monitoring** – Platforms must detect and remove harmful symbolic memes.

✓ **OSINT Research & Debunking** – Analysts need to track, expose, and counter disinformation memes.

6. Conclusion: Memes as a Digital Battlefield

Memes have evolved into a weapon for covert influence operations, using hidden symbolism, coded language, and psychological manipulation to push ideological narratives. OSINT investigators play a critical role in decoding these messages, exposing coordinated disinformation, and ensuring digital spaces remain free from propaganda-driven manipulation.

As AI-generated memes and deepfake images become more advanced, tracking and analyzing hidden messages in memes will become an even greater challenge for digital forensics and intelligence experts.

8.4 How Memes Are Used for Political & Ideological Manipulation

Memes are no longer just humorous internet jokes—they have become a powerful tool for political and ideological influence. Their ability to spread rapidly, evoke emotional responses, and simplify complex issues makes them ideal for propaganda, disinformation campaigns, and psychological manipulation. Political actors, extremist groups, and foreign influence campaigns leverage memes to sway public opinion, reinforce ideological beliefs, and polarize societies.

In this chapter, we will explore how memes are weaponized for political and ideological manipulation, the key strategies behind their spread, and how OSINT analysts can investigate and counter their influence.

1. Why Memes Are Effective for Manipulation

Memes are uniquely suited for influence operations due to their:

✓ **Emotional Impact** – Memes trigger anger, humor, fear, or outrage, making them more memorable.

✓ **Viral Nature** – Memes spread quickly through shares, reposts, and remixes, reaching millions.

✓ **Simplicity & Accessibility** – They distill complex issues into digestible, relatable content.

✓ **Low Detection Risk** – Unlike traditional propaganda, memes often evade fact-checking algorithms.

✓ **Cross-Platform Reach** – Memes circulate on multiple platforms, from social media to fringe forums.

📌 **Example:**

✓ During the 2016 U.S. elections, Russian disinformation campaigns used memes to stoke division between political groups, spreading false narratives through viral content.

2. Political & Ideological Meme Strategies

2.1 Polarization & Division

Political memes are designed to exaggerate ideological differences, creating an "us vs. them" mindset. They:

✓ **Demonize opponents** – Labeling the other side as "evil" or "stupid."

✓ **Create tribalism** – Reinforcing in-group loyalty and out-group hostility.

✓ **Amplify outrage** – Using sarcasm, exaggeration, and misleading claims to provoke emotional reactions.

☐ **OSINT Analysis Tools:**

✓ **Hoaxy** – Maps how politically divisive memes spread online.

✓ **Botometer** – Identifies bot networks amplifying polarizing memes.

📌 **Example**:

✓ During Brexit, memes painted opponents as either "ignorant nationalists" or "globalist traitors", further entrenching social divisions.

2.2 Propaganda & State-Controlled Narratives

Governments and political organizations use memes as soft propaganda to influence citizens.

✔ **Glorifying leaders** – Making politicians appear heroic, wise, or god-like.

✔ **Dismissing opposition** – Using humor to mock critics and delegitimize dissent.

✔ **Whitewashing controversies** – Shifting focus from real issues to ridicule-based distractions.

☐ **OSINT Analysis Tools:**

✔ **CrowdTangle** – Tracks how state-sponsored pages push memes.

✔ **Trend Analysis** – Identifies when government memes are coordinated across platforms.

📌 **Example:**

✔ In China, pro-government memes portray Xi Jinping as a wise, benevolent leader, while memes mocking dissenters go viral through controlled networks.

2.3 Memes as Disinformation Vehicles

Political memes are often used to spread misleading or outright false information.

✔ **Fabricated quotes & images** – Fake statements attributed to political figures.

✔ **Selective editing** – Images taken out of context to manipulate perceptions.

✔ **Conspiracy theories** – Memes push false narratives, making them seem credible.

☐ **OSINT Analysis Tools:**

✔ **InVID & FotoForensics** – Detect manipulated images and deepfake memes.

✔ **Reverse Image Search** – Finds the original context of altered memes.

📌 **Example:**

✓ A viral meme in 2020 falsely claimed a U.S. politician endorsed extremist groups, using a photoshopped tweet. OSINT analysts debunked it using metadata analysis.

2.4 Meme Warfare & Foreign Influence Operations

Foreign actors weaponize memes to influence elections, disrupt societies, and shape global narratives.

✓ **Exploiting existing social tensions** – Amplifying racial, political, or religious divisions.

✓ **Undermining trust in media & institutions** – Promoting anti-government or anti-science memes.

✓ **Creating confusion & doubt** – Mixing truth with lies to make people question reality.

☐ **OSINT Analysis Tools:**

✓ **Maltego & Graphika** – Map coordinated foreign influence campaigns.

✓ **Twitter Advanced Search** – Track which accounts first posted a meme.

📌 **Example**:

✓ Russian troll farms used memes to divide U.S. voters, posting content for both right-wing and left-wing audiences to increase political chaos.

3. Case Study: Meme Propaganda in the 2020 U.S. Elections

Step 1: Identifying Coordinated Memes

✓ OSINT researchers noticed identical memes being shared by thousands of new accounts.

Step 2: Reverse Image & Metadata Analysis

✓ The memes originated from a foreign-controlled network, not independent users.

Step 3: Network Mapping & Bot Detection

✓ Many meme-sharing accounts were automated bots, amplifying disinformation.

🔎 **Key Takeaway:**

✓ Memes were not an organic political movement—they were part of a foreign influence campaign aimed at destabilizing public trust.

4. OSINT Techniques for Investigating Political Memes

✓ **Reverse Image Search** – Finds original sources & modifications.

✓ **Hashtag & Trend Analysis** – Detects coordinated meme campaigns.

✓ **Social Media Forensics** – Identifies bots and troll farms pushing political memes.

✓ **Network Graphing Tools** – Maps how memes spread across communities.

5. Countering Political & Ideological Meme Manipulation

✓ **Digital Literacy & Education** – Teach people how memes can manipulate opinions.

✓ **Fact-Checking & OSINT Investigations** – Debunk fake memes before they spread further.

✓ **Platform Policies & AI Detection** – Social media sites need better controls against propaganda memes.

6. Conclusion: The Future of Political Meme Manipulation

As AI-generated content, deepfake memes, and hyper-targeted propaganda continue to evolve, political and ideological meme manipulation will become more sophisticated. OSINT analysts and fact-checkers must stay ahead by developing new detection techniques, understanding meme evolution, and educating the public on digital influence tactics.

Memes may seem like harmless internet jokes, but in the hands of disinformation actors, they shape elections, fuel division, and influence global geopolitics.

8.5 The Role of Imageboards & Underground Communities in Meme Culture

Imageboards and underground online communities have played a significant role in the evolution of meme culture, often serving as the birthplace of viral memes, ideological propaganda, and disinformation campaigns. These platforms—such as 4chan, 8kun, and obscure Telegram groups—provide an environment where anonymous users create, share, and weaponize memes to influence public discourse, recruit followers, and push political agendas.

This chapter explores how these underground spaces shape meme culture, how memes spread from these fringe platforms to mainstream social media, and how OSINT analysts can investigate and track their influence.

1. What Are Imageboards & Underground Communities?

Imageboards are anonymous, thread-based forums where users post images and comments without requiring accounts or personal identification. Some of the most well-known platforms include:

✓ **4chan** – One of the earliest and most influential imageboards, known for its role in meme creation, trolling, and disinformation campaigns.

✓ **8kun (formerly 8chan)** – A more extreme platform used by conspiracy theorists, extremist groups, and political agitators.

✓ **Telegram Channels** – Private and semi-private groups that coordinate meme-based influence campaigns.

✓ **Dark Web Forums** – Encrypted communities where fringe ideologies, propaganda, and extremist content are developed and spread.

These platforms often serve as testing grounds for memes, which later leak into mainstream spaces like Twitter, Facebook, and TikTok.

📌 **Example:**

✓ The "NPC Meme" (Non-Player Character) began as an inside joke on 4chan but later became a political weapon used to dehumanize opponents.

2. How Imageboards Influence Meme Culture

2.1 The "Meme Pipeline": From Imageboards to Mainstream

Memes often follow a pipeline from underground forums to global audiences:

1☐ **Creation** – Users on 4chan or similar platforms develop a new meme template, often laced with inside jokes, coded language, or extremist undertones.

2☐ **Amplification** – The meme is spread within the underground community, tested for virality, and refined.

3☐ **Troll Operations** – Users coordinate mass-posting campaigns, sending memes to Twitter, Reddit, and Facebook to manipulate public discourse.

4☐ **Mainstream Adoption** – Once a meme gains traction, influencers, media, and politicians unknowingly adopt it, often without understanding its origins.

☐ **OSINT Analysis Tools:**

✓ **KnowYourMeme** – Tracks the evolution and origin of memes.

✓ **4chan Archive & Telegram Scrapers** – Monitor trending memes in underground forums.

📌 **Example:**

✓ The "Pepe the Frog" meme started as an innocent cartoon but was later co-opted by extremist groups on imageboards before going mainstream.

2.2 Coordinated Meme-Based PsyOps (Psychological Operations)

Underground communities often use memes as psychological warfare tools to:

✓ **Destabilize political opponents** – Creating humiliating or misleading memes to discredit politicians or movements.

✓ **Promote extremist ideologies** – Embedding subtle ideological messages within humor to indoctrinate new users.

✓ **Exploit sensitive events** – Using tragic or controversial events to push conspiracy theories via memes.

☐ **OSINT Analysis Tools:**

✓ **CrowdTangle & Hoaxy** – Detect coordinated meme-based disinformation campaigns.
✓ **Botometer** – Identifies bot networks pushing memes in a synchronized manner.

📌 **Example**:

✓ The "QAnon" conspiracy movement originated on 8kun, where meme propaganda was used to attract new followers and spread false narratives.

2.3 The Role of Anonymity in Meme Radicalization

Imageboards thrive on anonymity, which encourages:

✓ **Unfiltered speech** – Users feel safe expressing radical ideas without consequences.
✓ **Groupthink & Echo Chambers** – Users reinforce each other's views, pushing extreme narratives further.
✓ **Gamification of Trolling** – Creating meme-based "raids" on social media platforms to manipulate public opinion.

☐ **OSINT Analysis Tools:**

✓ **Graphika & Maltego** – Map meme distribution networks.
✓ **Telegram Monitoring Tools** – Track private meme-sharing groups.

📌 **Example**:

✓ The "Clown World" meme, which mocks liberal ideologies, originated in 4chan's /pol/ board before spreading widely.

3. Case Study: Meme Warfare in the 2020 U.S. Elections

Step 1: Tracking Meme Origins

✓ OSINT analysts found highly politicized memes circulating on 4chan & Telegram before reaching Twitter.

Step 2: Identifying Coordinated Campaigns

✓ Researchers noticed newly created Twitter accounts mass-posting identical political memes.

Step 3: Mapping the Spread

✓ The memes were being amplified by bot accounts and influencers, making them appear organic.

🔎 **Key Takeaway:**

✓ Underground meme communities strategically manipulate elections by injecting polarizing memes into public discourse.

4. OSINT Techniques for Investigating Meme-Based Influence Operations

✓ **Reverse Image Search** – Determines where a meme first appeared.

✓ **Social Media Trend Analysis** – Tracks meme virality across platforms.

✓ **Telegram & Imageboard Monitoring** – Identifies coordinated meme production.

✓ **Metadata & Image Forensics** – Detects altered or deepfake memes.

5. Countering Meme-Driven Disinformation

✓ **Public Education on Meme Influence** – Teaching users how memes can be weaponized.

✓ **Platform Policy Adjustments** – Social media companies must detect & limit coordinated meme campaigns.

✓ **Fact-Checking & OSINT Investigations** – Exposing how underground communities manufacture viral narratives.

6. Conclusion: The Hidden Power of Underground Meme Communities

Imageboards and underground communities are not just internet subcultures—they are digital battlegrounds where memes are created, refined, and deployed for political and ideological warfare. OSINT analysts must closely monitor these spaces, track meme evolution, and expose coordinated influence operations before they reach mainstream platforms.

As AI-generated memes and encrypted communications become more sophisticated, tracking meme-driven manipulation will become even more critical in the fight against disinformation.

8.6 Case Study: A Meme-Driven Disinformation Campaign

Memes have become one of the most powerful tools for disinformation and influence operations, capable of shaping public perception, distorting reality, and even influencing political outcomes. In this case study, we will analyze a real-world meme-driven disinformation campaign, tracking its origins, spread, and impact while demonstrating OSINT techniques used to expose and counter it.

1. Background: The Disinformation Campaign

In 2020, as the U.S. presidential election neared, a viral meme falsely claimed that mail-in voting was a tool for widespread election fraud. The meme, designed to undermine trust in the electoral process, originated on 4chan's /pol/ board, then spread to Twitter, Facebook, and fringe-right Telegram groups.

🏛 **False Claim**: Mail-in ballots will be rigged by the opposition party to steal the election!

🎯 **Objective**: Erode confidence in the election outcome and suppress voter turnout.

2. Phase 1: The Meme's Origin & Creation

🔎 **Where it started:**

✓ **First posted on 4chan's /pol/** – Users brainstormed ways to spread doubt about mail-in ballots.

✓ **Trolls added graphics & statistics** – Users created fake statistics and misleading comparisons.

✓ **Anonymous users encouraged mass sharing** – Calls for "meme warfare" were posted to encourage viral spread.

☐ **OSINT Detection Methods:**

✓ **4chan Archive Tools** – Used to track original threads discussing mail-in ballot fraud.

✓ **Reverse Image Search** – Traced first known uploads of the meme.

📌 **Key Finding**: The meme was deliberately designed to mislead—fabricated statistics were inserted to make the false claim appear credible.

3. Phase 2: Amplification & Bot Networks

Once the meme was created, its spread was not organic—it was coordinated through bot networks and influence campaigns.

🔎 **How it spread:**

✓ **Telegram Channels & Private Groups** – Organized political groups spread the meme among followers.

✓ **Twitter Bot Networks** – Thousands of fake accounts posted identical versions of the meme, making it appear as a trending topic.

✓ **Facebook Pages & Political Influencers** – Certain fringe media outlets and activists shared the meme, adding more fabricated claims.

☐ **OSINT Detection Methods:**

✓ **Botometer** – Detected suspiciously high activity from new Twitter accounts sharing the meme.

✓ **CrowdTangle** – Tracked how fast the meme spread on Facebook and Instagram.

✓ **Hoaxy** – Mapped the network of accounts amplifying the meme.

📌 **Key Finding**: The meme was not spreading naturally—it was part of a planned operation to make election fraud seem real.

4. Phase 3: Mainstream Media Adoption

🔎 **When it hit the mainstream:**

✓ **Politicians & Commentators Cited the Meme** – Some political figures referenced the meme's false statistics in speeches.
✓ **News Outlets Covered the Controversy** – Some news stations reported on the public's growing distrust of mail-in voting, further amplifying the meme's impact.
✓ **Fact-Checkers Attempted Damage Control** – Organizations like Snopes and PolitiFact debunked the meme, but by then, millions had already seen it.

☐ **OSINT Detection Methods:**

✓ **Google Trends** – Showed spikes in searches related to "mail-in ballot fraud" after the meme's viral spread.
✓ **News API Searches** – Found how quickly mainstream media picked up the meme's narrative.

📌 **Key Finding**: By the time fact-checkers debunked the meme, its damage was already done—a significant portion of the public had internalized the false claim.

5. The Impact: How the Meme Shaped Public Perception

✓ **Surveys showed decreased trust in mail-in voting** – Polls found that 40% of certain political groups believed mail-in ballots were fraudulent.
✓ **Real-world consequences** – Some voters refused to use mail-in ballots, fearing their votes would not count.
✓ **Political violence risks** – The false claim contributed to post-election unrest and conspiracy theories.

📌 **Key Takeaway**: A single meme—created anonymously and spread through coordinated disinformation efforts—helped erode trust in an election process at a national scale.

6. OSINT Lessons from the Case Study

✓ 1. **Monitor Imageboards & Underground Platforms** – Many disinformation memes start on fringe sites before going mainstream.

✓ 2. **Use Reverse Image Search Early** – Finding the first appearance of a meme can reveal its original intent.

✓ 3. **Track Bot Activity & Network Coordination** – Many viral memes do not spread organically—they are pushed by influence operations.

✓ 4. **Cross-Check Information in Memes** – Many memes use fake statistics, edited images, or misleading claims.

✓ 5. **Be Aware of Meme-Based Psychological Operations** – Memes are used not just to entertain, but to influence elections, policies, and public sentiment.

7. Conclusion: The Growing Threat of Meme-Driven Disinformation

This case study illustrates the power of memes in shaping public opinion, particularly when combined with coordinated amplification efforts. As artificial intelligence improves meme generation and deepfake capabilities, disinformation campaigns will become even harder to detect.

📌 **Final Thought:**

OSINT analysts, journalists, and fact-checkers must stay ahead of meme-based disinformation operations—because in today's digital warfare, a well-timed meme can be more influential than a news article, a political speech, or even the truth itself.

9. Countering Disinformation with OSINT

In the battle against disinformation, OSINT (Open-Source Intelligence) provides a powerful arsenal for uncovering truth and exposing falsehoods. This chapter focuses on how analysts can leverage publicly available data to detect, debunk, and counter disinformation campaigns. We explore a range of OSINT techniques, including data mining, geolocation analysis, and social media tracking, to piece together the digital breadcrumbs left behind by those spreading misinformation. Additionally, we discuss the importance of collaboration with other fact-checkers and organizations in combating widespread disinformation. By mastering these methods, readers will gain the ability to not only expose false narratives but also effectively counter them, ensuring that truth prevails in the digital landscape.

9.1 Strategies for Identifying & Neutralizing Fake Narratives

In the battle against disinformation, identifying and neutralizing fake narratives is critical for protecting public discourse and ensuring information integrity. Fake narratives— whether they are fabricated news, manipulated facts, or distorted interpretations of real events—can be designed to mislead, divide, or manipulate audiences for political, ideological, or financial gain. This chapter explores OSINT strategies for detecting, analyzing, and countering disinformation narratives, equipping investigators, journalists, and analysts with effective countermeasures.

1. Understanding Fake Narratives

A fake narrative is an orchestrated attempt to present a distorted version of reality to achieve specific objectives. These narratives are often designed to:

✓ **Shape public opinion** – Influence how people think about an issue, event, or person.

✓ **Undermine trust** – Erode confidence in institutions, media, or political opponents.

✓ **Polarize communities** – Amplify divisions between social, political, or ethnic groups.

✓ **Create confusion** – Flood the information space with conflicting claims, making it difficult to discern truth.

📌 **Example**: A coordinated effort to spread misinformation about a pandemic might claim that vaccines contain microchips, causing vaccine hesitancy and public distrust.

2. OSINT Techniques for Identifying Fake Narratives

2.1 Monitoring the Spread of Disinformation

Fake narratives often follow predictable patterns of dissemination. OSINT tools can be used to track their origins and amplification tactics.

☐ **Tools & Techniques:**

✓ **Hoaxy & Botometer** – Detects bot-driven amplification of fake news.

✓ **Google Trends** – Identifies spikes in searches related to disinformation topics.

✓ **CrowdTangle** – Monitors how disinformation spreads on social media.

✓ **4chan & Telegram Monitoring** – Tracks early-stage narrative development in underground forums.

📌 **Example**: During an election, a rumor about widespread voter fraud may start on imageboards before being pushed to Twitter by bot networks.

2.2 Verifying Claims & Cross-Checking Information

Fact-checking is one of the most powerful defenses against fake narratives. Using OSINT methods, analysts can verify or debunk misleading claims.

☐ **Tools & Techniques:**

✓ **Reverse Image Search (Google, Yandex, TinEye)** – Detects misattributed or manipulated images.

✓ **InVID & ExifTools** – Analyzes metadata from videos and photos to detect alterations.

✓ **Wayback Machine** – Checks historical records of webpages to detect edited or removed content.

✓ **NewsGuard & Fact-Checking Sites** – Evaluates source credibility and claim accuracy.

📌 **Example**: A viral meme falsely claiming that a politician said something controversial can be debunked using original speech transcripts and video analysis.

2.3 Identifying Narrative Coordination & Bot Activity

Many disinformation campaigns use coordinated tactics, such as:

✔ **Hashtag manipulation** – Fake trends are created using bot-driven hashtags.

✔ **Engagement farming** – Fake accounts mass-like and share content to boost visibility.

✔ **Troll amplification** – Coordinated groups attack or promote content to manipulate discourse.

☐ **Tools & Techniques:**

✔ **Botometer** – Detects automated bot accounts spreading disinformation.

✔ **Trendsmap** – Tracks global and local social media trends.

✔ **Graphika & Maltego** – Maps relationships between accounts amplifying fake narratives.

📌 **Example**: A fake story about a terrorist attack may gain traction through thousands of automated tweets from newly created accounts.

3. Strategies for Neutralizing Fake Narratives

Once a fake narrative is identified, it must be neutralized before it gains widespread acceptance. This requires a combination of exposure, fact-checking, and strategic counter-messaging.

3.1 Exposing Disinformation Campaigns

✔ **Publish OSINT Findings** – Share evidence of manipulation with journalists, fact-checkers, and researchers.

✔ **Use Visual Proof** – Screenshots, metadata analysis, and network maps help expose the scale of disinformation campaigns.

✔ **Track & Attribute Sources** – Identifying the original sources of a fake narrative weakens its credibility.

📌 **Example**: OSINT investigators revealed that a false story about a U.S. military strike originated from a state-sponsored troll farm.

3.2 Counter-Messaging & Strategic Narratives

✓ **Prebunking vs. Debunking** – Prebunking (proactively educating the public) is often more effective than debunking after the fact.

✓ **Leverage Trusted Messengers** – Experts, journalists, and influencers can dismantle fake narratives more effectively than institutions alone.

✓ **Use Facts + Emotion** – Facts alone aren't always persuasive—combining truth with engaging storytelling improves impact.

📌 **Example**: When a fake claim about a disease outbreak spread, public health experts used myth-busting infographics and emotional testimonials to counteract the fear.

3.3 Encouraging Platform Accountability

✓ **Push for Social Media Moderation** – Platforms must be held accountable for allowing coordinated disinformation campaigns.

✓ **Report Fake Accounts & Networks** – Deplatforming key disinformation actors reduces their reach.

✓ **Advocate for Policy Changes** – Governments should enforce stronger disinformation tracking and response mechanisms.

📌 **Example**: A coalition of OSINT analysts exposed a bot network pushing election disinformation, leading to a mass takedown of fake accounts.

4. Case Study: Countering a Viral Fake Narrative

Scenario: A False Story About a U.S. Coup Attempt

☐ **OSINT Steps Taken:**

✓ **Reverse Image Search** – Revealed that the viral photos of "military takeover" were actually from a past protest.

✓ **Video Metadata Analysis** – Showed that "breaking news footage" was edited from an unrelated documentary.

✓ **Bot Network Detection** – Found that thousands of new Twitter accounts were spreading the story in a coordinated manner.

📌 **Outcome**:

✓ Fact-checking organizations debunked the claim within hours.

✓ Social media platforms flagged and removed manipulated content.

✓ Public officials reassured citizens, reducing panic.

5. Conclusion: The Ongoing Battle Against Fake Narratives

Disinformation campaigns are constantly evolving, and OSINT analysts, journalists, and fact-checkers must stay ahead by using a combination of technological tools, investigative techniques, and strategic counter-messaging.

✓ **Early detection is key** – The faster a fake narrative is identified, the less damage it can do.

✓ **Combining OSINT techniques is essential** – No single tool can stop disinformation; a multi-layered approach works best.

✓ **Public awareness is crucial** – Educating people on how fake narratives spread makes them less susceptible.

📌 **Final Thought:**

In an era where memes, misinformation, and fake narratives can shape global events, OSINT remains one of the most powerful weapons in the fight for truth.

9.2 Collaborating with Fact-Checkers & Investigative Journalists

Disinformation thrives in an environment where falsehoods spread faster than the truth, making collaboration between OSINT analysts, fact-checkers, and investigative journalists essential in countering fake narratives. By pooling resources, expertise, and verification methods, these groups can identify, expose, and neutralize disinformation before it causes significant harm. This chapter explores how OSINT professionals can work effectively with journalists and fact-checkers, the tools and techniques used in investigations, and strategies for disseminating verified information to the public.

1. Why Collaboration Is Essential in Fighting Disinformation

Disinformation campaigns are sophisticated, well-funded, and constantly evolving. No single group can combat them alone. By working together, OSINT analysts, fact-checkers, and investigative journalists can:

✓ **Verify information faster** – Fact-checkers specialize in debunking claims, while OSINT analysts provide technical evidence.

✓ **Trace the origins of fake narratives** – Investigative journalists uncover the broader context behind disinformation campaigns.

✓ **Expose disinformation networks** – OSINT techniques can map out connections between bad actors, bot networks, and propaganda sources.

✓ **Inform the public with credible reporting** – Journalists play a crucial role in ensuring accurate information reaches large audiences.

📌 **Example**: A viral claim about a fabricated protest in a foreign country was quickly debunked when OSINT analysts reverse-searched images and journalists contacted local sources for confirmation.

2. The Role of Each Group in Disinformation Investigations

2.1 OSINT Analysts

✓ **Collect and analyze open-source data** – Track fake news, doctored media, and suspicious activity.

✓ **Monitor bot networks & social media trends** – Detect coordinated influence operations.

✓ **Provide metadata analysis** – Verify authenticity of videos, images, and documents.

2.2 Fact-Checkers

✓ **Verify claims against credible sources** – Compare statements with historical records, experts, and data.

✓ **Use forensic tools to analyze media** – Detect deepfakes, manipulated images, and misleading edits.

✓ **Work with social media platforms** – Flag and report misleading or harmful content.

2.3 Investigative Journalists

✓ **Uncover the motives behind disinformation** – Investigate who benefits from fake narratives.

✓ **Conduct interviews & on-the-ground verification** – Speak with witnesses, experts, and insiders.

✓ **Publish findings to reach the public** – Ensure verified information is widely disseminated.

📌 **Example**: A network of fake political news websites was uncovered when OSINT analysts identified IP overlaps, fact-checkers debunked false articles, and journalists traced ownership records to a foreign influence operation.

3. OSINT Techniques for Collaboration in Fact-Checking

3.1 Identifying Fake News & Manipulated Media

☐ **Tools & Techniques:**

✓ **Google Reverse Image Search / TinEye** – Finds the original source of images.

✓ **InVID & ExifTool** – Extracts metadata from videos and photos to detect tampering.

✓ **Wayback Machine** – Checks if news articles or sources have been altered or deleted.

📌 **Example**: A viral photo claiming to show war crimes was debunked when metadata analysis revealed the image was from 2012, not 2023.

3.2 Mapping Disinformation Networks

☐ **Tools & Techniques:**

✔ **Maltego & Gephi** – Maps connections between fake accounts, websites, and influencers.

✔ **Hoaxy** – Visualizes how disinformation spreads on social media.

✔ **Botometer** – Detects automated bot accounts amplifying false narratives.

📌 **Example**: A fake news campaign about election fraud was traced to a coordinated bot network posting identical messages across platforms.

3.3 Verifying Online Claims with Cross-Referencing

☐ **Tools & Techniques:**

✔ **Google Fact Check Explorer** – Searches previous fact-checks on similar claims.

✔ **OSINT Telegram & Discord Communities** – Shares real-time disinformation tracking among analysts and reporters.

✔ **Cross-checking with primary sources** – Confirms events with official reports, eyewitness accounts, and experts.

📌 **Example**: A viral claim about a politician's resignation was debunked when journalists confirmed the official government website made no such announcement.

4. How to Build Effective Collaboration Between OSINT, Fact-Checkers & Journalists

4.1 Establish Secure Communication Channels

Disinformation actors often target investigators, journalists, and analysts. To collaborate effectively:

✔ Use encrypted messaging apps (e.g., Signal, ProtonMail) for sensitive discussions.

✔ Avoid sharing investigations publicly too early—disinformation networks adapt quickly.

✔ Verify new contacts before sharing information.

📌 **Example**: A fact-checking group collaborated with OSINT researchers via a private, secure Slack workspace to investigate deepfake videos.

4.2 Share Data & Findings in Real Time

Speed is crucial in disinformation investigations. Best practices include:

✔ Creating shared dashboards (e.g., Google Docs, Airtable, MISP Threat Intelligence Sharing).

✔ Using collaboration platforms like Bellingcat's Discord or First Draft's network.

✔ Tagging experts on Twitter to amplify findings among fact-checkers and journalists.

📌 **Example**: A disinformation campaign falsely claimed a political candidate had a secret bank account abroad—OSINT researchers quickly debunked it by tracing financial records and journalists published the findings.

4.3 Train & Educate Each Other

✔ OSINT analysts can teach journalists about metadata analysis, bot detection, and social media forensics.

✔ Journalists can train OSINT analysts in narrative-building, ethical reporting, and verifying human sources.

✔ Fact-checkers can educate both groups on fact-checking methodologies and common misinformation tactics.

📌 **Example**: A media organization trained OSINT investigators on ethical reporting guidelines, while OSINT experts taught journalists how to use reverse image search for verification.

5. Case Study: Collaborative Investigation of a Viral Fake News Story

Scenario:

A breaking news story claimed that a foreign government had launched a cyberattack against a major bank, causing public panic and financial instability.

Collaboration Process:

⬜⬜ OSINT Analysts:

✓ Used Shodan and VirusTotal to check for cyberattack indicators.

✓ Verified IP sources and metadata linked to the claim.

🔎 Fact-Checkers:

✓ Searched credible cybersecurity reports for evidence of an attack.

✓ Contacted government agencies and independent experts.

🖥 Investigative Journalists:

✓ Interviewed bank representatives and cybersecurity officials.

✓ Published findings in mainstream media to counter disinformation.

📌 **Outcome**: The claim was completely fabricated, originating from a foreign propaganda campaign to destabilize financial markets. The coordinated fact-checking and OSINT investigation stopped the narrative before it spread further.

6. Conclusion: Strengthening Collaboration for Future Investigations

Fighting disinformation requires a united front. By integrating OSINT techniques with fact-checking expertise and investigative journalism, teams can quickly debunk false claims, expose propaganda campaigns, and protect public discourse.

✓ **Information must be verified rapidly**—Disinformation spreads fast, so investigations must be faster.

✓ **Collaboration is key**—No single group can stop fake narratives alone.

✓ **Technology & human intelligence work best together**—Combining OSINT tools with journalistic expertise leads to the best results.

📌 **Final Thought**: In an era where disinformation is weaponized, OSINT, fact-checkers, and journalists must work together to ensure the truth is always louder than the lies.

9.3 Educating the Public on Media Literacy & OSINT Techniques

In the fight against disinformation, public awareness is one of the strongest defenses. While OSINT analysts, fact-checkers, and journalists work tirelessly to uncover the truth, their efforts are limited if the public cannot distinguish between credible information and fake narratives. Teaching media literacy and OSINT techniques empowers individuals to critically evaluate news, identify manipulated content, and avoid being misled by disinformation campaigns. This chapter explores the importance of media literacy, essential OSINT techniques for the public, and practical strategies for spreading awareness.

1. Why Media Literacy Is Critical in the Digital Age

Misinformation and disinformation spread because people often:

✔ Believe and share information without verification.

✔ Trust sources based on emotions rather than facts.

✔ Fall for clickbait headlines and sensationalized stories.

✔ Do not know how to investigate claims effectively.

A media-literate society is less susceptible to manipulation. When individuals can analyze news critically, question sources, and verify information, they become active participants in the information ecosystem rather than passive consumers.

📌 **Example**: A viral tweet claimed that a celebrity had died, leading to widespread panic. Those with basic OSINT skills quickly debunked it by checking official news sources and verifying social media posts from trusted individuals.

2. Key Media Literacy Concepts

2.1 Understanding Different Types of False Information

To educate the public, it's essential to distinguish between:

✔ **Disinformation** – False information deliberately spread to deceive (e.g., propaganda, fake news).

✓ **Misinformation** – False information shared without malicious intent (e.g., rumors, misinterpretations).

✓ **Malinformation** – True information twisted or selectively presented to mislead.

📌 **Example**: A doctored video of a political leader appearing to say something controversial could be disinformation. If someone shares it without knowing it's fake, it becomes misinformation.

2.2 Recognizing Manipulative Tactics

People should be aware of common disinformation tactics, including:

✓ **Emotional manipulation** – Stories designed to provoke anger, fear, or outrage.

✓ **Cherry-picking data** – Selecting only certain facts to support a misleading narrative.

✓ **Fake experts** – Presenting unqualified individuals as authorities on complex issues.

✓ **False equivalence** – Giving equal weight to credible sources and conspiracy theories.

📌 **Example**: A misleading article about climate change quotes a single scientist while ignoring the scientific consensus.

3. Teaching OSINT Techniques for Public Use

While full-scale OSINT investigations require expertise, basic verification techniques can help anyone fact-check information and avoid falling for fake news.

3.1 Reverse Image & Video Search

☐ **Tools:**

✓ **Google Reverse Image Search / TinEye** – Find the original source of an image.

✓ **InVID & ExifTool** – Extract metadata from videos and photos.

📌 **Example**: A viral photo claiming to show war damage was debunked when a user found the original image from a 2015 movie set.

3.2 Checking Website Credibility

Techniques:

✓ **Look at the URL and site design**—fake news sites often have misspellings or unusual domain names.

✓ **Check the About Us page**—legitimate news sources transparently disclose their editorial team.

✓ Use WHOIS lookup to find out who owns the website.

📌 **Example**: A website spreading false election results was exposed when an OSINT check showed it was registered only a month before the election.

3.3 Analyzing Social Media Accounts

Red Flags of Fake Accounts:

✓ Low follower count but high activity (suggests automation).

✓ Generic profile pictures (common in bot networks).

✓ Copy-pasting the same messages across multiple platforms.

📌 **Example**: A Twitter account spreading fake protest videos was revealed as a bot when users noticed it posted identical tweets every hour.

3.4 Cross-Referencing Information

How to Verify Claims:

✓ Compare the news across multiple reputable sources.

✓ Look for official confirmations from government agencies or experts.

✓ Use fact-checking websites like Snopes, PolitiFact, or Reuters Fact Check.

📌 **Example**: A viral hoax about a dangerous virus outbreak was debunked when users cross-checked with WHO and the CDC.

4. How to Promote Media Literacy & OSINT Awareness

4.1 Integrating OSINT Education in Schools

✓ Teach fact-checking skills as part of media studies and civics education.

✓ Introduce OSINT tools in research projects.

✓ Encourage students to investigate viral claims as exercises.

📌 **Example**: A university course on digital literacy teaches students how to verify online sources using OSINT tools.

4.2 Public Workshops & Community Training

✓ Host fact-checking workshops in libraries and community centers.

✓ Create online tutorials and YouTube videos explaining OSINT techniques.

✓ Partner with journalists and fact-checkers for public awareness campaigns.

📌 **Example**: A nonprofit organization runs free workshops teaching citizens how to analyze fake news and use reverse image search.

4.3 Social Media Campaigns Against Disinformation

✓ Share quick OSINT verification tips in engaging formats (memes, infographics, short videos).

✓ Collaborate with influencers and educators to reach younger audiences.

✓ Encourage people to question before sharing using slogans like "Stop, Verify, Share".

📌 **Example**: A viral TikTok campaign teaches users how to detect deepfake videos, making OSINT education accessible to millions.

4.4 Encouraging Critical Thinking Over Blind Trust

✓ Promote the habit of questioning sensational claims.

✓ Encourage the mindset of "trust, but verify".

✔ Teach that just because a story feels true doesn't mean it is.

✦ **Example**: A public awareness campaign explains how confirmation bias leads people to believe false news that aligns with their views.

5. Conclusion: Empowering Society Through OSINT & Media Literacy

Disinformation is a persistent and evolving threat, but an informed and vigilant public can resist manipulation. By equipping individuals with media literacy skills and basic OSINT techniques, we can create a society that:

✔ Thinks critically about the information they consume.

✔ Verifies news before sharing it.

✔ Recognizes manipulation tactics and refuses to be deceived.

✔ Becomes active participants in the fight against disinformation.

✦ **Final Thought**: Education is the most powerful weapon against disinformation. If every person learns how to fact-check, verify sources, and think critically, the spread of fake news will dramatically slow, weakening the influence of those who seek to deceive.

9.4 Tools & Techniques for Proactive Disinformation Monitoring

Disinformation campaigns are becoming more sophisticated, making it crucial for OSINT analysts, journalists, and cybersecurity professionals to monitor and counter false narratives before they spread widely. Proactive monitoring involves using advanced tools, AI-driven analysis, and network mapping techniques to detect disinformation in real-time. This chapter will explore the best tools and methodologies for tracking disinformation, identifying coordinated networks, and responding effectively.

1. Why Proactive Disinformation Monitoring Matters

While fact-checking is essential, reacting to disinformation after it has spread is often too late. By the time a false narrative is debunked, it may have already influenced public opinion, gone viral, or shaped political decisions. Proactive monitoring helps to:

✓ Identify emerging disinformation trends before they gain traction.

✓ Detect bot networks and coordinated campaigns in their early stages.

✓ Analyze changes in disinformation tactics used by malicious actors.

✓ Provide intelligence to policymakers, media, and fact-checkers to counter false narratives effectively.

📌 **Example**: During an election, OSINT analysts monitoring Twitter identified suspicious bot activity promoting a fake voter fraud narrative. By alerting fact-checkers early, they prevented widespread misinformation.

2. Essential Tools for Disinformation Monitoring

A range of OSINT tools can be used to track misleading narratives, manipulated media, and coordinated campaigns across platforms.

2.1 Social Media Monitoring Platforms

☐ Best tools for tracking real-time disinformation on social media:

✓ **Hoaxy** – Visualizes how misinformation spreads on Twitter.

✓ **CrowdTangle** – Tracks viral posts across Facebook, Instagram, and Reddit.

✓ **Bot Sentinel** – Detects bot activity and suspicious accounts.

✓ **Trendsmap** – Maps trending hashtags and keywords geographically.

✓ **Twitonomy** – Analyzes Twitter accounts for suspicious behavior.

📌 **Example**: OSINT researchers used Hoaxy to map the spread of a fake news article claiming a celebrity had died. The tool showed that most shares came from bot-like accounts, proving it was part of a disinformation campaign.

2.2 Image & Video Verification Tools

Disinformation often relies on manipulated images and deepfake videos. Detecting these requires specialized tools:

✔ **Google Reverse Image Search / TinEye** – Finds original sources of images.

✔ **InVID & ExifTool** – Extracts metadata from videos and photos.

✔ **Forensically** – Analyzes images for signs of manipulation (cloning, tampering).

✔ **Deepware Scanner** – Detects deepfake videos.

📌 **Example**: A viral video supposedly showing war crimes was debunked using InVID, which revealed the footage was actually from a 2015 action movie.

2.3 Bot & Network Analysis Tools

Disinformation campaigns often involve bot armies, troll farms, and coordinated networks pushing false narratives. Key tools for identifying these include:

✔ **Botometer** – Analyzes Twitter accounts for bot-like behavior.

✔ **Graphika** – Maps disinformation networks and influence campaigns.

✔ **Gephi** – A powerful tool for visualizing social media network connections.

✔ **OSoMe (Observatory on Social Media)** – Tracks coordinated activity on Twitter.

📌 **Example**: Researchers used Graphika to uncover a state-backed propaganda network amplifying false COVID-19 vaccine claims across Facebook and Twitter.

2.4 Keyword & Hashtag Monitoring

Tracking disinformation narratives requires monitoring specific keywords and hashtags that signal the emergence of new campaigns.

✔ **Google Alerts** – Sends notifications when specific terms appear online.

✔ **TweetDeck** – Monitors Twitter hashtags and mentions in real-time.

✔ **Mention** – Tracks brand mentions, keywords, and trends across platforms.

✔ **Talkwalker** – Monitors online discussions and identifies fake engagement.

📌 **Example**: During a referendum, analysts used TweetDeck to monitor hashtags related to election fraud. They noticed a sudden spike in bot-generated tweets, indicating a coordinated campaign.

3. Advanced Techniques for Detecting Disinformation

While tools help automate the process, effective disinformation monitoring requires human intelligence and investigative techniques.

3.1 Identifying Coordinated Behavior

Disinformation campaigns often involve multiple accounts working together to amplify false narratives. Analysts should look for:

✓ Accounts posting identical content at the same time.

✓ Unusual spikes in engagement from low-follower accounts.

✓ Hashtags that suddenly trend without organic discussion.

📌 **Example**: A network of sockpuppet accounts was exposed when investigators noticed dozens of Twitter profiles tweeting identical conspiracy theories within seconds of each other.

3.2 Analyzing Fake News Websites

Some disinformation campaigns rely on fabricated news sites designed to look legitimate. Techniques for spotting them include:

✓ Checking WHOIS records to see when and who registered the domain.

✓ Looking at the site's history using the Wayback Machine.

✓ Analyzing writing style and grammar for inconsistencies.

📌 **Example**: A fake news website spreading anti-vaccine propaganda was discovered when researchers found it had been registered just a month before a major election.

3.3 Geolocation & Metadata Analysis

Many disinformation campaigns use old or misattributed images and videos. To verify authenticity:

✓ Use Google Earth or Sentinel Hub to geolocate images.

✓ Check metadata with ExifTool to see if an image has been altered.

✓ Compare timestamps and weather conditions in the image with historical data.

📌 **Example**: A viral photo claiming to show protests in a foreign country was debunked when analysts compared street signs and landmarks to Google Maps, revealing it was from a different location.

4. Strategies for Effective Disinformation Response

Once disinformation is detected, action must be taken to prevent its spread and minimize its impact.

4.1 Engaging Fact-Checkers & Journalists

✓ Alert fact-checking organizations (e.g., Snopes, PolitiFact, BBC Reality Check).

✓ Provide evidence-backed reports to journalists covering disinformation.

✓ Work with media outlets to publish corrections quickly.

📌 **Example**: When a false story about a terrorist attack began trending, fact-checkers debunked it within hours by tracing the original image to a 2013 gas explosion.

4.2 Amplifying Correct Information

✓ Use the same hashtags and platforms where the disinformation is spreading.

✓ Encourage influencers, journalists, and trusted figures to share fact-checked content.

✓ Educate the public on OSINT techniques to verify claims themselves.

📌 **Example**: During a pandemic, OSINT analysts debunked a fake vaccine side effect claim by amplifying expert research and verified reports.

4.3 Reporting & Removing Harmful Content

✓ Report coordinated disinformation to platforms like Twitter, Facebook, and YouTube.

✓ Submit evidence of bot networks to cybersecurity agencies.

✔ Use legal mechanisms to take down fake news websites in extreme cases.

📌 **Example**: A network of coordinated bot accounts spreading election misinformation was reported to Twitter, leading to mass suspensions.

5. Conclusion: The Future of Proactive Disinformation Monitoring

Disinformation will continue to evolve, using more sophisticated AI-generated content, deepfakes, and bot-driven amplification. Proactive monitoring is no longer optional—it is a necessity. By combining:

✔ Advanced OSINT tools for detection,

✔ Human-led investigative techniques, and

✔ Strategic responses to limit the spread,

We can stay ahead of disinformation actors and safeguard the integrity of public discourse.

📌 **Final Thought**: The battle against disinformation is ongoing, but the more we monitor, expose, and counter false narratives in real-time, the harder it becomes for malicious actors to manipulate the public.

9.5 Government & Tech Company Responses to Disinformation

The fight against disinformation is a global challenge, with both governments and technology companies playing crucial roles in countering false narratives. While governments focus on policy, regulations, and law enforcement, tech companies are responsible for content moderation, algorithm adjustments, and platform security. However, their responses often face criticism due to concerns over censorship, transparency, and effectiveness. This chapter examines the approaches, successes, and shortcomings of government and tech industry efforts to combat disinformation.

1. Government Responses to Disinformation

Governments worldwide have taken various steps to address disinformation, ranging from legislation and regulatory frameworks to public awareness campaigns and intelligence operations.

1.1 Legislation & Regulatory Measures

Many countries have introduced laws to curb the spread of disinformation, particularly during elections and crises.

✓ **European Union (EU)** – Digital Services Act (DSA) & Code of Practice on Disinformation

- Requires tech companies to remove harmful content and increase transparency in content moderation.
- Imposes fines for failing to address misinformation.

✓ **United States** – Countering Foreign Influence & Disinformation

- Cybersecurity and Infrastructure Security Agency (CISA) monitors disinformation threats.
- Foreign Malign Influence Center (FMIC) tracks foreign propaganda campaigns.
- Debate over content moderation vs. free speech concerns remains unresolved.

✓ **United Kingdom** – Online Safety Bill

- Holds social media platforms accountable for harmful content.
- Encourages transparency in AI-generated disinformation and deepfake content.

📌 **Example**: The EU's Code of Practice on Disinformation led platforms like Google and Facebook to implement fact-checking measures, reducing the spread of false election-related content.

1.2 Intelligence & Cybersecurity Operations

Governments also use intelligence agencies and cybersecurity teams to track and counter disinformation threats.

✓ **Russia's Disinformation Networks Targeting Elections**

- U.S. intelligence agencies uncovered Russian-backed campaigns spreading fake news via social media bots.
- The FBI and NSA worked with tech companies to take down coordinated inauthentic networks.

✔ China's Influence Operations on Social Media

- The U.S. and EU exposed China's coordinated efforts to shape narratives about COVID-19, Taiwan, and Western politics.
- OSINT and cyber-intelligence teams identified fake accounts amplifying government-backed messaging.

📌 **Example**: In 2020, the U.S. Cyber Command launched counter-operations against foreign disinformation networks, disabling their infrastructure before election day.

1.3 Public Awareness & Media Literacy Campaigns

Governments also invest in educating the public to increase media literacy and critical thinking.

✔ Finland's National Media Literacy Program

- Integrates media literacy education into schools, training students to identify fake news.
- Teaches fact-checking skills and source verification to combat misinformation.

✔ Taiwan's Rapid Response to Disinformation

- Established a fact-checking task force to debunk false narratives within hours.
- Uses humor and viral memes to counter disinformation before it spreads.

📌 **Example**: Taiwan's fact-checking teams worked with Facebook and local influencers to quickly debunk COVID-19 vaccine misinformation, preventing public panic.

2. Tech Company Responses to Disinformation

Social media and tech companies are often at the center of disinformation battles, as their platforms serve as primary distribution channels for fake news. Their responses include content moderation, algorithmic adjustments, and partnerships with fact-checkers.

2.1 Content Moderation & Policy Enforcement

- Tech giants have introduced strict content moderation policies to remove or flag false information.

✓ Facebook (Meta) – Fact-Checking & AI Detection

- Third-party fact-checking partnerships (e.g., PolitiFact, Snopes).
- AI systems detect and label misleading content, especially related to elections and health crises.

✓ Twitter/X – Warning Labels & Reduced Visibility

- Introduced "misleading information" labels for false claims.
- Uses de-amplification strategies to prevent fake news from trending.

✓ YouTube – Removal of Harmful Misinformation

- Takes down videos spreading medical misinformation, election lies, and conspiracy theories.
- Enhances recommendation algorithms to prioritize verified sources.

📌 **Example**: Facebook's fact-checking program reduced engagement with fake news by 80%, but critics argue that false content still spreads before moderation catches up.

2.2 Algorithmic Adjustments to Reduce Fake News

Tech companies have adjusted their algorithms to limit disinformation's reach.

✓ Google Search & YouTube Ranking Adjustments

- Prioritizes trusted sources (BBC, Reuters, FactCheck.org).
- Demotes websites known for clickbait and misinformation.

✔ **Facebook's Engagement-Based Ranking Changes**

- Reduced engagement-based virality of news articles to prevent clickbait amplification.

✔ **Twitter's Anti-Bot Measures**

- Uses AI to detect and suspend automated bot accounts involved in disinformation campaigns.

📌 **Example**: YouTube's algorithm update reduced the recommendation of conspiracy theory videos by 70% but faced backlash for censoring controversial political content.

2.3 Partnerships with Fact-Checkers & NGOs

Tech companies collaborate with independent organizations to improve fact-checking.

✔ **Google's Fact-Check Explorer** – Helps users verify claims using reputable fact-checking sources.
✔ **Facebook's Third-Party Fact-Checking Program** – Works with AFP, Reuters, and Snopes to flag false stories.
✔ **Twitter's Community Notes (formerly Birdwatch)** – Allows users to provide context to misleading tweets.

📌 **Example**: During the COVID-19 pandemic, Google promoted WHO and CDC resources, while Facebook labeled misleading health claims with fact-checking links.

3. Challenges & Criticism of Government & Tech Responses

Despite these efforts, government and tech responses to disinformation face significant challenges.

✔ **Free Speech vs. Censorship**

- Critics argue that government regulations and tech moderation limit free expression.

- Some laws (e.g., Russia's "Fake News Law") are used to suppress dissent instead of stopping misinformation.

✔ Slow Response Time

- Fact-checking and moderation often happen too late, after a false narrative has already spread widely.
- AI detection is not always accurate, leading to false positives and missed threats.

✔ Disinformation Adapts Quickly

- Malicious actors change tactics, using deepfakes, encrypted messaging apps, and decentralized platforms to evade detection.

✔ Lack of Platform Accountability

- Tech companies profit from engagement, meaning controversial content—including misinformation—remains lucrative.
- Transparency reports often lack full details on enforcement actions.

📌 **Example**: Twitter's content moderation weakened after policy changes in 2023, leading to an increase in misinformation and coordinated disinformation campaigns.

4. The Future of Disinformation Countermeasures

Disinformation will continue evolving, and governments and tech companies must adapt. Future countermeasures may include:

✔ Stronger AI-driven disinformation detection (real-time deepfake analysis).

✔ Increased transparency from social media platforms (better data-sharing with researchers).

✔ Improved international cooperation to combat state-sponsored propaganda.

✔ More advanced OSINT investigations to track emerging disinformation threats.

★ **Final Thought**: While progress has been made, no single approach will eliminate disinformation. The fight requires a combination of technology, policy, and public awareness to create a more informed digital society.

9.6 Case Study: How OSINT Helped a Community Combat Fake News

Disinformation and fake news don't just affect global politics—they impact local communities, businesses, and even personal relationships. This case study explores how a small town leveraged OSINT (Open-Source Intelligence) techniques to combat a viral fake news story that threatened its local economy and public trust. By using fact-checking methods, digital forensics, and community collaboration, the town was able to debunk false claims, hold bad actors accountable, and restore confidence in local institutions.

1. The Fake News Crisis: A Local Business Under Attack

In early 2023, the small town of Brookhaven, known for its tourism and small businesses, found itself at the center of a rapidly spreading fake news scandal. A viral social media post claimed that a popular local bakery, Maple & Crust, was using expired ingredients and had been secretly shut down by health inspectors. The post included:

✓ A photo of a "health notice" taped to the bakery's door.

✓ A "customer testimonial" detailing alleged food poisoning.

✓ Claims that the owners had bribed officials to reopen without a proper inspection.

Within 24 hours, the post had been shared over 50,000 times, leading to:

● Mass cancellations of orders at the bakery.
● Protests and negative online reviews, harming its reputation.
● Local news stations reporting the claims without verifying them.

The business owners denied all allegations, but by then, the damage was done. The community was divided, with some defending the bakery while others demanded its closure.

2. Mobilizing the OSINT Community

Realizing the need for evidence-based verification, a local group of tech-savvy volunteers and investigative journalists formed a team to analyze the claims using OSINT techniques. Their goal was simple: determine if the accusations were real or fabricated.

2.1 Fact-Checking the "Health Notice" Photo

The first step was analyzing the photo of the alleged health violation notice posted on the bakery's door. Using reverse image search and metadata analysis, the team found:

✓ The same photo had appeared months earlier in an unrelated news article about a different restaurant's closure in another state.

✓ Metadata inspection showed the image was edited and cropped, suggesting manipulation.

✓ Local health department records showed no recent violations for the bakery.

🔎 **Conclusion**: The image was fake and repurposed to support the false claim.

2.2 Investigating the "Customer Testimonial"

A Facebook user named "Emily J. Thompson" had posted a detailed story about suffering from food poisoning after eating at Maple & Crust. The OSINT team conducted a deep dive into her profile and found:

✓ Newly created account (less than a week old).

✓ No previous activity before the viral post.

✓ Profile picture was a stock photo (found via reverse image search).

✓ No verifiable connections to the local community.

🔎 **Conclusion**: The account was a sock puppet—a fake identity created to spread misinformation.

2.3 Tracking the Source of the Fake News

To uncover who started the rumor, the OSINT team used:

✓ Keyword analysis to trace the earliest mentions of the story.

✓ Social media analytics tools to track where and how the post spread.

✓ IP tracing and network analysis to look for coordinated activity.

Findings:

● The first tweet spreading the bakery rumor came from an account linked to a competing bakery in a nearby town.
● Multiple bot accounts amplified the story, retweeting and reposting it within minutes of its first appearance.
● The bakery owner's business competitor had a history of using fake reviews and negative press tactics.

🔎 **Conclusion**: This was a targeted smear campaign designed to damage Maple & Crust's reputation for competitive advantage.

3. Community Action & Damage Control

Once the OSINT team gathered enough evidence, they launched a community fact-checking campaign to counteract the fake news.

3.1 Presenting Evidence to Local Media & Authorities

✓ The findings were shared with local journalists, who issued a corrective report exposing the fake claims.

✓ The local health department publicly confirmed the bakery had no violations.

✓ Law enforcement opened an investigation into the competitor's involvement in the smear campaign.

📌 **Impact**: Local news channels retracted their initial reports and issued corrections, helping undo some of the damage.

3.2 Coordinated Online Counter-Disinformation Effort

The OSINT team worked with social media platforms to report fake accounts and misleading content.

✓ Twitter (X) and Facebook removed the sock puppet accounts after the report was filed.

✓ Google's fact-checking labels were applied to the false claims, reducing their spread.

✓ Community members flooded review sites with legitimate positive testimonials, restoring the bakery's online reputation.

📌 **Impact**: The bakery regained trust, and orders returned to normal within weeks.

3.3 Lessons for the Community: How to Spot Fake News

To prevent future incidents, the OSINT team launched a media literacy campaign, teaching residents how to:

✓ Verify sources before sharing content.

✓ Use reverse image search to check photo authenticity.

✓ Identify sock puppet accounts and coordinated disinformation efforts.

✓ Report false claims on social media platforms.

📌 **Impact**: Schools and community groups integrated OSINT techniques into digital literacy workshops.

4. The Aftermath & Lasting Impact

By leveraging OSINT and community collaboration, Brookhaven was able to neutralize a disinformation attack before it caused irreversible damage. The case also highlighted:

✓ The power of fake news to disrupt local economies and businesses.

✓ The importance of quick, evidence-based debunking before false claims spread too far.

✓ The need for ongoing digital literacy education to build community resilience against disinformation.

📌 **Final Thought**: This case proves that OSINT is not just for intelligence agencies—it can empower everyday citizens to defend truth and accountability in their communities.

10. Case Study: Disinformation in Elections

Elections have long been a prime target for disinformation campaigns, with malicious actors attempting to sway voter opinions, undermine trust in democratic processes, and manipulate electoral outcomes. In this case study, we dissect real-world examples of disinformation in recent elections, analyzing the tactics used to spread false information and the platforms exploited to amplify these messages. Through an OSINT lens, we'll trace the digital trail of these campaigns, uncovering the role of fake news, deepfakes, social media manipulation, and foreign interference. By studying these high-profile examples, readers will gain a deeper understanding of how disinformation can shape political landscapes and the critical role of OSINT in defending electoral integrity.

10.1 Historical Examples of Election Disinformation

Election disinformation is not a new phenomenon—it has been used for centuries to manipulate public opinion, suppress voter turnout, and influence electoral outcomes. While the tactics have evolved with technology, the core goal remains the same: to deceive, mislead, and manipulate the electorate for political gain. This section explores historical cases of election disinformation, highlighting key strategies used and their impact on democracy.

1. Early Election Disinformation: The 19th & 20th Centuries

Before the digital age, election disinformation spread through newspapers, pamphlets, and word of mouth. Some of the earliest recorded examples include forged documents, character assassinations, and outright lies designed to sway voters.

1.1 The 1828 U.S. Presidential Election – "Coffin Handbill" Smear Campaign

📌 **Target**: Andrew Jackson
📌 **Tactic**: Fake propaganda pamphlets
📌 **Impact**: One of the dirtiest elections in U.S. history

During the 1828 U.S. presidential race between Andrew Jackson and John Quincy Adams, Adams' supporters distributed sensational pamphlets called "Coffin Handbills". These flyers falsely accused Jackson of executing six soldiers without trial and suggested he was a bloodthirsty tyrant.

✔ **Disinformation Strategy:**

- Used fake witness accounts to paint Jackson as a murderer.
- Printed dramatic imagery of coffins to stir emotional outrage.
- Spread rapidly through handbills and newspapers across the country.

📌 **Outcome**: Despite the smear campaign, Jackson won the presidency, but the election set a precedent for negative campaigning based on disinformation.

1.2 The 1940 U.S. Election – Fake Nazi Propaganda Hoax

📌 **Target**: Franklin D. Roosevelt
📌 **Tactic**: Forged documents to link opponent to Nazi Germany
📌 **Impact**: Increased distrust in media and political figures

During Franklin D. Roosevelt's campaign for a third term, forged letters and documents were circulated, falsely claiming that his opponent, Wendell Willkie, was secretly supported by Nazi Germany.

✔ **Disinformation Strategy:**

- Fake letters were "leaked" to newspapers, giving them an air of legitimacy.
- Opponents amplified the story through radio broadcasts and editorials.
- Fear of foreign influence in U.S. elections made the public more susceptible.

📌 **Outcome**: The disinformation failed to stop Roosevelt's re-election, but it fueled public paranoia about foreign interference—a theme that persists in modern elections.

2. Cold War Election Disinformation (1950s–1980s)

During the Cold War, both the United States and the Soviet Union engaged in election interference and propaganda to shape global political landscapes.

2.1 Soviet "Active Measures" – Disinformation in Foreign Elections

📌 **Targets**: Multiple countries, including the U.S., France, and Germany
📌 **Tactic**: Fake news, forged documents, and planted media stories

📌 **Impact**: Widespread political destabilization

The KGB (Soviet intelligence agency) used "Active Measures" to manipulate elections worldwide by:

✔ Planting fake stories in foreign newspapers (which were later cited as "evidence" by other media).

✔ Forging documents to discredit political candidates.

✔ Promoting conspiracy theories to undermine trust in democratic institutions.

📌 **Example**: In 1983, the Soviet Union spread false claims that the U.S. government created the AIDS virus to target minorities—an effort to damage America's global reputation and create domestic unrest.

2.2 1972 Chilean Election – U.S. Disinformation Against Salvador Allende

📌 **Target**: Salvador Allende (socialist candidate)
📌 **Tactic**: Fake news, bribery, and media manipulation
📌 **Impact**: Election interference contributed to a military coup

The CIA conducted a covert disinformation campaign to prevent the election of socialist candidate Salvador Allende in Chile. Their efforts included:

✔ Funding false media reports that portrayed Allende as a Soviet puppet.

✔ Spreading fear-mongering propaganda about communism.

✔ Encouraging business strikes and economic instability to weaken public confidence.

📌 **Outcome**: Allende won the election but was overthrown in a U.S.-backed coup in 1973. This case exemplifies how disinformation can be part of larger geopolitical power struggles.

3. Digital Age Disinformation (2000s–Present)

With the rise of social media, artificial intelligence, and bots, election disinformation has become faster, more sophisticated, and harder to detect.

3.1 2016 U.S. Presidential Election – Russian Disinformation Operations

✦ **Target**: U.S. electorate (favoring Trump over Clinton)

✦ **Tactic**: Social media manipulation, fake news websites, and bot networks

✦ **Impact**: Increased polarization and loss of trust in democratic institutions

The Russian Internet Research Agency (IRA) orchestrated an elaborate campaign to influence the 2016 U.S. election. Their tactics included:

✓ Creating fake social media accounts that posed as real Americans.

✓ Spreading conspiracy theories and divisive content on Facebook, Twitter, and Instagram.

✓ Organizing real-life protests and counter-protests to escalate tensions.

✦ **Outcome**: While it's unclear whether Russian disinformation changed the election outcome, it successfully deepened social divisions and mistrust in the media.

3.2 2018 Brazilian Election – WhatsApp Disinformation Network

✦ **Target**: Brazilian voters (favoring Jair Bolsonaro)

✦ **Tactic**: Mass messaging, doctored images, and viral hoaxes

✦ **Impact**: Misinformation influenced millions of voters

During Brazil's 2018 presidential election, supporters of far-right candidate Jair Bolsonaro used WhatsApp disinformation networks to spread fake news at an unprecedented scale.

✓ Manipulated images showing his opponent involved in corruption.

✓ Hoax stories about voter fraud to undermine trust in the election process.

✓ Coordinated bot networks spreading divisive memes and messages.

✦ **Outcome**: Bolsonaro won, but WhatsApp was forced to crack down on automated messaging and misinformation campaigns in subsequent elections.

4. Lessons from Historical Election Disinformation

Election disinformation has evolved, but some key lessons remain constant:

✓ Fake news spreads fastest when it aligns with existing fears or biases.

✓ Disinformation campaigns often rely on emotion, not facts, to manipulate voters.

✓ Foreign and domestic actors exploit digital platforms to amplify propaganda.

✓ Transparency, media literacy, and OSINT techniques are essential for countering election misinformation.

📌 **Final Thought**: As technology advances, election disinformation will only become more sophisticated. Understanding historical examples helps us recognize and combat future attempts to manipulate democracy.

10.2 Investigating Fake Accounts & Coordinated Campaigns

The spread of disinformation in elections often relies on fake accounts, bot networks, and coordinated influence campaigns. These operations are designed to manipulate public opinion, amplify divisive narratives, and create the illusion of widespread support or opposition for a political cause. This section explores how to identify and investigate fake accounts, detect coordinated disinformation efforts, and use OSINT techniques to track their origins.

1. The Role of Fake Accounts in Election Disinformation

Fake accounts serve multiple purposes in disinformation campaigns, including:

✓ Amplifying propaganda by making false narratives trend.

✓ Harassing political opponents and discouraging voter participation.

✓ Creating a false sense of public opinion by artificially inflating engagement.

✓ Spreading misinformation rapidly across social media platforms.

These accounts can be operated by individuals, political operatives, or state-sponsored actors to influence elections.

1.1 Types of Fake Accounts

◆ **Bots**: Automated accounts programmed to like, share, and comment on posts at scale.

◆ **Sock Puppets**: Fake personas controlled by real people to manipulate discussions.

◆ **Trolls**: Accounts used to provoke arguments, spread misinformation, or attack opponents.

◆ **Cyborg Accounts**: Hybrid accounts that combine human and bot activity to appear more credible.

2. OSINT Techniques for Detecting Fake Accounts

Identifying fake accounts is crucial in uncovering coordinated disinformation campaigns. Investigators can use OSINT techniques to analyze suspicious accounts and networks.

2.1 Profile Analysis: Spotting Red Flags

When analyzing a potentially fake account, look for the following signs:

✔ Low-quality profile information (generic names, stock photos, missing bios).

✔ Recently created account with high activity in a short time.

✔ Unusual engagement patterns, such as excessive retweets but few original posts.

✔ Repetitive or copy-pasted content used across multiple accounts.

🔍 **Example**: Using a reverse image search, investigators found that a Twitter account claiming to be a "concerned American voter" was actually using a stock photo from a Russian website.

2.2 Behavior Analysis: Identifying Automation & Coordination

Fake accounts often follow predictable patterns that can be detected using engagement metrics and time analysis.

✔ Posting at unnatural intervals (e.g., tweeting every minute 24/7).

✔ Coordinated activity, where multiple accounts post the same message simultaneously.

✔ Following and engaging with only specific political pages or hashtags.

✔ Language inconsistencies, such as switching between languages or unnatural phrasing.

🔍 **Example**: In the 2020 U.S. election, researchers identified a bot network spreading election fraud claims by analyzing accounts that tweeted identical content within seconds of each other.

2.3 Network Mapping: Exposing Coordinated Campaigns

Coordinated disinformation campaigns often involve networks of fake accounts amplifying each other. OSINT investigators use network analysis tools to map these connections.

✓ **Graph Analysis**: Mapping retweets, shares, and mentions to identify central nodes in a disinformation network.

✓ **Hashtag Tracking**: Examining which accounts are pushing certain hashtags to detect coordinated pushes.

✓ **Follower Overlap**: Investigating whether multiple fake accounts follow the same small group of influencers.

☐ **Tools for Network Analysis:**

◆ **Hoaxy** – Visualizes how fake news spreads.
◆ **Graphika** – Maps social media influence networks.
◆ **TweetDeck & Trendsmap** – Tracks hashtag and keyword trends.

🔍 **Example**: During the 2019 Indian elections, researchers used network analysis to detect thousands of fake accounts boosting a specific political candidate. The accounts all followed the same set of influencers, revealing a coordinated strategy.

3. Investigating Bot Networks & Coordinated Campaigns

3.1 Using Bot Detection Tools

Fake accounts can be analyzed with bot detection algorithms that assess their behavior and likelihood of automation.

✓ **Botometer** – Checks if a Twitter account is a bot.

✓ **Twitonomy** – Analyzes Twitter engagement patterns.

✓ **Bot Sentinel** – Detects political bots spreading misinformation.

🔍 **Example**: In the 2018 Brazilian election, investigators found that over half of the pro-Bolsonaro tweets were generated by bots, artificially amplifying political narratives.

3.2 Tracking Influence Operations Using OSINT

To uncover who is behind a disinformation campaign, investigators use OSINT techniques such as:

✓ **Domain analysis**: Checking websites spreading fake news using Whois lookup & domain history tools.

✓ **Metadata extraction**: Examining images and videos shared by fake accounts for clues.

✓ **Cross-platform tracking**: Identifying similar fake personas across different social media sites.

🔍 **Example**: In the 2022 French elections, investigators used domain analysis to uncover that a website publishing anti-Macron fake news stories was registered in Russia and linked to past disinformation efforts.

4. Case Study: Exposing a Coordinated Election Disinformation Operation

During the 2019 European Parliament elections, an OSINT team uncovered a massive bot-driven disinformation campaign targeting European voters.

4.1 The Discovery

✓ Thousands of new Twitter accounts were created just weeks before the election.

✓ Accounts posted identical anti-EU narratives, claiming the elections were rigged.

✓ Hashtags like #EUCorrupt and #EuroFraud were artificially boosted.

4.2 The Investigation

✓ Using bot detection tools, researchers found that 70% of the accounts were automated.

✓ Network analysis showed the campaign originated from a single Russian-linked group.

✓ Metadata analysis of images found fake voter fraud photos that had been used in past elections.

4.3 The Outcome

✓ Social media platforms removed thousands of fake accounts.

✓ European authorities issued a public warning about the disinformation campaign.

✓ The case highlighted the growing threat of election interference via social media.

5. Preventing & Countering Election Disinformation Campaigns

5.1 Steps Social Media Platforms Can Take

✓ Implement stricter verification for political accounts.

✓ Develop AI-driven bot detection to remove fake accounts.

✓ Label state-sponsored content and disinformation warnings.

5.2 How Investigators & Journalists Can Help

✓ Use OSINT tools to detect and expose fake accounts.

✓ Report findings to social media platforms and fact-checking organizations.

✓ Educate the public on how to spot and report fake accounts.

5.3 What the Public Can Do

✓ Be skeptical of viral political claims, especially from unknown sources.

✓ Use fact-checking tools before sharing information.

✓ Report suspicious accounts and campaigns to social media platforms.

Fake accounts and coordinated disinformation campaigns have become a major threat to democracy, influencing elections through deception and manipulation. However, OSINT techniques provide powerful tools for exposing these operations. By combining bot detection, network analysis, and digital forensics, investigators can track, analyze, and dismantle disinformation campaigns before they cause widespread harm.

✦ **Final Thought**: As election disinformation grows more sophisticated, vigilance, transparency, and digital literacy will be essential in protecting the integrity of democratic elections worldwide.

10.3 Tracking Election Misinformation Across Social Media

The rapid spread of election misinformation on social media platforms has become one of the most significant threats to democratic processes worldwide. False claims about voter fraud, ballot tampering, candidate scandals, and manipulated results can undermine public trust in elections and influence voter behavior. This chapter explores how to track, analyze, and counter election misinformation using OSINT techniques.

1. How Election Misinformation Spreads on Social Media

Election-related misinformation spreads rapidly due to a combination of algorithmic amplification, psychological biases, and coordinated influence campaigns.

1.1 Key Factors Driving Misinformation Spread

✔ **Virality & Algorithmic Boosting** – Platforms like Facebook, Twitter, and TikTok prioritize engagement-driven content, often promoting sensational misinformation over factual reports.

✔ **Echo Chambers & Confirmation Bias** – Users tend to follow like-minded communities, reinforcing their existing beliefs and making them more susceptible to election-related falsehoods.

✔ **Coordinated Disinformation Campaigns** – State actors, political groups, and troll farms use fake accounts, bots, and meme warfare to manipulate public perception.

✔ **Lack of Fact-Checking on Private Channels** – WhatsApp, Telegram, and Signal are popular for spreading election misinformation, as messages circulate in encrypted, closed groups with minimal moderation.

1.2 Common Types of Election Misinformation

◆ **False Voter Fraud Claims** – Example: "Dead people are voting" or "Thousands of fake ballots were found."

◆ **Misleading Poll Data** – Example: Fake surveys designed to demoralize or encourage voters.

◆ **Deepfake Videos & AI-Generated Content** – Manipulated media falsely showing candidates making controversial statements.

◆ **Fake Endorsements & Scandals** – Fabricated stories about political candidates receiving secret funding or engaging in corruption.

◆ **Election Boycotts & Voter Suppression** – False claims that voting locations are closed, ballots won't be counted, or elections are postponed.

2. OSINT Techniques for Tracking Election Misinformation

Investigators, fact-checkers, and analysts can monitor, verify, and debunk election-related falsehoods using various OSINT methods and tools.

2.1 Monitoring Social Media Platforms for Misinformation Trends

Tracking election misinformation requires constant surveillance of social platforms where political discussions are taking place.

📌 **Key Platforms to Monitor:**

✓ **Twitter/X** – Real-time political debates, hashtags, and bot activity.

✓ **Facebook & Instagram** – Fake news articles, viral election hoaxes, meme-based disinformation.

✓ **TikTok & YouTube** – Misinformation spread through short videos, deepfakes, and influencer-led narratives.

✓ **WhatsApp, Telegram, Discord** – Private group discussions with minimal moderation.

📌 **OSINT Tools for Monitoring:**

◆ **CrowdTangle** – Tracks trending election-related content on Facebook and Instagram.
◆ **Hoaxy** – Maps the spread of election misinformation across social networks.

- ◆ **Trendsmap** – Identifies trending political hashtags on Twitter/X.
- ◆ **OSINT Telegram Scraper** – Monitors disinformation in Telegram groups.

🔍 **Example**: Ahead of the 2022 Brazilian elections, analysts used CrowdTangle to track viral misinformation falsely claiming that electronic voting machines were rigged.

2.2 Identifying Suspicious Hashtags & Viral Narratives

Disinformation campaigns often rely on coordinated hashtag manipulation to make false narratives go viral.

📌 **Signs of Coordinated Misinformation Campaigns:**

✓ Hashtags appear suddenly & gain traction unnaturally fast.

✓ Thousands of accounts tweet identical messages simultaneously.

✓ Engagement comes mostly from newly created or bot-like accounts.

📌 **Methods for Tracking Election-Related Hashtags:**

- ◆ **TweetDeck** – Monitors hashtag activity in real-time.
- ◆ **Ritetag** – Analyzes hashtag popularity and associated accounts.
- ◆ **Botometer** – Detects bot-driven engagement in trending topics.

🔍 **Example**: During the 2020 U.S. election, the hashtag #StopTheSteal was artificially boosted by bot networks, falsely claiming the election was rigged.

2.3 Verifying Viral Election-Related Images & Videos

Many election-related falsehoods use misleading or doctored images to deceive voters.

📌 **Common Manipulation Tactics:**

✓ Old images repurposed as "evidence" for current events.

✓ Photoshop edits adding or removing key details.

✓ Deepfake videos making candidates say false statements.

📌 **OSINT Tools for Verifying Images & Videos:**

◆ **Google Reverse Image Search** – Checks if an image has been used in previous contexts.

◆ **InVID-WeVerify** – Analyzes metadata & breaks down video frames for verification.

◆ **TinEye** – Tracks altered versions of an image across the web.

🔍 **Example**: A viral image of "ballot boxes dumped in a river" during the 2020 U.S. elections was debunked using reverse image search, revealing it was actually from a 2016 Philippines election.

2.4 Analyzing Fake News Websites & Clickbait Sources

Many election misinformation campaigns rely on fake news websites designed to look like legitimate media outlets.

📌 **How to Identify Fake News Websites:**

✓ Check domain registration (Whois lookup).

✓ Analyze writing style (excessive sensationalism, lack of sources).

✓ Look for connections to known disinformation networks.

📌 **Tools for Investigating Suspicious Websites:**

◆ **Whois Lookup** – Identifies who owns a website.

◆ **Wayback Machine** – Shows historical changes to misleading websites.

◆ **Domain Big Data** – Tracks website registration details.

🔍 **Example**: In the 2019 UK elections, researchers found a network of fake news sites spreading anti-Labour propaganda, all registered under the same owner.

3. Countering Election Misinformation with OSINT

3.1 Fact-Checking & Debunking False Claims

Fact-checkers play a crucial role in countering election misinformation by verifying and debunking false narratives.

📌 **Trusted Fact-Checking Organizations:**

✓ **Snopes** – Debunks viral misinformation.

✓ **PolitiFact** – Focuses on political claims and statements.

✓ **Reuters Fact Check** – Verifies election-related stories globally.

📌 **How to Debunk Election Misinformation:**

✓ Find the original source of a claim.

✓ Use OSINT tools to verify images, videos, and statistics.

✓ Cross-check information with reliable news outlets.

3.2 Reporting Disinformation & Coordinated Campaigns

Social media platforms and election watchdogs rely on user reports to take action against misinformation.

📌 **Where to Report Election Misinformation:**

✓ **Twitter/X & Facebook Report Features** – Flags false election content.

✓ **Election Integrity Watchdogs (e.g., First Draft, EIP)** – Tracks misinformation trends.

✓ **Government Election Offices** – Some countries have portals to report election fraud rumors.

🔍 **Example**: Ahead of the 2022 Philippine elections, Facebook removed thousands of fake accounts tied to disinformation campaigns after investigative journalists reported coordinated activity.

Election misinformation on social media poses a serious threat to democracy, shaping public perception and influencing voter behavior. However, OSINT techniques provide powerful tools to track, analyze, and debunk false narratives.

📌 **Key Takeaways:**

✓ Social media platforms are the primary battlegrounds for election disinformation.

✓ OSINT tools help monitor trends, verify content, and track coordinated campaigns.

✓ Fact-checking, reporting, and public awareness are critical in countering false narratives.

As misinformation tactics evolve, proactive monitoring and digital literacy will be essential in safeguarding election integrity worldwide.

10.4 Analyzing Manipulated Polls & Fake Political Endorsements

Public opinion polls and political endorsements play a critical role in shaping voter perceptions and election outcomes. However, manipulated polls and fake endorsements have become powerful tools in disinformation campaigns. These tactics can mislead voters, create false narratives, and manipulate public sentiment in favor of or against a candidate or party. This section explores how OSINT techniques can help detect, analyze, and debunk manipulated polls and fabricated political endorsements.

1. How Poll Manipulation and Fake Endorsements Influence Elections

1.1 The Impact of Polls & Endorsements on Voter Behavior

✓ **Psychological Influence** – Voters often want to support a "winning" candidate (bandwagon effect) or may feel discouraged if their preferred candidate appears to be losing (suppression effect).

✓ **Media Amplification** – News organizations frequently report on polls and endorsements, giving false or manipulated data a wider audience.

✓ **Fundraising & Campaign Strategy** – Donors and strategists adjust spending and messaging based on polling trends, making fraudulent polls a tool to shift resources.

✓ **Voter Suppression & Mobilization** – Fake polls may be designed to demoralize opposition voters or energize certain groups based on misleading data.

1.2 Common Manipulation Tactics in Polling

⚙ Poll Manipulation Methods:

⬧ Fake or Misleading Sample Sizes – Polls may use small, unrepresentative samples to exaggerate a candidate's popularity.

⬧ Leading or Misleading Questions – Questions are worded to influence responses rather than collect neutral data.

⬧ Cherry-Picked Data – Only certain poll results are publicized while others are ignored.

⬧ Fabricated Polls – Entirely fake polls attributed to non-existent or obscure polling firms.

⬧ Bot-Driven Online Polls – Automated scripts or paid click farms artificially inflate online poll numbers.

☐ **Example**: In the 2016 U.S. election, multiple unreliable online polls circulated on social media falsely claiming that one candidate had a "90% chance" of winning, misleading voters about the actual race dynamics.

1.3 How Fake Political Endorsements Spread

⚙ Common Fake Endorsement Tactics:

⬧ Deepfake Videos & AI-Generated Endorsements – Public figures are falsely shown endorsing a candidate.

⬧ Fake Quotes & Doctored Images – Graphics and memes falsely attribute endorsements or criticisms to celebrities, politicians, or business leaders.

⬧ Social Media Bots & Trolls – Automated accounts spread fabricated endorsements to manipulate public perception.

⬧ Hijacking Real Statements – A real statement is taken out of context to imply an endorsement that doesn't exist.

☐ **Example**: In the 2022 Brazilian election, fake news circulated on WhatsApp claiming that soccer star Neymar had endorsed a candidate, using a doctored image, when in reality, he had made no public statement.

2. OSINT Techniques for Detecting Poll & Endorsement Manipulation

2.1 Investigating Polling Sources

📌 **Key Steps to Verify Poll Authenticity:**

✓ **Check the Polling Organization** – Is the poll conducted by a reputable firm (e.g., Gallup, Pew Research, YouGov)?

✓ **Analyze the Sample Size & Methodology** – Are the respondents randomly selected? Are demographic factors (age, race, region) considered?

✓ **Compare with Other Polls** – Does this poll align with trends from multiple sources, or does it stand out suspiciously?

✓ **Look for Funding & Political Bias** – Who commissioned the poll? Political PACs and partisan groups often fund push polls designed to sway opinions.

📌 **OSINT Tools for Poll Analysis:**

◆ **FiveThirtyEight Poll Tracker** – Aggregates and rates the reliability of political polls.
◆ **Roper Center for Public Opinion Research** – Archives historical poll data for cross-checking.
◆ **Wayback Machine** – Tracks changes in poll results over time, exposing potential manipulation.

☐ **Example**: During the 2019 UK elections, analysts found that several polls promoting one party's overwhelming lead were conducted by a nonexistent research firm created just weeks before the election.

2.2 Reverse Image & Video Search for Fake Endorsements

📌 **How to Detect Fake Endorsement Images & Videos:**

✓ **Reverse Image Search** – Check if an image has been altered or repurposed using Google Reverse Image Search or TinEye.

✓ **Metadata Analysis** – Inspect the file's metadata using tools like ExifTool to detect manipulations.

✓ **Deepfake Detection** – Use AI-based tools like Deepware Scanner or Reality Defender to check for synthetic media.

✔ **Cross-Reference Statements** – Verify endorsement claims on official websites or verified social media accounts.

📌 **OSINT Tools for Verifying Political Endorsements:**

◆ **InVID-WeVerify** – Extracts keyframes from videos to check for manipulation.
◆ **Fotoforensics** – Analyzes image alterations and inconsistencies.
◆ **Politwoops** – Tracks deleted tweets from politicians to catch inconsistencies.

☐ **Example**: In the 2020 U.S. elections, a doctored video falsely showed a prominent activist endorsing a candidate. OSINT researchers used InVID to trace the video back to its original, unedited version, exposing the deception.

2.3 Tracking Social Media Amplification of Fake Polls & Endorsements

📌 **Red Flags for Coordinated Disinformation Campaigns:**

✔ **Hashtags & Memes Repeating the Same Poll Data** – Does one specific poll get unusually high engagement compared to others?
✔ **Bot-Generated Engagement** – Does the content receive suspiciously similar comments & shares from newly created accounts?
✔ **Network Analysis of Spreading Accounts** – Are certain users or groups pushing identical narratives across platforms?

📌 **OSINT Tools for Monitoring Disinformation Trends:**

◆ **Botometer** – Detects bot-driven activity promoting fake polls.
◆ **CrowdTangle** – Tracks how fake endorsements spread across social media.
◆ **Hoaxy** – Maps the connections between accounts sharing disinformation.

☐ **Example**: In the 2022 French presidential election, Twitter bots were found artificially inflating engagement on a fake poll claiming a candidate had already secured victory.

3. Countering Poll & Endorsement Disinformation with OSINT

3.1 Fact-Checking & Public Awareness

✓ Use fact-checking platforms like Snopes, PolitiFact, and Reuters Fact Check to verify poll data and endorsements.

✓ Educate the public on how manipulated polling works and why endorsements should be verified from primary sources.

✓ Encourage media literacy to help voters spot disinformation before spreading it further.

3.2 Reporting Manipulated Polls & Endorsements

✓ Flag disinformation on social media platforms using reporting tools.

✓ Submit evidence of fake polls or endorsements to investigative journalists and election watchdog groups.

✓ Advocate for transparency in polling methodology to reduce the impact of manipulated surveys.

☐ **Example**: In the 2020 Indian elections, a coalition of fact-checkers successfully debunked a fake endorsement campaign that falsely claimed Bollywood celebrities supported a political party.

Manipulated polls and fake political endorsements can significantly impact election outcomes by distorting public perception and misleading voters. However, OSINT provides powerful tools to verify polling data, detect fake endorsements, and counter disinformation campaigns.

📌 **Key Takeaways:**

✓ Poll manipulation is often driven by biased sampling, misleading questions, or outright fabrication.

✓ Fake endorsements frequently rely on deepfakes, doctored images, or taken-out-of-context statements.

✓ OSINT tools can verify polling sources, detect media manipulation, and track disinformation spread.

By staying vigilant and applying OSINT techniques, analysts and citizens alike can help protect election integrity and ensure informed voting decisions.

10.5 The Impact of Disinformation on Voter Behavior

Disinformation has become a powerful tool for influencing elections, shaping public perceptions, and manipulating voter behavior. By spreading false narratives, misleading claims, and emotional propaganda, disinformation campaigns can suppress voter turnout, shift political allegiances, and polarize societies. This section explores how disinformation affects voter behavior, the psychological mechanisms behind it, and how OSINT techniques can help identify and counter these deceptive tactics.

1. How Disinformation Influences Voter Behavior

Election disinformation is strategically designed to exploit emotions, reinforce biases, and create confusion. Some of the key ways disinformation impacts voters include:

1.1 Suppressing Voter Turnout

🔍 **Disinformation tactics designed to discourage voting:**

◆ **False information about voting procedures** – Disinformation campaigns spread wrong dates, locations, or voter ID requirements to confuse voters.
◆ **Claims that voting is pointless** – Narratives that an election is "rigged" or "already decided" can discourage participation.
◆ **Targeted misinformation** – Minority communities or opposition supporters are often deliberately misled to keep them away from the polls.

☐ **Example**: In the 2020 U.S. election, misleading social media posts falsely claimed that mail-in ballots would not be counted, discouraging early voting.

1.2 Shaping Public Perception of Candidates

🔍 **Disinformation tactics to discredit or elevate candidates:**

◆ **Fake scandals & smear campaigns** – Fabricated allegations (e.g., corruption, criminal activity) are spread to damage reputations.

◆ **Deepfake videos & AI-generated content** – Manipulated videos falsely depict candidates making controversial statements.

◆ **Manipulated search results** – Coordinated efforts boost or bury certain stories online to control narratives.

☐ **Example**: In the 2022 Brazilian election, deepfake videos circulated showing a candidate "admitting" to fraud, despite no such confession ever happening.

1.3 Reinforcing Political Polarization

🔊 **Disinformation tactics that widen societal divisions:**

◆ **Echo chambers & filter bubbles** – Social media algorithms reinforce biases by only showing content that aligns with pre-existing beliefs.

◆ **Inciting outrage & fear** – Fake news often uses highly emotional language to deepen ideological divides.

◆ **False comparisons & misleading statistics** – Disinformation distorts reality by presenting biased, out-of-context comparisons.

☐ **Example**: In the Brexit referendum, disinformation campaigns spread false economic statistics, claiming that leaving the EU would free up £350 million per week for healthcare funding.

2. The Psychology Behind Disinformation's Effectiveness

Voters are especially vulnerable to disinformation due to cognitive biases and emotional triggers. Understanding these psychological mechanisms is key to developing countermeasures.

2.1 Confirmation Bias

✔ People favor information that confirms their existing beliefs and dismiss contradictory evidence.

✔ Disinformation campaigns exploit this by tailoring fake news to specific ideological groups.

✔ Echo chambers reinforce bias by surrounding people with like-minded opinions.

☐ **Example**: During the 2016 U.S. election, Facebook groups tailored disinformation content to specific political demographics, making it more likely to be believed and shared.

2.2 The Illusory Truth Effect

✓ People are more likely to believe false information if they see it repeatedly.

✓ Disinformation campaigns flood social media with repetitive messaging, making lies appear credible.

✓ This is especially powerful when combined with visual elements (memes, videos).

☐ **Example**: Russian influence campaigns used bot networks to repeatedly post false narratives about election fraud, making them seem more credible over time.

2.3 Fear & Emotional Manipulation

✓ Disinformation is often designed to provoke fear, anger, or outrage because emotional content spreads faster.

✓ Messages that trigger strong emotional responses are more likely to be shared, regardless of their accuracy.

☐ **Example**: In the 2019 Indian elections, viral WhatsApp messages falsely claimed violent attacks were planned against a religious group, increasing tensions and influencing voter sentiment.

3. OSINT Techniques for Detecting & Countering Election Disinformation

To combat disinformation's impact on voter behavior, OSINT analysts use a variety of investigative techniques and digital forensics tools.

3.1 Identifying Disinformation Campaigns

✓ **Network Analysis**: Mapping who is sharing false claims and detecting coordinated activity.

✓ **Keyword Monitoring**: Tracking viral election-related falsehoods before they spread further.

✓ **Bot Detection**: Identifying automated accounts amplifying disinformation.

📌 **Useful OSINT Tools:**

◆ **Hoaxy** – Visualizes the spread of disinformation across Twitter.
◆ **Botometer** – Detects automated social media accounts.
◆ **CrowdTangle** – Monitors trending narratives and disinformation spread.

☐ **Example**: Analysts used CrowdTangle to track the spread of election fraud conspiracies on Facebook during the 2020 U.S. election.

3.2 Verifying Election Claims with OSINT

✓ **Reverse Image Search**: Detects doctored images, deepfakes, and misleading visuals.

✓ **Fact-Checking Statements**: Compares claims against official records & independent sources.

✓ **Metadata Analysis**: Examines document & media metadata to uncover forgery.

📌 **Useful OSINT Tools:**

◆ **Google Reverse Image Search & TinEye** – Detects manipulated photos.
◆ **InVID-WeVerify** – Analyzes videos for signs of tampering.
◆ **Politifact, Snopes, BBC Reality Check** – Fact-checking election-related claims.

☐ **Example**: In the 2022 French elections, fact-checkers used InVID to debunk a viral video falsely showing ballot tampering.

3.3 Preventing the Spread of Election Disinformation

✓ **Public Awareness Campaigns** – Educating voters on how disinformation works.

✓ **Social Media Reporting** – Flagging fake news & manipulative ads.

✓ **Media Literacy Training** – Teaching people how to fact-check election content.

📌 **Example**: Estonia successfully reduced election disinformation by launching media literacy initiatives and providing citizens with OSINT training.

4. Conclusion: Protecting Election Integrity with OSINT

Election disinformation is designed to exploit human psychology, distort reality, and influence voter behavior. By understanding how these tactics work and leveraging OSINT techniques, analysts and fact-checkers can help counter false narratives and protect democracy.

📌 Key Takeaways:

✓ Disinformation influences voter behavior through suppression, false narratives, and polarization.

✓ Psychological factors like confirmation bias and emotional manipulation make people vulnerable to fake news.

✓ OSINT tools can track, analyze, and debunk election-related disinformation.

✓ Public awareness and media literacy are critical to preventing disinformation's spread.

By applying OSINT methodologies, election watchdogs, journalists, and digital investigators can play a critical role in safeguarding election integrity and empowering voters with the truth.

10.6 Case Study: OSINT in Action Against Election Disruption

Election disinformation has become a powerful tool for manipulating public opinion, suppressing voter turnout, and disrupting democratic processes. In recent years, open-source intelligence (OSINT) investigators have played a critical role in detecting, exposing, and mitigating disinformation campaigns designed to influence elections. This case study explores a real-world example where OSINT techniques were successfully used to counteract an election disruption campaign, revealing the tactics used, the investigative process, and the impact of the findings.

1. Background: The Election & the Disinformation Campaign

In the months leading up to the 2020 U.S. Presidential Election, intelligence agencies and independent OSINT analysts began noticing unusual online activity designed to spread false election narratives. The disinformation efforts were multi-layered and sophisticated, involving:

◆ Fake news articles falsely claiming widespread voter fraud.
◆ Social media bot networks amplifying these false narratives.
◆ Manipulated videos and images designed to discredit mail-in voting.
◆ Coordinated hashtag campaigns targeting swing-state voters.

These tactics were designed to undermine public trust in the electoral process and create chaos. While mainstream media covered some of these incidents, OSINT investigators played a crucial role in uncovering the full scale of the operation.

2. OSINT Investigators Detect Suspicious Activity

2.1 Tracking Social Media Amplification

Investigators used OSINT tools to track how disinformation was spreading across social media platforms.

📌 **Key Observations:**

✓ Hashtags like #StopTheSteal and #RiggedElection were suddenly trending, despite minimal organic engagement.

✓ Thousands of new Twitter accounts with low follower counts were posting identical messages.

✓ Suspicious Facebook groups emerged, filled with misleading election content.

📌 **OSINT Tools Used:**

◆ **Hoaxy** – To visualize how false narratives were spreading.
◆ **Botometer** – To identify bot accounts pushing election disinformation.
◆ **CrowdTangle** – To analyze how viral misinformation was performing on Facebook.

☐ **Finding**: Investigators uncovered a coordinated effort by thousands of bot accounts, primarily originating from foreign actors, to flood social media with false claims about voting fraud.

2.2 Verifying Manipulated Content & Fake News

Another key component of the disinformation campaign involved doctored images, deepfake videos, and fake news articles designed to mislead voters. OSINT investigators conducted forensic analysis to debunk these claims.

📌 **Example 1: Fake Ballot Dumping Video**

▶ A video surfaced on Twitter, allegedly showing election workers discarding ballots in a dumpster.

☐ **OSINT Analysis:**

✔ Investigators conducted a reverse image search (using InVID & Google Images) and found that the video was actually from a different country and unrelated to the U.S. election.

✔ Metadata analysis of the video's timestamps revealed that it was recorded months before the election.

✔ Geolocation tools confirmed that the location was not in the U.S.

✅ **Result**: Fact-checkers debunked the video, and social media platforms flagged it as misinformation.

📌 **Example 2: Fake News Claiming Voting Machines Changed Votes**

▶ A viral article falsely claimed that electronic voting machines in key states were switching votes.

☐ **OSINT Analysis:**

✔ The website publishing the article was found to be a newly registered domain with no history.

✓ The supposed "evidence" in the article was an out-of-context video from a decade-old software glitch, unrelated to the current election.

✓ Using WHOIS lookup and domain registration tracking, investigators traced the website's origin to a foreign-linked disinformation network.

✅ **Result**: The website was reported, and multiple fact-checking organizations exposed it as fake.

2.3 Mapping the Disinformation Network

To uncover the broader coordination behind these disinformation efforts, OSINT analysts conducted network analysis.

📌 **Findings:**

✓ Many of the social media accounts spreading false claims were linked to previous disinformation campaigns in past elections.

✓ The same actors were using multiple fake identities to appear as "concerned citizens" while actually being part of a coordinated influence operation.

✓ Troll farms from foreign locations were traced back to specific organizations involved in past election interference efforts.

📌 **OSINT Tools Used:**

♦ **Maltego** – For mapping connections between accounts, websites, and domains.
♦ **Graphika** – For analyzing coordinated disinformation networks.
♦ **DomainTools** – To track website registrations and ownership history.

✅ **Result**: The findings were shared with journalists, fact-checkers, and intelligence agencies, leading to the shutdown of several disinformation networks before Election Day.

3. Impact of the OSINT Investigation

The OSINT-led exposure of these disinformation efforts had significant consequences:

✓ **Social media platforms took action** – Many of the bot accounts, fake websites, and misleading hashtags were flagged or removed.

✓ **Voters became more informed** – Fact-checking organizations used the findings to educate the public about election misinformation.

✓ **Government agencies acted** – Cybersecurity teams monitored and countered foreign disinformation attempts in real time.

✓ **Journalists amplified the findings** – Major news outlets reported on the disinformation campaign, helping to reduce its overall effectiveness.

By applying OSINT techniques, digital forensics, and network analysis, investigators were able to expose and mitigate an organized attempt to disrupt a major election.

4. Lessons Learned & Future OSINT Strategies

4.1 The Importance of Real-Time OSINT Monitoring

✓ Continuous monitoring of social media trends, deepfake content, and fake news sites is essential to stay ahead of disinformation campaigns.

4.2 The Role of Public Awareness

✓ Educating voters on how to recognize fake news and disinformation is one of the strongest defenses against manipulation.

4.3 Strengthening Cross-Industry Collaboration

✓ OSINT analysts, journalists, fact-checkers, and intelligence agencies must work together to detect, verify, and counteract election-related misinformation.

4.4 The Need for More Advanced Detection Tools

✅ As AI-generated content and deepfakes become more sophisticated, OSINT tools must evolve to detect them more effectively.

5. Conclusion: OSINT as a Powerful Weapon Against Election Disinformation

This case study highlights how OSINT investigators played a crucial role in uncovering and countering election disinformation efforts. By leveraging social media tracking, digital forensics, and network analysis, they successfully exposed a coordinated attempt to manipulate voter behavior and disrupt democratic processes.

As election disinformation tactics continue to evolve, OSINT techniques will remain a critical defense against digital propaganda, false narratives, and voter manipulation. By staying vigilant, enhancing investigative methods, and promoting media literacy, OSINT analysts can help ensure more transparent and fair elections in the future.

🔎 Key Takeaways:

✔ OSINT investigators tracked, verified, and exposed a coordinated disinformation campaign.

✔ Disinformation tactics included fake news, deepfake videos, bot amplification, and manipulated hashtags.

✔ Social media monitoring, digital forensics, and network analysis were essential in countering election disruption.

✔ Collaboration with fact-checkers, journalists, and cybersecurity experts strengthened the impact of the investigation.

This case study serves as a powerful example of how OSINT can be used to protect democracy and uphold election integrity in an era of digital disinformation. 🚨

11. Ethical Dilemmas in Disinformation Investigations

As OSINT analysts work to uncover and counter disinformation, they often face complex ethical dilemmas that can challenge their methods and decision-making. This chapter explores the ethical considerations involved in disinformation investigations, such as privacy concerns, the potential for unintended consequences, and the responsibility to avoid spreading false information while debunking it. We discuss the fine line between vigilance and overreach, the impact of exposing sources and methods, and the ethical boundaries of surveillance and data collection. By examining these challenges, readers will gain insight into the importance of maintaining ethical integrity in their work and navigating the moral complexities that arise when combating disinformation in the digital age.

11.1 The Ethics of Investigating & Exposing Fake News Creators

In the battle against disinformation, OSINT investigators, journalists, and fact-checkers often face ethical dilemmas when uncovering the identities of fake news creators and exposing their tactics. While transparency and accountability are crucial for maintaining public trust in information, there are risks associated with publicly identifying individuals or groups behind disinformation campaigns. This section explores the ethical considerations, potential consequences, and best practices when investigating and exposing fake news creators.

1. The Importance of Ethical Investigations

OSINT investigations into fake news networks, coordinated disinformation efforts, and propaganda operations can reveal critical information about who is responsible for spreading falsehoods and how these efforts are orchestrated. However, ethical dilemmas arise in balancing public interest, privacy rights, and the risk of unintended consequences.

Key Ethical Questions:

- When is it justified to expose fake news creators?
- What risks do investigators face when revealing identities?

- How do we ensure accuracy before making accusations?
- What are the legal and moral implications of publishing findings?

Failing to navigate these issues carefully can lead to reputational damage, legal action, or even retaliation against investigators.

2. Balancing Transparency & Privacy Rights

A core ethical dilemma in exposing fake news creators is the balance between transparency and individual privacy.

📌 Scenario 1: A Political Disinformation Network

✅ **Ethical Justification**: If an organized group is spreading deliberate lies to influence an election, exposing them serves the public interest.
🏛 **Ethical Risk**: If an OSINT investigator wrongly identifies a person as part of the network, they could face serious consequences.

📌 Scenario 2: An Individual Sharing Misinformation

✅ **Ethical Justification**: Educating the public about misinformation sources is crucial.
🏛 **Ethical Risk**: If a private citizen unknowingly shares false information, publicly exposing them could lead to harassment, doxxing, or even legal repercussions.

Best Practice:

- Differentiate between malicious actors and uninformed individuals.
- Prioritize exposing coordinated disinformation networks over individual missteps.
- Ensure any exposure aligns with legal and ethical standards.

3. Risks of Misidentification & Unintended Harm

OSINT investigations are highly dependent on accuracy, and errors in attribution can cause irreversible harm.

Case Study: A Misidentification Incident

In 2021, an OSINT researcher mistakenly identified a Twitter user as part of a foreign disinformation network. The person faced harassment and threats, only for it to be revealed later that they had no connection to the campaign.

How to Avoid Misidentification:

✓ Verify findings across multiple independent sources.

✓ Use digital forensics and metadata analysis to confirm authenticity.

✓ Avoid rushing to conclusions without strong evidence.

● **Golden Rule**: "If you don't have 100% certainty, do NOT expose an identity."

4. Legal & Ethical Boundaries of OSINT Investigations

Investigating fake news creators often involves gathering publicly available information, but ethical concerns arise when investigations infringe on privacy, break platform policies, or involve hacking into private accounts.

📌 **What's Ethical?**

✅ Using WHOIS lookups, domain registration tracking, and social media analysis to identify coordinated networks.

✅ Fact-checking claims, using reverse image searches, and verifying metadata to debunk misinformation.

📌 **What's Unethical & Possibly Illegal?**

✗ Hacking into private emails, accounts, or databases.

✗ Doxxing individuals (publishing private addresses, phone numbers, etc.).

✗ Spreading false accusations based on weak or circumstantial evidence.

◆ **Best Practice**: Always operate within ethical and legal boundaries and ensure that investigations are rooted in fact-based analysis rather than personal bias.

5. The Role of Responsible Reporting & Fact-Checking

Once an OSINT investigator uncovers a disinformation network or fake news creator, deciding how to present the findings is just as important as the investigation itself.

Responsible Reporting Guidelines:

✓ Ensure absolute accuracy before publishing any findings.

✓ Provide clear evidence (screenshots, metadata, archived links, etc.).

✓ Avoid personal attacks and focus on the broader impact of disinformation.

✓ Consider the consequences of exposure—both for the creator and the investigator.

When NOT to Expose a Fake News Creator:

▶ If the individual is a private citizen who unknowingly shared misinformation.
▶ If the evidence is inconclusive or circumstantial.
▶ If the exposure could lead to harassment or violence.

6. The Consequences of Exposing Fake News Creators

While exposing disinformation actors can be crucial for public awareness and accountability, it can also come with risks:

◆ **For the Investigator:**

⚠ Retaliation & harassment from the disinformation network.
⚠ Legal threats or lawsuits from exposed individuals.
⚠ Being targeted by disinformation campaigns attempting to discredit their work.

◆ **For the Exposed Individuals:**

⚠ Loss of reputation or employment.
⚠ Harassment or threats from the public.
⚠ Potential legal action (if linked to criminal activities).

Ethical Considerations Before Exposing Someone:

✅ Is the exposure necessary for public interest and safety?

✅ Have all findings been verified and cross-checked?

✅ Are there ways to expose the disinformation campaign without endangering individuals?

◆ **Best Practice**: When possible, report findings to trusted organizations (journalists, fact-checkers, government agencies) rather than publishing sensitive information independently.

7. Conclusion: A Responsible Approach to Investigating Fake News Creators

Ethical OSINT investigations require a balance between exposing harmful disinformation and respecting privacy rights. Investigators must be meticulous in verifying findings, cautious in their approach, and mindful of unintended consequences.

✔ Prioritize uncovering disinformation networks rather than targeting individuals.

✔ Use ethical OSINT techniques and avoid privacy violations.

✔ Verify all evidence rigorously before making public claims.

✔ Consider the potential harm before exposing fake news creators.

✔ Engage with responsible journalists and fact-checking organizations for ethical reporting.

By following ethical best practices, OSINT investigators can continue to play a vital role in fighting disinformation while upholding journalistic integrity and human rights. 🚨

11.2 The Fine Line Between Censorship & Content Moderation

As misinformation and disinformation proliferate online, governments, social media platforms, and regulatory bodies have implemented various content moderation strategies to curb the spread of harmful narratives. However, the increasing control over online speech has led to a critical debate: Where does content moderation end, and censorship begin? Striking the right balance is essential to maintaining freedom of expression while preventing the manipulation of public discourse.

This section explores the ethical, legal, and societal challenges of moderating online content, examining the risks of overreach, political bias, and the unintended consequences of content regulation.

1. What Is Content Moderation?

Content moderation refers to the process of monitoring, reviewing, and managing user-generated content (UGC) on digital platforms to ensure compliance with community guidelines, legal regulations, and ethical standards.

Types of Content Moderation:

◆ **Pre-Moderation**: Content is reviewed before being published. (Example: YouTube's automated review system for harmful content.)
◆ **Post-Moderation**: Content is published first but can be flagged and removed if it violates policies. (Example: Facebook's fact-checking labels.)
◆ **Automated Moderation**: AI-powered systems detect and remove content based on predefined algorithms. (Example: Twitter's misinformation detection tools.)
◆ **User-Flagged Moderation**: Users report content that is then reviewed by moderators. (Example: Reddit's reporting system.)

💡 **Key Question**: At what point does content moderation cross into censorship, stifling legitimate debate?

2. The Dangers of Overreach: When Moderation Becomes Censorship

Censorship occurs when governments, corporations, or institutions suppress information, ideas, or viewpoints—often under the pretext of "protecting the public."

🔊 **Red Flags That Indicate Censorship:**

● **Suppressing dissenting voices**: Removing opinions simply because they challenge mainstream narratives.
● **Excessive reliance on AI & algorithms**: Automated moderation tools misinterpreting satire, political discourse, or legitimate criticism.

● **Selective enforcement:** Rules being applied inconsistently, often influenced by political or corporate biases.

● **Mass deplatforming**: Banning users or organizations without transparency on why decisions were made.

📌 **Case Study: COVID-19 Information & Moderation Controversy**

During the COVID-19 pandemic, platforms like Facebook, YouTube, and Twitter aggressively moderated content to combat misinformation. While some removals were justified (e.g., false claims about cures), others were more controversial, such as censoring discussions on lab leak theories, which were later recognized as valid hypotheses.

This example highlights how over-moderation can stifle legitimate discussions and lead to public distrust in information gatekeepers.

3. Political Bias in Moderation: Who Decides What Is "Misinformation"?

One of the biggest concerns in content moderation is subjectivity—who determines what is harmful, misleading, or dangerous?

Challenges of Political Bias in Moderation:

◆ **Polarized enforcement**: Some voices are silenced while others are given a platform, often based on political leanings.

◆ **Pressure from governments & corporations**: Platforms may comply with government directives or corporate interests rather than uphold neutrality.

◆ **The "Ministry of Truth" Problem**: When one entity has unchecked control over information, the risk of authoritarian censorship increases.

📌 **Example: The Twitter Files Leak**

Internal documents leaked in 2022 revealed how Twitter employees engaged in politically motivated content moderation, often under pressure from government officials and advocacy groups. This raised concerns about social media platforms acting as gatekeepers of political discourse.

💡 **Key Takeaway**: Content moderation should not be weaponized to silence political opposition or dissent.

4. The Consequences of Under-Moderation: The Spread of Harmful Content

While over-moderation risks censorship, under-moderation allows harmful content to flourish. Platforms that fail to enforce their own guidelines can become breeding grounds for:

⚠ Disinformation & fake news that manipulates public opinion.

⚠ Hate speech & extremist content that incites violence.

⚠ Scams, fraud, and exploitation targeting vulnerable users.

⚠ AI-generated misinformation & deepfakes used to deceive audiences.

📌 Case Study: The Role of Facebook in the Rohingya Crisis

In Myanmar, Facebook failed to moderate hate speech and incitements to violence, contributing to the persecution of the Rohingya Muslim minority. The platform later admitted that it played a role in fueling ethnic violence.

💡 **Lesson**: Platforms must strike a balance—moderating harmful content without infringing on free expression.

5. The Role of AI in Content Moderation: Strengths & Weaknesses

AI and machine learning have become essential tools in content moderation, but they come with limitations.

Pros of AI-Based Moderation:

✓ Scalability: Can process billions of posts faster than human moderators.

✓ Consistency: Enforces rules uniformly (when trained properly).

✓ Rapid response: Can detect viral misinformation trends in real time.

Cons of AI-Based Moderation:

✗ **Context blindness**: AI struggles to understand satire, nuance, and cultural differences.

✗ **False positives & negatives**: Legitimate content may be removed, while harmful content slips through.

✗ Algorithmic biases: Training data can reflect societal biases, leading to unfair enforcement.

📌 Example: YouTube's Demonetization Controversy

YouTube's AI-based moderation system demonetized many independent journalists and political commentators, often flagging their content as "controversial", while allowing mainstream media outlets to cover similar topics without penalties.

💡 Solution: A hybrid approach—AI for scalability, human moderation for contextual decision-making.

6. Finding the Right Balance: Ethical Principles for Content Moderation

To prevent both censorship and the spread of harmful content, platforms must implement transparent, fair, and accountable moderation policies.

Best Practices for Ethical Content Moderation:

✅ **Transparency**: Platforms should clearly define content policies and explain why content is removed.

✅ **Accountability**: Users should have appeal mechanisms when their content is flagged.

✅ **Neutrality**: Moderation policies should be consistent, apolitical, and not influenced by external pressures.

✅ **User control**: Platforms should allow users to customize content filters, rather than imposing one-size-fits-all rules.

7. Conclusion: The Need for Nuanced Moderation

The challenge of content moderation vs. censorship is a delicate balancing act. While combating disinformation is essential, overzealous moderation can stifle free speech, suppress dissent, and create distrust in media platforms.

✓ Over-moderation can lead to censorship, political bias, and loss of public trust.

✓ Under-moderation allows harmful content, misinformation, and hate speech to spread unchecked.

✓ AI should complement—not replace—human moderation.

✓ Transparency, fairness, and accountability are key to ethical content moderation.

💡 **Final Thought**: The digital space must remain a place for open dialogue, where harmful content is addressed, but diverse perspectives are not silenced. Striking this balance is the real challenge of the information age. 🔎

11.3 Privacy Concerns in Identifying Disinformation Actors

The battle against disinformation requires uncovering bad actors who manipulate public discourse. However, identifying these individuals or groups comes with serious ethical and legal challenges, particularly regarding privacy rights, surveillance concerns, and potential misuse of OSINT techniques. While OSINT analysts, journalists, and researchers aim to expose disinformation campaigns, their work must be balanced against the risk of violating individual privacy and ethical boundaries.

This section explores the privacy risks, ethical dilemmas, and best practices in tracking disinformation actors while respecting legal frameworks and human rights.

1. Why Privacy Matters in Disinformation Investigations

The digital world thrives on anonymity—a double-edged sword. While anonymity protects whistleblowers, activists, and vulnerable individuals, it also enables troll farms, fake news peddlers, and state-sponsored disinformation actors to operate unchecked.

◆ OSINT investigators often rely on publicly available information, but does that mean everything should be exposed?
◆ Where is the line between exposing harmful deception and violating privacy rights?

Key Privacy Risks in Disinformation Investigations

⚠ **Doxxing & Unintended Harm**: Exposing a suspected disinformation actor's identity could lead to harassment, violence, or legal repercussions—even if they turn out to be innocent.

⚠ **Mass Surveillance & Government Overreach**: Governments may exploit disinformation investigations to justify intrusive surveillance measures against opposition voices.

⚠ **Collateral Damage**: Investigations may unintentionally expose private individuals, journalists, or researchers, creating a chilling effect on free speech.

⚠ **Legal Consequences**: Some investigative methods may violate data protection laws, such as the GDPR (General Data Protection Regulation) or US privacy laws.

📌 **Case Study: The Russia-Linked Twitter Bot Hunt**

In 2017, journalists and researchers attempted to track Russian bot networks on Twitter. However, many accounts flagged as bots belonged to real people, leading to false accusations and reputational damage. This incident highlighted the risk of misidentification in OSINT investigations.

💡 **Lesson**: Privacy concerns must be carefully managed to prevent misattribution and harm to innocent individuals.

2. Ethical Dilemmas in Exposing Disinformation Actors

Ethical OSINT investigations must consider the impact of exposing individuals or organizations involved in disinformation campaigns.

The Key Ethical Questions:

◆ Does the public's right to know outweigh an individual's right to privacy?
◆ When does an OSINT investigation cross the line into targeted harassment?
◆ Should disinformation actors be exposed publicly, or should findings be shared with authorities and platforms privately?

Scenarios Where Exposure Is Justified vs. Risky

Scenario	Public Exposure Justified?	Privacy Concerns?
A government agency spreading election disinformation	☑ Yes, if evidence is strong	⚠ Possible political retaliation
A bot network pushing fake news at scale	☑ Yes, if it's a coordinated operation	⚠ Risk of false positives
A single anonymous account posting misinformation	✗ Not always—better to focus on **patterns, not individuals**	☑ High risk of privacy violation
A journalist unknowingly amplifying false information	✗ No—better to correct misinformation without targeting individuals	☑ Risk of reputational harm

📌 Example: Exposing "Fake Experts" in COVID-19 Misinformation

During the pandemic, OSINT researchers uncovered fake doctors and scientists spreading medical disinformation. While exposing false credentials was in the public interest, some legitimate scientists were falsely accused, damaging careers.

💡 **Lesson**: Investigators must verify claims rigorously before making public accusations.

3. Legal Boundaries: What OSINT Investigators Can and Cannot Do

OSINT operates in a gray area of the law, where publicly available data is fair game, but privacy laws still apply.

Key Legal Frameworks Affecting OSINT Investigations

🔒 GDPR (General Data Protection Regulation) [EU]

- Protects personal data; investigators must justify data collection.
- Personal data cannot be processed without legitimate interest.

🔒 US Privacy Laws (e.g., Stored Communications Act, CFAA)

- Unauthorized access to private accounts or data breaches is illegal.
- Even scraping public data can violate terms of service (e.g., LinkedIn lawsuit against web scrapers).

📜 UN Human Rights Guidelines on Digital Privacy

- Investigations must respect human rights and due process.
- Exposing individuals should be proportionate to the harm caused.

📌 Example: The Cambridge Analytica Scandal

Investigators exposed how Cambridge Analytica harvested Facebook data for political disinformation. However, the exposure also revealed millions of private user profiles, raising questions about whether the investigation itself violated privacy laws.

💡 **Lesson**: Investigators must ensure their methods do not violate the same privacy principles they seek to protect.

4. Best Practices for Ethical & Privacy-Conscious OSINT Investigations

To balance privacy with investigative integrity, OSINT researchers should follow these best practices:

A. Minimize Harm (The "Need-to-Know" Principle)

◆ **Prioritize systemic threats over individuals**—focus on networks, patterns, and trends rather than personal details.

◆ **Avoid public exposure unless absolutely necessary**—consider sharing findings with fact-checkers, platforms, or legal authorities instead.

B. Verify Before You Amplify

◆ Cross-check evidence before making accusations—misidentifications can ruin reputations.

◆ Use multiple OSINT techniques (metadata analysis, linguistic patterns, network mapping) to confirm identities.

C. Use Legally and Ethically Sound Data Collection Methods

◆ **Respect terms of service**—avoid unauthorized scraping of data.

◆ **Do not use hacked or leaked data**—even if it exposes disinformation actors.

◆ Anonymize sensitive data when sharing findings to protect bystanders.

📌 Example: Bellingcat's Ethical Approach to Disinformation Investigations

The investigative group Bellingcat follows strict guidelines:

✓ Publicly available information only.

✓ No hacking or unauthorized access.

✓ Verification through multiple independent sources.

💡 Lesson: Ethical OSINT can expose disinformation networks without violating privacy rights.

5. Conclusion: The Balance Between Accountability & Privacy

◆ Identifying disinformation actors is crucial, but investigators must avoid unethical tactics.
◆ Doxxing and false accusations can undermine credibility and cause real-world harm.
◆ OSINT should focus on patterns and networks rather than targeting individuals unless absolutely necessary.
◆ Transparency, due diligence, and respect for privacy laws are essential for ethical investigations.

💡 Final Thought: The fight against disinformation must not become an excuse for mass surveillance, privacy violations, or online witch hunts. Ethical OSINT ensures that truth is revealed without compromising human rights. 🔎

11.4 How Disinformation Investigators Can Be Targeted

Investigating disinformation is a high-stakes endeavor. Researchers, journalists, and OSINT analysts working to expose fake news networks, bot armies, and influence campaigns often become targets themselves. Disinformation actors—including state-sponsored groups, troll farms, and criminal networks—actively try to intimidate, discredit, or silence those who expose their operations.

This section explores the risks faced by disinformation investigators, the tactics used to target them, and strategies for protecting oneself in an increasingly hostile information battlefield.

1. Why Disinformation Investigators Are Targeted

Disinformation thrives in shadows, and those who work to uncover the truth threaten powerful interests. Investigators may be targeted for:

♦ **Exposing government-backed disinformation campaigns** – Some regimes use OSINT and digital forensics to suppress dissent, making investigators prime targets.
♦ **Revealing the tactics of troll farms and influence networks** – Disrupting these operations can trigger retaliatory harassment.
♦ **Debunking viral falsehoods** – High-profile fact-checkers often face online mobs and smear campaigns.
♦ **Tracking down financial backers of disinformation** – Investigating funding sources of fake news sites may provoke legal and digital attacks.

📌 **Example: The Case of Bellingcat**

Investigative group Bellingcat, known for exposing Russian military operations and disinformation, has been targeted by hacking attempts, smear campaigns, and even death threats.

💡 **Lesson**: Powerful disinformation actors don't play fair—investigators must be prepared for retaliation.

2. Common Tactics Used to Target Investigators

A. Online Harassment & Doxxing

📌 **What It Is:**

- Investigators are bombarded with threats, insults, and harassment on social media.
- Doxxing (publicly exposing personal details like addresses, phone numbers, or family information) is used to intimidate.

📌 **Real-World Example:**

- Fact-checkers from PolitiFact and Snopes have been doxxed and harassed after debunking conspiracy theories.

- Female journalists face highly gendered harassment, including threats of sexual violence.

◆ **Defense Strategies:**

✓ Use privacy protection services to remove personal data from public databases.

✓ Avoid posting identifiable information on personal social media accounts.

✓ Use pseudonyms when possible for OSINT research.

B. Smear Campaigns & Disinformation Attacks

📌 **What It Is:**

- Attackers create fake news stories, doctored images, or AI-generated videos to discredit investigators.
- False allegations (e.g., "foreign agent," "paid shill," "criminal past") are spread online.
- Trolls use keyword hijacking—flooding search results with negative stories about the investigator.

📌 **Real-World Example:**

Investigative journalist Maria Ressa, who exposed disinformation campaigns in the Philippines, was falsely accused of fraud and cyber-libel in state-controlled media.

◆ **Defense Strategies:**

✓ Monitor mentions of your name using Google Alerts or OSINT tools like Social Searcher.

✓ Use right-to-be-forgotten laws (where applicable) to request takedowns of false content.

✓ Document defamation attempts for possible legal action.

C. Cyber Attacks & Digital Espionage

📌 **What It Is:**

- Phishing emails attempt to steal login credentials.
- Spyware and malware are sent via fake news links.
- Man-in-the-middle attacks intercept sensitive communications.

📌 **Real-World Example:**

The Pegasus spyware was used against journalists investigating disinformation networks, allowing attackers to access their private conversations and contacts.

◆ **Defense Strategies:**

✔ Use end-to-end encrypted messaging apps (e.g., Signal, ProtonMail).

✔ Enable two-factor authentication (2FA) on all accounts.

✔ Avoid clicking suspicious links or downloading unknown files.

D. Legal Threats & SLAPP Lawsuits

📌 **What It Is:**

- Strategic Lawsuits Against Public Participation (SLAPPs) are used to intimidate journalists and researchers with costly legal battles.
- Investigators are accused of defamation, hacking, or violating privacy laws when exposing disinformation networks.

📌 **Real-World Example:**

A U.S. media outlet was sued for investigating a disinformation network promoting COVID-19 conspiracy theories. Even though the claims were true, the lawsuit drained their resources.

◆ **Defense Strategies:**

✔ Consult with legal experts before publishing investigations.

✔ Use libel insurance if working for a news organization.

✔ Keep detailed records of all findings to defend against false claims.

E. Physical Threats & Surveillance

📌 **What It Is:**

- In authoritarian regimes, investigators may face intimidation, surveillance, or even arrest.
- Undercover agents may infiltrate OSINT communities to track researchers.

📌 **Real-World Example:**

Journalists in Russia and China investigating disinformation have been followed, detained, or even assassinated.

◆ **Defense Strategies:**

✓ Avoid using real names when traveling for sensitive research.

✓ Meet sources in safe locations and avoid discussing work in public.

✓ Consider digital self-defense training from groups like Access Now or CPJ (Committee to Protect Journalists).

3. How to Protect Yourself as a Disinformation Investigator

A. Strengthen Digital Security

- Use a separate "burner" device for high-risk investigations.
- Store sensitive documents in air-gapped (offline) systems.
- Use a password manager and rotate passwords regularly.

B. Manage Your Online Footprint

- Google yourself regularly to see what information is public.
- Remove personal details from data broker sites (use services like DeleteMe).
- Use alias emails for OSINT work instead of personal accounts.

C. Build a Support Network

- Join investigative journalism or OSINT communities for protection.

- ◆ Work with trusted colleagues rather than conducting solo investigations.
- ◆ Document all threats and report harassment to relevant platforms.

D. Use Secure Communication Channels

- ◆ Encrypt emails using PGP encryption.
- ◆ Use anonymous VPNs and Tor when researching sensitive topics.
- ◆ Avoid discussing investigations over insecure social media platforms.

4. Conclusion: Staying Resilient in the Face of Threats

Disinformation actors target investigators because truth threatens their operations. From online harassment and smear campaigns to cyberattacks and legal threats, the risks are real—but they can be mitigated.

- ◆ Strengthening digital security, online privacy, and legal awareness is crucial.
- ◆ Investigators should work in teams and maintain strong professional networks.
- ◆ Resilience, preparation, and ethical OSINT practices will help investigators continue exposing disinformation without becoming victims themselves.

💡 **Final Thought**: In the fight against disinformation, truth-seekers must protect themselves as fiercely as they pursue the facts. □□

11.5 The Responsibility of OSINT Analysts in Media Investigations

The role of OSINT (Open-Source Intelligence) analysts in media investigations is more critical than ever. As disinformation spreads rapidly across social media, news websites, and encrypted messaging platforms, analysts must balance truth-seeking with ethical responsibility. The power to expose disinformation networks, identify false narratives, and verify media content comes with significant obligations.

This section explores the responsibilities of OSINT analysts in media investigations, including accuracy, ethical considerations, source verification, and the impact of their findings on public discourse and policy decisions.

1. The Power & Influence of OSINT in Media Investigations

OSINT analysts work at the intersection of journalism, intelligence, and cybersecurity, uncovering critical information that influences news reporting, public opinion, and even government policies.

A. The Role of OSINT in Fact-Checking & Investigations

✓ **Identifying disinformation campaigns** – Tracking fake news sources, bot networks, and propaganda efforts.

✓ **Verifying digital media** – Using metadata analysis, reverse image searching, and AI-detection tools to confirm authenticity.

✓ **Tracking viral narratives** – Monitoring how falsehoods spread and who benefits from their amplification.

✓ **Unmasking fake personas** – Investigating sock puppets, troll farms, and state-sponsored actors behind misinformation.

💡 **Example**: During the Russia-Ukraine conflict, OSINT analysts exposed fake videos and staged war footage, preventing misleading narratives from gaining traction.

B. The Influence of OSINT Findings on Public Perception

When OSINT analysts publish findings, they shape how people interpret events, trust media, and engage with information. A single investigation can:

◆ Expose a political disinformation campaign.
◆ Prevent false narratives from influencing elections.
◆ Uncover coordinated propaganda efforts by foreign actors.

However, with great influence comes great responsibility. Analysts must be mindful of misinterpretation, bias, and potential harm caused by their investigations.

2. Key Responsibilities of OSINT Analysts in Media Investigations

A. Commitment to Accuracy & Truth

📌 **Why It Matters:**

- Inaccurate OSINT findings can cause reputational damage, misinformation, and even geopolitical tensions.
- Mistakes in image verification or source attribution can lead to false accusations.

📌 **Best Practices:**

✓ Cross-check findings with multiple independent sources.

✓ Avoid rushing to publish results without thorough verification.

✓ Use standardized methodologies to ensure reliability.

💡 **Example**: In 2018, an OSINT analyst wrongly identified an individual as a suspect in an assassination attempt, leading to harassment of an innocent person. This case highlights the need for careful verification before publicizing findings.

B. Ethical Considerations in OSINT Investigations

📌 **Challenges Analysts Face:**

◆ Should all information uncovered be made public, or does some data pose security risks?
◆ Is it ethical to track private individuals even if they spread disinformation?
◆ How can analysts avoid bias in their investigations?

📌 **Ethical Best Practices:**

✓ Follow the Principles of Ethical OSINT – do not dox, harass, or manipulate findings.

✓ Respect privacy laws and avoid collecting personally identifiable information (PII) without cause.

✓ Be transparent about sources and methods when publishing investigations.

💡 **Example:**

During the COVID-19 pandemic, some OSINT analysts tracked anti-vaccine misinformation networks. While exposing their tactics was crucial, leaking personal details of individual influencers would have crossed ethical lines.

C. Avoiding Bias & Confirmation Bias

📌 **The Problem:**

- OSINT analysts may subconsciously look for evidence that confirms their beliefs while ignoring contradictory data.
- Political or ideological bias can affect which stories analysts choose to investigate and how they present findings.

📌 **How to Stay Objective:**

✔ Use structured analytic techniques (e.g., Analysis of Competing Hypotheses) to test different explanations.

✔ Seek peer review—having other analysts challenge findings helps remove bias.

✔ Consider alternative explanations before drawing conclusions.

💡 **Example**: An OSINT team investigating election fraud allegations must analyze data from all sides, not just one political party, to ensure unbiased reporting.

D. Protecting Sources & Sensitive Information

📌 **Risks in Media Investigations:**

- Whistleblowers and sources who provide OSINT analysts with sensitive information can face retaliation.
- Revealing too much investigative detail can allow disinformation actors to adapt and avoid detection.

📌 **Best Practices:**

✔ Use secure communication channels (e.g., Signal, ProtonMail) when working with sources.

✔ Anonymize or obfuscate certain details to protect whistleblowers.

✔ Disclose only necessary information to support conclusions while minimizing risk.

💡 **Example**: In an investigation into Chinese state-sponsored disinformation, OSINT researchers redacted sensitive information to avoid exposing sources within China.

E. Considering the Consequences of OSINT Findings

📌 **Potential Risks:**

- **Public backlash or political consequences** – OSINT findings that expose government involvement in disinformation can lead to diplomatic crises.
- **Legal implications** – Analysts must avoid violating privacy laws or defamation regulations.
- **Misinformation feedback loops** – Incorrect findings can fuel conspiracy theories if misinterpreted.

📌 **Mitigation Strategies:**

✓ Clearly define the limits of OSINT findings—what is fact vs. speculation.

✓ Include context and disclaimers when findings are not 100% verified.

✓ Work with fact-checkers and legal experts before publishing high-risk investigations.

💡 **Example:**

An OSINT analyst investigating a viral video of a supposed military attack must ensure their findings don't escalate tensions by wrongly attributing blame.

3. The Future of OSINT in Media Investigations

As technology evolves, OSINT analysts will play an even bigger role in countering disinformation and verifying media content. However, AI-generated fake news, deepfakes, and synthetic media will make the job more challenging.

A. The Growing Need for OSINT Collaboration

✓ Journalists, fact-checkers, and OSINT analysts must work together to combat disinformation.

✓ Cross-industry partnerships (tech companies, governments, NGOs) can improve fact-checking efforts.

B. Training the Next Generation of Ethical OSINT Analysts

✓ OSINT must be taught with a focus on critical thinking, ethics, and responsible information use.

✓ Organizations should create ethical guidelines for OSINT in media investigations.

4. Conclusion: The Weight of Responsibility

Being an OSINT analyst in media investigations is not just about exposing falsehoods—it's about ensuring truth is presented responsibly. The ability to influence public discourse means OSINT analysts must be accurate, ethical, and aware of the consequences of their findings.

- Strive for accuracy & verification.
- Maintain ethical integrity & avoid bias.
- Protect sources & consider legal implications.
- Think about the long-term impact of your investigations.

💡 **Final Thought**: In the battle against disinformation, OSINT analysts must be as responsible with the truth as they are relentless in uncovering it.

11.6 Case Study: Ethical Challenges in a High-Stakes Disinformation Probe

In early 2022, an OSINT team uncovered a large-scale disinformation campaign spreading false narratives about a political crisis in Eastern Europe. The operation involved bot networks, manipulated videos, and fabricated news articles, designed to influence international perception. As the OSINT analysts dug deeper, they faced several ethical dilemmas:

- Should they expose the identities of those behind the campaign, potentially putting lives at risk?

- What if their findings unintentionally aided one political side over another?
- How could they ensure their investigation didn't itself become a tool for further disinformation?

This case study explores the ethical challenges faced in high-stakes OSINT investigations, the tough decisions analysts had to make, and the lessons learned about responsibility in digital intelligence.

1. The Discovery: Uncovering a Disinformation Network

In February 2022, OSINT analysts monitoring social media trends and foreign influence operations detected a coordinated fake news campaign about military actions in a conflict zone. The campaign involved:

✓ Doctored satellite images showing supposed troop movements that never happened.

✓ AI-generated "eyewitness" accounts spreading false battlefield reports.

✓ A surge in bot activity amplifying the fake narratives on Twitter and Telegram.

✓ Fabricated government statements attributed to officials who had never made them.

At first, the OSINT team thought they were dealing with random misinformation, but after deeper investigation, they traced the source to a sophisticated influence operation linked to a state-sponsored group.

2. Ethical Dilemma #1: To Reveal or Not to Reveal Identities?

Through OSINT techniques like reverse image searching, linguistic analysis, and metadata tracking, the team identified key individuals running the campaign. However, publishing their names raised serious ethical concerns:

Arguments for Exposure:

✓ **Accountability** – Holding disinformation actors accountable could deter future campaigns.

✓ **Public Interest** – The public deserved to know who was manipulating them.

✓ **Transparency** – Naming the perpetrators could pressure social media platforms to act.

Arguments Against Exposure:

✕ **Risk of Retaliation** – The identified individuals could be targets of physical or digital harm.

✕ **Legal & Privacy Concerns** – Accusations could lead to defamation lawsuits if the evidence was not airtight.

✕ **Possible Misidentification** – Even small errors in OSINT analysis could wrongly implicate innocent people.

Decision & Outcome:

After consulting legal experts and digital rights groups, the OSINT team chose not to publicly name the individuals but instead provided the evidence to international fact-checking organizations and cybersecurity researchers for further action.

💡 **Lesson**: Sometimes the responsible choice is to withhold certain information, even if exposure seems justified.

3. Ethical Dilemma #2: Avoiding Political Bias

The disinformation campaign was designed to favor one political faction over another in the conflict. The OSINT team worried that publishing their findings could:

◆ Be perceived as taking sides, damaging their credibility.

◆ Be weaponized by media or political groups to serve their own agendas.

◆ Influence real-world diplomatic relations between nations.

How the Team Maintained Objectivity:

✓ Focused only on verifiable digital evidence (not speculation or political opinions).

✓ Used neutral language in their reports to avoid emotive or politically charged terms.

✓ Sought independent verification from other OSINT analysts before publishing.

✓ Released findings simultaneously to multiple media outlets to prevent selective reporting.

💡 **Lesson**: Disinformation investigations must be driven by facts, not political agendas.

4. Ethical Dilemma #3: The Risk of Amplifying Disinformation

By exposing the fake news operation, the OSINT team risked unintentionally amplifying the false narratives. Sometimes, debunking a fake claim can:

- Bring more attention to the lie than it originally had.
- Cause people to repeat or believe the disinformation even more due to the "backfire effect."
- Give disinformation actors a chance to refine their tactics based on what was exposed.

Strategies to Minimize Harm:

✓ Focused on explaining tactics rather than repeating false claims.

✓ Used content moderation techniques—reporting findings directly to platforms instead of making them viral.

✓ Provided contextual framing—clearly distinguishing between falsehoods and verified facts.

💡 **Lesson**: Fighting disinformation requires careful messaging—exposing the truth without spreading the lie further.

5. Ethical Dilemma #4: Engaging with Fake News Sources

To gain deeper insights into the disinformation campaign, the OSINT analysts infiltrated private social media groups and forums where the false narratives were being coordinated. However, this raised an ethical concern:

- Should OSINT analysts pretend to be supporters of the disinformation campaign to gather intelligence?
- Is it ethical to mislead or deceive bad actors for investigative purposes?

Decision & Outcome:

✓ The team used passive monitoring instead of engaging directly.

✓ They avoided creating fake identities or engaging in deception, which could compromise their ethical standing.

✓ Instead, they relied on pattern analysis, network mapping, and digital forensics to track activities.

🔆 **Lesson**: OSINT investigators must balance effectiveness with ethical integrity.

6. The Aftermath & Broader Impact

After weeks of investigation, the OSINT team compiled their findings into a comprehensive report that was shared with:

- Journalists & fact-checking organizations to raise awareness.
- Social media platforms to help remove disinformation actors.
- Cybersecurity agencies to strengthen defenses against future campaigns.

✓ Major social media platforms removed thousands of fake accounts.

✓ International media used the findings to debunk major falsehoods.

✓ Government agencies took action against state-sponsored influence operations.

However, the investigation also drew negative consequences:

✗ Some disinformation actors doxxed the OSINT analysts, attempting to intimidate them.

✗ Critics accused the investigation of being biased, despite its neutral approach.

✗ The campaign did not fully disappear—it simply evolved into more sophisticated tactics.

Conclusion: The Weight of Ethical Responsibility

This case study highlights how OSINT investigations into disinformation require constant ethical decision-making. OSINT analysts must navigate privacy concerns, political neutrality, risk mitigation, and responsible reporting—all while ensuring that their findings do not do more harm than good.

Key Takeaways for OSINT Analysts:

✓ **Verify rigorously** – A small mistake can have massive consequences.

✅ **Think before exposing identities** – Weigh the risks of naming individuals.

✅ **Remain neutral** – Avoid giving the impression of political bias.

✅ **Minimize amplification of falsehoods** – Frame findings carefully.

✅ **Protect yourself** – Disinformation actors often retaliate against investigators.

💡 **Final Thought**: Ethical OSINT analysis is not just about finding the truth—it's about ensuring that truth is revealed responsibly.

12. The Future of OSINT in Media Verification

As the digital landscape continues to evolve, so too does the role of OSINT in media verification. In this chapter, we explore the future of open-source intelligence in combating disinformation, focusing on emerging technologies, trends, and methodologies that will shape the way we verify information. From AI-powered tools for detecting deepfakes to advanced algorithms for tracking disinformation across multiple platforms, we examine the innovations that are enhancing the accuracy and speed of OSINT investigations. We also discuss the increasing importance of collaboration between analysts, journalists, and tech companies in the fight for truth. By understanding these future developments, readers will be equipped to stay ahead of evolving threats and continue to ensure the integrity of information in the digital age.

12.1 Emerging AI & Machine Learning Tools for Fake News Detection

As disinformation campaigns grow more sophisticated, so do the tools used to detect them. Artificial Intelligence (AI) and Machine Learning (ML) have become critical in identifying fake news, deepfakes, and coordinated influence campaigns. These technologies can process massive amounts of data, detect patterns invisible to the human eye, and provide real-time analysis of suspicious content.

This section explores the latest AI-driven tools, how they work, their limitations, and their future role in combating digital deception.

1. How AI & Machine Learning Help Detect Fake News

AI-driven fake news detection operates in three main ways:

1️⃣ **Text Analysis** – AI analyzes language patterns, sentiment, and writing styles to identify misleading or machine-generated content.
2️⃣ **Image & Video Forensics** – ML algorithms detect manipulated media, including deepfakes and altered images.
3️⃣ **Network Analysis** – AI maps coordinated disinformation campaigns, tracking fake accounts and bot activity.

These methods allow AI systems to identify falsehoods faster and more efficiently than traditional fact-checking.

2. AI-Powered Fake News Detection Tools

Several AI-based tools have emerged to fight disinformation. Some of the most notable include:

◆ Google's BERT & T5 (Language Processing Models)

- Can detect misleading information in text-based content.
- Identifies inconsistencies, contradictions, and sentiment shifts in articles.
- Used in Google's fact-checking efforts to flag unreliable sources.

◆ Meta's AI Disinformation Detection System

- Detects coordinated inauthentic behavior across Facebook and Instagram.
- Uses pattern recognition to track bot networks and fake engagement.
- Can flag deepfake videos and manipulated images.

◆ Microsoft's Video Authenticator

- Analyzes subtle facial distortions, lighting inconsistencies, and unnatural blinks to detect deepfakes.
- Assigns a confidence score to videos to indicate potential manipulation.

◆ Twitter's (Now X) Birdwatch & AI Content Moderation

- Uses community-driven AI to verify misleading claims.
- Detects fake trends and bot-generated tweets.
- Works with fact-checking organizations to label false content.

◆ Fake News Detection APIs (Like Factual.ai & ClaimBuster)

- Scans articles and posts in real-time, assigning credibility scores.
- Flags sensationalist language, false claims, and biased reporting.
- Integrates with news outlets and fact-checking sites.

These tools enhance the capabilities of OSINT analysts by providing automated detection, allowing investigators to focus on verification and contextual analysis.

3. How AI Detects Fake Text-Based Content

AI models analyze linguistic features, credibility signals, and semantic inconsistencies in news articles, tweets, and blog posts.

✓ **Natural Language Processing (NLP)** – Detects repetitive phrasing, unnatural sentence structures, and biased wording.

✓ **Machine Learning Classification** – Compares articles to known disinformation databases to find similarities.

✓ **Sentiment Analysis** – Flags content that uses emotionally charged, manipulative language often found in fake news.

✓ **Source Validation** – Cross-checks sources against fact-checking databases to identify unverified claims.

For example, GPT-4-powered models can now detect AI-generated propaganda articles by analyzing linguistic fingerprints left by synthetic text.

4. Detecting Deepfakes & Synthetic Media with AI

Deepfake detection requires specialized AI-driven forensic tools that analyze:

✓ **Facial & Motion Inconsistencies** – AI detects unnatural eye movements, blinking patterns, and facial distortions.

✓ **Audio & Lip Syncing Errors** – AI compares voice patterns and lip movements for mismatches.

✓ **Metadata & Pixel-Level Analysis** – AI tools like Forensic.ai scan for compression artifacts, inconsistent shadows, and cloned pixels.

◆ **Example**: Researchers at MIT developed an AI that detects deepfake videos with 96% accuracy by analyzing microexpressions—tiny facial movements that AI struggles to replicate.

5. AI for Identifying Coordinated Disinformation Networks

AI can also track fake accounts and bot-driven disinformation campaigns by analyzing:

✓ **Posting Patterns** – AI detects accounts that post at unnatural frequencies, indicating automation.

✓ **Hashtag Manipulation** – Tracks how fake news spreads using coordinated hashtags.

✓ **Account Behavior Clustering** – Identifies groups of fake accounts interacting with each other to amplify false narratives.

◆ **Example**: Twitter's AI once removed 200,000 accounts linked to a state-backed disinformation operation using network analysis.

6. Limitations & Challenges of AI in Fake News Detection

Despite its advancements, AI is not perfect in identifying fake news.

✗ **False Positives & Negatives** – AI can flag real news as fake or fail to detect subtle disinformation.
✗ **Adversarial Attacks** – Disinformation actors train AI to bypass detection by tweaking language and formatting.
✗ **Bias in AI Training Data** – AI models reflect the biases of the datasets they are trained on, which can affect neutrality.
✗ **Lack of Context Understanding** – AI struggles with sarcasm, satire, and evolving political narratives.

◆ **Example**: AI models trained on Western news sources may misinterpret regional dialects, humor, or cultural references in non-English content.

✓ **Solution**: AI should be used alongside human analysts for verification.

7. The Future of AI in Fake News Detection

The next generation of AI-driven fake news detection will focus on:

🚀 **Explainable AI (XAI)** – AI models that explain their reasoning, making decisions more transparent.
🚀 **Multimodal AI** – AI that combines text, video, and audio analysis for better verification.
🚀 **Blockchain for Content Authentication** – Using blockchain to verify media authenticity at the moment of creation.

🛠 **Decentralized AI Fact-Checking** – Open-source AI tools that crowdsource disinformation detection.

💡 The ultimate goal: AI should become a trusted partner for OSINT analysts, fact-checkers, and journalists—not a replacement, but a powerful tool for digital truth verification.

Conclusion: AI as a Double-Edged Sword

While AI is revolutionizing fake news detection, it also presents new ethical and technological challenges. The arms race between AI-driven disinformation and AI-based detection will continue to evolve, requiring constant innovation.

Key Takeaways:

✓ AI is transforming fact-checking with automated text analysis, deepfake forensics, and bot detection.

✓ Tools like Google's BERT, Microsoft's Video Authenticator, and AI-powered fact-checkers are improving accuracy.

✓ AI has limitations—human oversight is still crucial for context, bias detection, and verification.

✓ The future lies in multimodal AI, blockchain verification, and decentralized fact-checking.

💡 **Final Thought**: The fight against fake news is no longer just about human intuition—it's about leveraging AI responsibly to uncover the truth in a digital world filled with deception.

12.2 The Role of Blockchain & Cryptographic Proof in Media Verification

In an era where fake news, deepfakes, and manipulated media spread rapidly, traditional verification methods are struggling to keep up. Blockchain technology and cryptographic proof offer a new way to securely authenticate digital content by ensuring its integrity, source, and time of creation.

By leveraging decentralized ledgers, cryptographic hashing, and digital signatures, blockchain provides a tamper-proof record of media history, making it a powerful tool for OSINT analysts, journalists, and fact-checkers.

This section explores how blockchain enhances media verification, its practical applications, and the challenges it faces.

1. How Blockchain Secures Digital Content

Blockchain is a distributed, immutable ledger that records transactions across a network of computers. Once data is added, it cannot be altered or deleted without consensus, making it ideal for proving the authenticity of digital content.

Here's how it applies to media verification:

✓ **Timestamping & Provenance Tracking** – Media files are hashed and stored on a blockchain, creating an immutable proof of when and where they were created.

✓ **Tamper Detection** – If an image, video, or document is altered, its hash changes, making manipulation detectable.

✓ **Decentralized Authentication** – Unlike centralized verification systems, blockchain is resistant to censorship and manipulation.

✓ **Smart Contracts for Verification** – Self-executing smart contracts can automatically verify content authenticity using predefined conditions.

◆ **Example**: A news agency uploads a video to a blockchain-based verification system. If anyone tries to alter the footage, its cryptographic fingerprint no longer matches, exposing the modification.

2. Cryptographic Proof: Ensuring Integrity & Authenticity

Cryptographic proof strengthens blockchain-based verification by ensuring data integrity and authenticity through:

◆ **Cryptographic Hashing**

A hash function converts digital content into a unique string of characters. Even a small change completely alters the hash, revealing tampering.

✓ **Example**: A video is hashed and stored on a blockchain. If altered, even by a single pixel, the new hash will not match the original, signaling manipulation.

◆ **Digital Signatures & Public Key Infrastructure (PKI)**

✓ Content creators can use private keys to digitally sign their work, proving authorship.

✓ Viewers can verify authenticity using the creator's public key.

✓ This ensures only verified sources can publish authenticated content.

◆ **Example**: A journalist uploads a verified photo to a blockchain with a digital signature. Anyone can verify its authenticity using the journalist's public key.

◆ **Zero-Knowledge Proofs (ZKPs) for Privacy-Preserving Verification**

✓ ZKPs allow verification without revealing sensitive details (e.g., the identity of a whistleblower).

✓ Useful for protecting investigative journalists, activists, and OSINT analysts.

◆ **Example**: A whistleblower submits a document proving corruption. Using ZKPs, they verify its authenticity without revealing personal details.

3. Real-World Applications of Blockchain in Media Verification

Several projects are already leveraging blockchain and cryptographic proof for fact-checking and media authentication:

◆ **Truepic (Blockchain for Photo & Video Verification)**

- Uses cryptographic hashing and secure metadata storage to ensure media authenticity.
- Records time, location, and device information on the blockchain.
- Prevents deepfake and manipulated content from spreading.

◆ **The New York Times' "The News Provenance Project"**

- Explores how blockchain can track media origins and prevent misattribution of content.
- Stores metadata, edits, and publication history on an immutable ledger.

◆ **Starling Lab (Blockchain for Human Rights & OSINT)**

- Uses cryptographic proof and decentralized storage to document war crimes and human rights violations.
- Ensures footage remains unaltered and admissible in court.

◆ **Adobe Content Authenticity Initiative (CAI)**

- Partners with Microsoft and Twitter to use blockchain for tracking content edits and proving media authenticity.
- Embeds cryptographic proof into images and videos at the moment of creation.

These projects highlight how blockchain restores trust in digital content and enhances OSINT investigations.

4. How OSINT Analysts Can Use Blockchain for Verification

OSINT professionals can integrate blockchain-based tools into their investigations to:

✓ **Verify Source Authenticity** – Check whether an image or video matches its blockchain-stored hash.

✓ **Analyze Digital Signatures** – Confirm if content was signed by a legitimate journalist, agency, or whistleblower.

✓ **Detect Tampering** – Compare hashes to identify manipulated content.

✓ **Track Information Flow** – Use blockchain to map the spread of misinformation and its origin.

◆ **Example**: During an election, an OSINT analyst verifies a viral video's timestamp and metadata using blockchain, exposing it as manipulated footage from a different year.

5. Challenges & Limitations of Blockchain-Based Verification

Despite its potential, blockchain faces several challenges in media verification:

✗ **Scalability Issues** – Storing large media files on the blockchain is expensive and slow.
✓ **Solution**: Use off-chain storage (IPFS, Arweave) with blockchain-stored hashes for verification.

✗ **Adoption Barriers** – Journalists, fact-checkers, and social media platforms must integrate blockchain verification systems.
✓ **Solution**: Collaboration with tech companies, governments, and media organizations.

✗ **Potential for Misinformation on Blockchain** – If false content is uploaded with a cryptographic signature, it gains false legitimacy.
✓ **Solution**: Implement reputation systems and verification processes for trusted sources.

◆ **Example**: A deepfake creator uploads synthetic content with a digital signature, misleading users. A trusted verification protocol is needed to prevent abuse.

6. The Future of Blockchain & Cryptographic Proof in OSINT

The next wave of blockchain-based media verification will focus on:

🖋 **Decentralized Fact-Checking Networks** – Using blockchain to crowdsource media verification across independent analysts.
🖋 **AI & Blockchain Integration** – AI verifies content while blockchain stores unalterable proof of authenticity.
🖋 **NFT-Based Media Provenance** – News agencies may mint verified content as NFTs, ensuring permanent ownership and authenticity records.
🖋 **Blockchain for Legal & Investigative Use** – Courts may accept blockchain-stored digital evidence for cases involving disinformation, cybercrime, and OSINT investigations.

💡 **The ultimate goal**: To create a trusted, decentralized, and tamper-proof ecosystem for digital media verification.

Conclusion: Blockchain as the Future of Truth Verification

Blockchain and cryptographic proof offer a groundbreaking way to combat misinformation by ensuring content integrity, authenticity, and traceability.

Key Takeaways:

✔ Blockchain creates an immutable record of media authenticity, preventing manipulation.

✔ Cryptographic proof (hashing, digital signatures, ZKPs) ensures data integrity & privacy.

✔ Real-world projects (Truepic, CAI, NYT) are already using blockchain for fact-checking.

✔ OSINT analysts can track misinformation origins and verify digital evidence using blockchain.

✔ Challenges remain, but the future of media verification is decentralized, transparent, and cryptographically secured.

💡 **Final Thought**: As digital deception grows more advanced, blockchain and cryptographic proof may become the gold standard for media verification, restoring trust in the age of misinformation.

12.3 How Disinformation Tactics Are Evolving

Disinformation is not a static phenomenon—it evolves alongside technological advancements, social media trends, and global events. While traditional tactics like propaganda and media manipulation remain relevant, new methods are constantly emerging, driven by advancements in artificial intelligence, automation, and psychological warfare.

This section explores how disinformation tactics are evolving, the role of AI and deepfakes, the increasing sophistication of social media influence campaigns, and what OSINT analysts need to watch for in the future.

1. The Shift from Manual to Automated Disinformation

In the past, disinformation campaigns relied heavily on human propagandists, fake news websites, and traditional media outlets. Today, they are increasingly automated, using AI-driven chatbots, content generators, and algorithmic manipulation to spread false narratives at an unprecedented scale.

◆ AI-Generated Fake Content

✔ AI models like ChatGPT and Llama can generate convincing fake news articles, fabricated social media posts, and biased narratives at scale.

✔ Synthetic media tools can create deepfake videos and AI-generated voices, making it harder to distinguish real from fake.

✦ **Example**: A fake news website uses an AI to generate thousands of fabricated articles per day, each slightly modified to bypass fact-checking algorithms.

◆ Deepfake Propaganda & AI-Generated Personas

✔ AI can create hyper-realistic deepfakes, making it possible to fabricate videos of politicians, celebrities, or journalists saying things they never said.

✔ AI-generated personas can masquerade as real activists, journalists, or influencers, giving credibility to fake narratives.

✦ **Example**: A deepfake video of a world leader announcing a fake policy is released before an election, misleading voters.

2. The Rise of Hyper-Personalized Disinformation

Social media platforms use sophisticated algorithms to personalize content, creating echo chambers and reinforcing users' existing biases. Disinformation actors now exploit this to micro-target individuals and manipulate public opinion more effectively.

◆ Algorithmic Manipulation

✔ Disinformation campaigns hijack recommendation algorithms to spread content that reinforces specific narratives.

✔ Bots and trolls engage with posts to boost visibility, tricking algorithms into promoting disinformation as "popular content."

◆ **Example**: A coordinated disinformation campaign spams engagement on misleading health-related posts, making them trend on social media.

◆ AI-Driven Behavioral Manipulation

✓ AI analyzes user data to craft highly persuasive content, tailored to exploit an individual's emotions, fears, or biases.

✓ This leads to precision-targeted disinformation campaigns, where users receive different false narratives based on their online behavior.

◆ **Example**: A voter in the U.S. is targeted with disinformation tailored to their political views, while another in Europe receives a completely different but equally manipulative message.

3. Weaponizing Virality: How Disinformation is Engineered to Spread

Disinformation campaigns are now designed for maximum virality, leveraging memes, manipulated hashtags, and viral challenges to amplify reach.

◆ Meme Warfare & Viral Trends

✓ Disinformation actors use memes and short-form content to simplify complex issues into emotionally charged messages.

✓ Viral challenges and hoaxes are deployed to create artificial controversies that capture media attention.

◆ **Example**: A fake news meme about a political scandal spreads rapidly because it is funny, shocking, and easy to share, despite being false.

◆ Hijacking Trending Topics & Social Movements

✓ Disinformation agents exploit real social issues by inserting false narratives into trending discussions.

✓ Hashtags are manipulated to create artificial popularity for false claims.

◈ **Example**: A fake grassroots movement is engineered by bots spamming a manipulated hashtag, tricking real users into amplifying it.

4. Disinformation in the Age of Generative AI

AI is making it easier, cheaper, and faster to create disinformation at scale. Key developments include:

◆ AI-Generated Fake News & Synthetic Media

✔ AI tools can write realistic but false news articles, opinion pieces, and social media comments with little effort.

✔ Fake news websites can be automated, publishing thousands of articles per day to flood information spaces.

◈ **Example**: A fully AI-generated news website creates false geopolitical stories, influencing international tensions.

◆ AI-Generated Deepfake Audio & Video

✔ Fake news anchors, political leaders, and celebrities can be fabricated using deepfake technology.

✔ Real footage can be edited to distort meaning, making fabricated statements appear legitimate.

◈ **Example**: A deepfake video of a world leader declaring war causes panic before it is debunked.

◆ AI-Powered Chatbots for Disinformation

✔ AI-powered bots can converse with real users, reinforcing false narratives in comment sections, forums, and social media.

✓ These bots are increasingly difficult to detect, mimicking real human behavior and engagement patterns.

◆ **Example**: An AI-driven chatbot army floods social media, pushing anti-vaccine propaganda by engaging in realistic debates.

5. The Future of Disinformation Warfare: What's Next?

The next generation of disinformation tactics will become even more sophisticated, exploiting emerging technologies and new vulnerabilities. Here's what to expect:

◆ **Synthetic Influencers & AI-Powered Personas**

✓ AI will generate entire fake influencers with realistic faces, voices, and opinions to spread disinformation.
✓ These influencers will gain followers, build trust, and slowly introduce false narratives.

◆ **Example**: A fake AI-generated political analyst gains credibility over time before spreading manipulated election narratives.

◆ **Deepfake-as-a-Service (DFaaS)**

✓ Criminal groups and state actors will offer deepfake technology as a service, making disinformation campaigns accessible to anyone.
✓ This will make fake news campaigns more affordable and scalable.

◆ **Example**: A political candidate hires a DFaaS provider to create deepfake videos smearing their opponent.

◆ **AI-Powered Disinformation Ecosystems**

✓ Future campaigns will combine deepfake video, AI-written articles, and synthetic voices into fully automated propaganda machines.

✓ AI will monitor user engagement and optimize content in real-time for maximum psychological impact.

◆ **Example**: A state-backed AI system analyzes social media in real time and automatically adjusts disinformation narratives to counter fact-checking efforts.

6. How OSINT Analysts Can Combat Evolving Disinformation

To counter these new threats, OSINT professionals must adapt their investigative techniques and leverage advanced tools:

✓ **AI-Powered Verification Tools** – Use AI for deepfake detection, synthetic media analysis, and metadata verification.

✓ **Blockchain for Content Provenance** – Track media authenticity using blockchain-stored cryptographic proof.

✓ **Reverse Image & Video Search** – Continuously verify visual content using forensic analysis tools.

✓ **Behavioral Analysis of Bots & AI Personas** – Identify automated disinformation networks through pattern recognition.

◆ **Example**: An OSINT analyst detects a fake AI-generated journalist account by analyzing linguistic patterns and metadata inconsistencies.

Conclusion: The Never-Ending Battle Against Disinformation

Disinformation tactics are evolving at an alarming rate, driven by AI, automation, and psychological targeting. The fight against fake news, deepfakes, and propaganda will require continuous adaptation, better tools, and international cooperation.

Key Takeaways:

✓ Disinformation is becoming AI-driven, hyper-personalized, and automated.

✓ Fake news is evolving into synthetic media, deepfake influencers, and AI-powered propaganda.

✓ OSINT analysts must stay ahead of emerging tactics, using AI verification, blockchain, and behavioral analysis.

✓ The war on disinformation is ongoing and ever-changing, requiring constant vigilance and innovation.

💡 **Final Thought**: In the battle against digital deception, knowledge, technology, and transparency will be our greatest weapons.

12.4 The Battle Against Synthetic Media & AI-Generated Fakes

The rise of synthetic media and AI-generated content has transformed the landscape of digital disinformation. From deepfake videos to AI-written articles and synthetic voices, fake content is becoming more realistic, more accessible, and harder to detect. This rapid evolution has made it easier than ever for bad actors—state-sponsored groups, propagandists, cybercriminals, and conspiracy theorists—to fabricate and spread false information at scale.

As AI-generated disinformation becomes more sophisticated, OSINT analysts, fact-checkers, and digital forensics experts must develop new tools and strategies to detect and counter these threats. This chapter explores the growing challenge of synthetic media, real-world examples of AI-generated fakes, detection methods, and the ongoing battle to protect digital truth.

1. What is Synthetic Media?

◆ **Definition & Types of AI-Generated Fakes**

Synthetic media refers to content created or altered using artificial intelligence, including:

✓ **Deepfake Videos**: AI-generated videos where a person's face is swapped or their voice is cloned to fabricate statements or actions.

✓ **AI-Generated Text:** Automated news articles, blog posts, or social media comments written by AI, often designed to manipulate public opinion.

✔ **Synthetic Voices (Voice Cloning):** AI models that can replicate a person's voice, making it possible to generate realistic fake phone calls or speeches.

✔ **AI-Generated Images:** Fake profile pictures, altered satellite images, or fabricated news photos that are difficult to distinguish from real ones.

◆ **Example:** A deepfake video of a political leader falsely announcing war could trigger panic, market instability, or even diplomatic crises before it is debunked.

2. How AI-Generated Fakes Are Used in Disinformation Campaigns

◆ Political Manipulation & Election Interference

✔ Deepfake videos of politicians spreading false statements before elections.

✔ Fake AI-generated "news" articles amplifying misinformation about candidates.

✔ Synthetic social media accounts pushing divisive narratives to manipulate voters.

◆ **Example:** A deepfake video of a presidential candidate "admitting" to election fraud spreads on social media just days before voting, causing mass confusion.

◆ Fake News & Media Deception

✔ AI-written fake news stories designed to look credible.

✔ Fake "expert opinions" created with AI-generated personas.

✔ Deepfake news anchors delivering false information.

◆ **Example:** A state-backed propaganda network uses an AI-generated journalist persona to spread fabricated geopolitical reports.

◆ Fraud & Cybercrime

✔ Voice cloning used for CEO fraud (impersonating executives to authorize wire transfers).

✔ Deepfake videos used for blackmail and extortion.

✓ AI-generated images and documents used to create fake identities for scams.

◆ **Example**: Cybercriminals use AI to clone a CEO's voice and trick an employee into transferring millions of dollars to a fraudulent account.

3. Tools & Techniques for Detecting AI-Generated Fakes

As synthetic media becomes more realistic, OSINT analysts must use advanced techniques to verify the authenticity of digital content.

◆ **Deepfake Detection Tools**

✓ **Deepware Scanner & Deepfake-o-meter** – AI-powered tools that analyze facial inconsistencies and detect manipulated videos.

✓ **Microsoft Video Authenticator** – Detects subtle deepfake artifacts like mismatched lip-sync and irregular lighting.

✓ **Reality Defender** – A real-time deepfake detection tool used by journalists and fact-checkers.

◆ **Example**: OSINT analysts use Deepware Scanner to detect that a viral video of a celebrity making offensive remarks was AI-generated.

◆ **Reverse Image & Video Search**

✓ **Google Reverse Image Search & TinEye** – Identifies whether an image has been altered or fabricated.

✓ **InVID & Forensically** – Tools for analyzing video metadata and image manipulation traces.

✓ **PhotoDNA** – Helps detect AI-generated fake profile pictures and manipulated visuals.

◆ **Example**: Investigators use InVID to verify that a "live war footage" video was actually from a 2014 video game, not real-world combat.

◆ **Voice Cloning & Synthetic Audio Detection**

✓ **Resemble AI & Sonantic** – Tools used to detect voice cloning and synthesized speech patterns.

✓ **Adobe Project VoCo Detector** – Helps identify synthetically altered voices.

⬥ **Example**: Fact-checkers use Resemble AI to confirm that an audio recording of a government official "ordering election fraud" was AI-generated.

◆ **AI-Written Content Detection**

✓ **GPTZero & AI Text Classifier** – Detect AI-generated text in news articles, blog posts, and social media.

✓ **GLTR (Giant Language Model Test Room)** – Analyzes statistical patterns in writing to spot AI-generated content.

⬥ **Example**: Journalists use GPTZero to uncover that an entire network of "independent news websites" was actually run by AI chatbots.

4. The Future of Synthetic Media & AI-Generated Fakes

◆ **What's Next in Disinformation Warfare?**

✓ **Deepfake-as-a-Service (DFaaS)** – Companies offering deepfake generation tools for hire.

✓ **Fully AI-Generated Fake Influencers** – Synthetic personalities with thousands of followers spreading propaganda.

✓ **AI-Created Fake Podcasts & News Shows** – AI hosts generating automated but convincing media.

⬥ **Example**: A state-backed disinformation campaign creates a completely AI-generated journalist, complete with deepfake video interviews, podcasts, and news articles.

◆ **AI vs. AI: The Next Stage of Fact-Checking**

✓ AI-driven disinformation will be countered by AI-powered verification tools.

✓ Blockchain-based authentication will help verify real vs. fake content.

✓ Governments and tech companies will deploy automated disinformation tracking systems.

♦ **Example**: Future AI tools could analyze news in real-time, detecting synthetic media and flagging potential disinformation before it spreads.

5. Strategies for Combating AI-Generated Disinformation

✓ **Strengthening AI-Detection Algorithms** – Governments and researchers must develop more advanced AI-detection tools.

✓ **Promoting Digital Literacy** – Educating the public on how to spot deepfakes and AI-generated misinformation.

✓ **Implementing Content Authentication** – Using watermarking and blockchain verification to certify authentic media.

✓ **Regulating Deepfake Abuse** – Governments must enforce policies to prevent malicious deepfake usage.

♦ **Example**: The EU introduces a legal framework requiring social media platforms to detect and label deepfake content.

Conclusion: The Never-Ending Battle Against AI-Driven Disinformation

The rise of synthetic media presents one of the biggest challenges in modern information warfare. As AI-generated fakes become more sophisticated and widespread, the battle between disinformation actors and digital truth-seekers will only intensify.

Key Takeaways:

✓ AI-generated fakes are rapidly improving, making detection harder.

✓ Deepfake videos, synthetic voices, and AI-generated text are used in political, media, and cybercrime disinformation.

✓ OSINT analysts must leverage deepfake detection tools, metadata analysis, and AI-driven verification.

✔ Governments, tech companies, and fact-checkers must collaborate to regulate and counter synthetic media threats.

💡 **Final Thought**: The war on AI-driven disinformation will require a combination of technology, policy, and digital literacy to preserve truth in the digital age.

12.5 Strengthening Global Collaboration Against Disinformation

Disinformation is no longer a localized issue—it is a global threat with the power to manipulate public opinion, disrupt elections, incite violence, and undermine trust in institutions. As disinformation campaigns become more coordinated and sophisticated, countering them requires international collaboration among governments, technology companies, fact-checkers, journalists, and OSINT analysts.

No single country, organization, or platform can effectively combat disinformation alone. Strengthening global partnerships in intelligence sharing, policy-making, technology development, and public awareness is essential to staying ahead of state-sponsored propaganda, fake news networks, and AI-generated synthetic media.

This chapter explores the key players in the fight against disinformation, the challenges of international cooperation, successful case studies of collaboration, and strategies to strengthen global efforts in tackling this ever-evolving threat.

1. Key Players in Global Disinformation Efforts

◆ Governments & International Organizations

✔ **United Nations (UN):** Advocates for digital literacy, ethical AI use, and regulation of online misinformation.
✔ **European Union (EU):** Implements laws like the Digital Services Act (DSA) to regulate online platforms and fight fake news.
✔ **NATO's StratCom COE**: Monitors and counters state-backed disinformation campaigns in geopolitics.

✓ **Five Eyes Alliance (FVEY):** Intelligence-sharing network (U.S., U.K., Canada, Australia, New Zealand) that tracks global disinformation threats.

◆ **Example**: The EU vs. Disinfo project investigates and debunks pro-Kremlin disinformation narratives across Europe.

◆ **Social Media & Tech Companies**

✓ **Google, Meta (Facebook), Twitter/X, TikTok, YouTube**: Implement fact-checking partnerships and AI-powered fake news detection.

✓ **Microsoft & OpenAI**: Develop tools for detecting AI-generated content and deepfakes.

✓ **NewsGuard & FactCheck.org**: Monitor and rate the credibility of news sources to help users identify disinformation.

◆ **Example**: Twitter (X) and Meta partnered with fact-checkers during the 2022 elections to label misleading political content.

◆ **OSINT Analysts, Journalists & Fact-Checkers**

✓ **Bellingcat**: Investigates war crimes and exposes state-sponsored fake news.

✓ **The Atlantic Council's DFRLab**: Tracks disinformation trends and coordinated influence operations.

✓ **First Draft & Snopes**: Verify news stories and train journalists in fake news detection techniques.

◆ **Example**: OSINT investigators used geolocation analysis to debunk Russia's claims about Ukrainian military actions.

2. Challenges in Global Disinformation Cooperation

◆ **Differences in Regulations & Free Speech Laws**

✓ Countries have different definitions of "disinformation", making policy alignment difficult.

✓ Authoritarian regimes may weaponize "fake news" laws to suppress free speech, complicating global cooperation.

◆ **Example**: The U.S. prioritizes free speech, while the EU enforces stricter platform regulations, leading to policy conflicts.

◆ **Lack of Standardized Detection Methods**

✓ Fact-checking methods vary across regions, leading to inconsistent debunking of fake news.

✓ Limited data-sharing agreements prevent real-time international threat tracking.

◆ **Example**: A disinformation campaign spreads on WhatsApp in India, but global fact-checkers struggle to analyze it due to encrypted messages.

◆ **State-Sponsored Disinformation & Political Barriers**

✓ Governments that use disinformation as a tool are unlikely to cooperate in global counter-disinformation initiatives.

✓ Cyber warfare tactics make it hard to trace and attribute fake news operations to state actors.

◆ **Example**: Intelligence agencies struggle to publicly expose Russian or Chinese disinformation campaigns without escalating diplomatic tensions.

◆ **Misinformation Spread via Encrypted & Decentralized Platforms**

✓ WhatsApp, Telegram, Signal and decentralized social networks make fake news tracking harder due to encryption.

✓ Misinformation spreads faster in private groups, where fact-checkers have limited visibility.

◆ **Example**: During the COVID-19 pandemic, WhatsApp groups became hotspots for vaccine misinformation, making regulation difficult.

3. Case Studies: Successful Global Collaboration Against Disinformation

◆ EU & U.S. Joint Effort to Counter Russian Disinformation (2022)

✓ The EU's East StratCom Task Force worked with U.S. intelligence agencies to track and debunk pro-Russian propaganda during the Ukraine war.

✓ Tech companies were pressured to demonetize state-backed Russian media outlets like RT and Sputnik.

✓ OSINT analysts and journalists exposed fake war footage and deepfake videos of Ukrainian leaders surrendering.

◆ **Result**: Coordinated efforts weakened Russia's information warfare strategy, reducing its global reach.

◆ WHO's Global Fight Against COVID-19 Misinformation (2020-2021)

✓ The World Health Organization (WHO) partnered with Facebook, Twitter, and Google to flag and remove COVID-19 falsehoods.

✓ AI-driven monitoring tools helped detect viral anti-vaccine conspiracy theories.

✓ Fact-checking collaborations across countries helped counter misinformation in multiple languages.

◆ **Result**: Millions of false claims about COVID-19 treatments and vaccines were debunked before they reached wider audiences.

4. Strengthening Global Disinformation Defense Strategies

◆ Improving International Intelligence Sharing

✓ Enhance collaboration between governments, cybersecurity firms, and social media platforms.

✓ Develop cross-border data-sharing agreements for tracking coordinated fake news networks.

◆ **Example**: The Five Eyes alliance expands intelligence-sharing to track foreign influence operations in real-time.

◆ **Standardizing Fake News & Deepfake Detection Tools**

✓ Create global AI-powered fact-checking systems that verify viral content across multiple platforms.

✓ Implement watermarking and digital provenance to distinguish real vs. AI-generated content.

◆ **Example**: Tech companies adopt blockchain-based verification for news footage, preventing fake war videos from going viral.

◆ **Regulating Social Media & Encrypted Messaging Apps**

✓ Push for mandatory transparency reports on disinformation takedowns.

✓ Enforce penalties for platforms that allow unmoderated fake news to spread.

◆ **Example**: The EU's Digital Services Act forces tech giants to label and remove disinformation at scale.

◆ **Expanding Media Literacy & Public Awareness Campaigns**

✓ Governments, educators, and journalists must train citizens in fact-checking skills.

✓ Schools should teach digital literacy to counter youth exposure to disinformation.

◆ **Example**: Finland's national media literacy program has made it one of the most resilient countries against fake news.

Conclusion: A Global Fight for Digital Truth

Disinformation is a borderless challenge that requires borderless solutions. Strengthening international cooperation between governments, tech platforms, OSINT analysts, and civil society is crucial in the fight against fake news, deepfakes, and synthetic media threats.

Key Takeaways:

✓ No single entity can combat disinformation alone—collaboration is essential.

✓ Governments, tech companies, and fact-checkers must standardize detection tools.

✓ State-backed disinformation campaigns pose major challenges to global cooperation.

✓ Education and media literacy remain the strongest defense against misinformation.

💡 **Final Thought**: The future of disinformation warfare will be shaped by how effectively the world collaborates to expose, debunk, and neutralize digital deception before it undermines democracy, public trust, and global stability.

12.6 Preparing for the Future: Skills & Tools for the Next Generation of OSINT Investigators

As disinformation tactics evolve, so must the skill set of Open-Source Intelligence (OSINT) investigators. The rise of AI-generated content, deepfakes, synthetic media, and bot-driven influence campaigns presents new challenges that demand advanced technical expertise, critical thinking, and adaptability.

Future OSINT investigators will need to master emerging tools, refine analytical techniques, and navigate ethical dilemmas in an increasingly complex information environment. This chapter explores the core skills, essential tools, and future trends shaping the next generation of disinformation investigators.

1. Essential Skills for Future OSINT Analysts

◆ **Advanced Digital Forensics & Data Analysis**

✓ Understanding metadata, hash values, and forensic footprints in digital media.

✓ Using AI-assisted analytics to detect manipulated images, videos, and documents.

✓ Mastering network analysis to track botnets and coordinated disinformation campaigns.

◈ **Example**: Future analysts will need to reverse-engineer AI-generated deepfakes by identifying pixel inconsistencies, shadow mismatches, and unnatural facial movements.

◆ AI & Machine Learning for Disinformation Detection

✓ Training AI models to recognize pattern anomalies in fake news content.

✓ Leveraging automated language models to analyze misinformation trends at scale.

✓ Developing custom AI classifiers for detecting synthetic propaganda and AI-generated disinformation.

◈ **Example**: OSINT investigators will rely on neural networks to detect text patterns that mimic GPT-generated disinformation narratives.

◆ Blockchain & Cryptographic Verification Techniques

✓ Understanding blockchain-based provenance tracking for verifying digital content.

✓ Using cryptographic watermarking to authenticate news footage and social media posts.

✓ Applying hash verification techniques to confirm unaltered document integrity.

◈ **Example**: Investigators will trace news videos to their original source using blockchain-ledger timestamps, ensuring authenticity.

◆ Advanced Social Media Intelligence (SOCMINT)

✓ Mapping fake engagement campaigns and bot networks across platforms.

✓ Conducting sentiment analysis to detect emerging misinformation narratives.

✔ Using natural language processing (NLP) to decode coded messages in extremist and conspiracy networks.

◆ **Example**: Analysts will monitor Telegram, Discord, and dark web forums for early warning signs of coordinated disinformation operations.

◆ **Ethical & Legal Expertise in Digital Investigations**

✔ Navigating privacy laws, cybersecurity policies, and ethical dilemmas in online investigations.

✔ Understanding OSINT best practices to avoid data manipulation and bias.

✔ Engaging in responsible disclosure when exposing high-risk disinformation actors.

◆ **Example**: Future investigators will balance exposure of disinformation networks while protecting individuals' privacy rights.

2. Essential OSINT Tools for Future Investigators

◆ **AI-Powered Deepfake & Synthetic Media Detection**

✔ **Deepware Scanner** – Identifies AI-generated deepfake videos.

✔ **Microsoft's Video Authenticator** – Analyzes subtle deepfake distortions in facial movements.

✔ **Truepic** – Uses cryptographic verification to confirm image authenticity.

◆ **Future Use**: Analysts will deploy real-time deepfake detection algorithms to verify breaking news footage before misinformation spreads.

◆ **Advanced Reverse Image & Video Search Tools**

✔ **Google Reverse Image Search** – Identifies original sources of manipulated images.

✔ **InVID & WeVerify** – Extracts metadata and frames from suspicious videos for verification.

✓ **Sensity AI** – Detects AI-generated face-swaps and synthetic media.

◆ **Future Use**: OSINT specialists will rely on enhanced image forensics tools with AI-driven tampering detection.

◆ **Dark Web & Encrypted Platform Monitoring**

✓ **ShadowDragon & Maltego** – Maps disinformation networks across social media & the dark web.

✓ **Hunchly** – Tracks online misinformation actors & digital footprints.

✓ **Telegram Open Network (TON) Scraper** – Extracts fake news narratives from encrypted messaging groups.

◆ **Future Use**: Investigators will track misinformation narratives spreading via private Telegram & WhatsApp groups in real time.

◆ **OSINT Automation & Threat Intelligence Platforms**

✓ **SpiderFoot** – Automates cyber threat intelligence & digital footprint analysis.

✓ **Shodan** – Scans servers, IoT devices & state-sponsored botnets linked to disinformation campaigns.

✓ **TweetBeaver & Hoaxy** – Detects bot-driven fake news amplification on Twitter/X.

◆ **Future Use**: AI-powered tools will automate disinformation tracking at a scale unmanageable by human analysts alone.

3. Future Trends in Disinformation & OSINT Investigations

◆ **The Rise of AI-Generated Disinformation Armies**

✓ AI-powered fake personas will produce hyper-realistic fake news at scale.

✓ Automated propaganda campaigns will flood social media with tailored misinformation.

✓ AI-assisted deepfake political figures will be used for election interference & diplomatic deception.

◆ **Counter-OSINT**: Investigators will develop real-time AI detection tools to analyze linguistic anomalies & AI-generated voice cloning.

◆ Decentralized Disinformation Networks

✓ Blockchain-based media networks may be weaponized to distribute untraceable fake news.

✓ Peer-to-peer encrypted networks (e.g., IPFS, Mastodon, Nostr) will make disinformation harder to track.

✓ Decentralized AI models will remove traditional moderation barriers, making regulation difficult.

◆ **Counter-OSINT**: Analysts will build machine-learning classifiers to detect suspicious blockchain-stored propaganda content.

◆ The Expansion of "Metaverse" Misinformation

✓ Disinformation will spread via immersive AR/VR platforms like Meta's Horizon Worlds.

✓ Synthetic influencers & AI-generated avatars will push political and ideological misinformation.

✓ Deepfake VR simulations could be used to alter historical narratives & fabricate real-world events.

◆ **Counter-OSINT**: Investigators will develop VR-based forensic tools to analyze synthetic reality manipulations.

4. Preparing the Next Generation of OSINT Investigators

◆ Investing in OSINT Education & Training

✓ Expanding OSINT training programs in universities, cybersecurity courses, and journalism schools.

✓ Hosting global OSINT hackathons to develop AI-assisted misinformation tracking tools.

✓ Creating specialized OSINT certifications for government, media, and law enforcement professionals.

◆ **Example**: Bellingcat & the DFRLab already train journalists and analysts in OSINT methodologies.

◆ Enhancing Global Collaboration Against Disinformation

✓ Building international OSINT task forces to track cross-border misinformation networks.

✓ Strengthening partnerships between governments, private sector, and fact-checking organizations.

✓ Promoting open-source AI development for fake news detection & synthetic media forensics.

◆ **Example**: The EU, U.S., and tech companies are already developing joint AI-driven misinformation tracking initiatives.

Conclusion: The Future of OSINT & Disinformation Investigations

Disinformation threats are rapidly evolving, and future OSINT analysts must be equipped with cutting-edge skills and tools to counter AI-driven deception, synthetic media manipulation, and algorithmic propaganda.

Key Takeaways:

✓ OSINT investigators must master AI-driven forensics, machine learning, and blockchain verification.

✓ Emerging threats include AI-generated disinformation armies, deepfake political figures, and metaverse misinformation.

✓ Global collaboration, education, and tech innovation will be essential in preparing the next generation of OSINT professionals.

💡 **Final Thought**: The battle for truth in the digital age will depend on how well we equip OSINT investigators with the skills, tools, and strategies needed to counter the next wave of global disinformation warfare.

In today's digital world, disinformation and fake news are more prevalent than ever, influencing public opinion, manipulating narratives, and even impacting national security. With the rise of social media, misinformation spreads at an unprecedented rate, making it increasingly difficult to distinguish fact from fiction. Open-Source Intelligence (OSINT) provides the tools and methodologies needed to detect, analyze, and counter disinformation campaigns effectively.

Investigating Disinformation & Fake News with OSINT is a comprehensive guide to identifying false narratives, tracking their sources, and understanding the tactics used to spread misinformation. Whether you are a journalist, investigator, researcher, or security professional, this book equips you with the skills to uncover the truth and combat digital deception.

What You'll Learn in This Book

- **Understanding Disinformation & Misinformation**: Learn the key differences and why they matter in OSINT investigations.
- **Identifying Fake News & Manipulated Media**: Discover techniques to verify sources, fact-check articles, and detect doctored images or videos.
- **Tracking the Spread of Disinformation**: Use OSINT tools to map how false narratives originate and propagate across platforms.
- **Investigating Bot Networks & Troll Farms**: Uncover automated accounts and coordinated influence campaigns used to amplify fake news.
- **Social Media Analysis for Disinformation Investigations**: Learn how to monitor Twitter, Facebook, Reddit, and other platforms for misleading content.
- **Deepfakes & Synthetic Media Detection**: Identify AI-generated images, videos, and voices used in misinformation campaigns.
- **Reverse Image & Video Search Techniques**: Verify visual content to determine its authenticity and original source.
- **Geolocation & Timeline Analysis**: Use OSINT to confirm when and where images, videos, and events actually occurred.
- **Psychological & Political Tactics in Disinformation**: Understand the techniques used to manipulate public opinion and decision-making.
- **Countering Disinformation & Promoting Media Literacy**: Learn strategies for debunking false claims and educating others on media manipulation.

With real-world case studies, hands-on exercises, and expert methodologies, Investigating Disinformation & Fake News with OSINT is an essential resource for anyone looking to uncover the truth in an era of digital deception. Whether you're tracking propaganda campaigns, verifying viral stories, or investigating online hoaxes, this book will sharpen your ability to detect and combat misinformation.

Thank you for reading **Investigating Disinformation & Fake News with OSINT**. In an age where misinformation can shape opinions, policies, and even elections, your commitment to uncovering the truth is more important than ever. By learning these OSINT techniques, you are strengthening your ability to identify and counter false narratives, making the internet a more reliable space for accurate information.

We encourage you to use these skills ethically and responsibly. The fight against disinformation is ongoing, and every investigator, journalist, and researcher plays a crucial role in promoting truth and accountability.

We greatly appreciate your time, curiosity, and dedication to intelligence gathering. If you found this book valuable, we'd love to hear your feedback! Your insights help us improve future editions and continue providing high-quality resources for OSINT professionals.

Stay critical, stay ethical, and keep investigating.

Continue Your OSINT Journey

Expand your skills with the rest of The **OSINT Analyst Series**:

- **OSINT Foundations**: The Beginner's Guide to Open-Source Intelligence
- **The OSINT Search Mastery**: Hacking Search Engines for Intelligence
- **OSINT People Finder**: Advanced Techniques for Online Investigations
- **Social Media OSINT**: Tracking Digital Footprints
- **Image & Geolocation Intelligence**: Reverse Searching and Mapping
- **Domain, Website & Cyber Investigations with OSINT**
- **Email & Dark Web Investigations**: Tracking Leaks & Breaches
- **OSINT Threat Intel**: Investigating Hackers, Breaches, and Cyber Risks
- **Corporate OSINT**: Business Intelligence & Competitive Analysis
- **OSINT for Deep & Dark Web**: Techniques for Cybercrime Investigations
- **OSINT Automation**: Python & APIs for Intelligence Gathering
- **OSINT Detective**: Digital Tools & Techniques for Criminal Investigations
- **Advanced OSINT Case Studies**: Real-World Investigations
- **The Ethical OSINT Investigator**: Privacy, Legal Risks & Best Practices

We look forward to seeing you in the next book!

Happy investigating!